1991

THE MOTHER EARTH
HANDBOOK

THE MOTHER EARTH HANDBOOK

What You Need to Know and Do—
at Home, in Your Community,
and through Your Church—
to Help Heal Our Planet Now

Edited by Judith S. Scherff

Foreword by Kent Foerster

CONTINUUM • NEW YORK

1991

The Continuum Publishing Company
370 Lexington Avenue, New York, NY 10017

Printed in the United States of America
Typesetting output: TEXSource, Houston

This book is printed on recycled paper.

Library of Congress Cataloging-in-Publication Data

The Mother Earth handbook : what you need to know and do—at home, in
  your community, and through your church—to help heal our planet now
  / edited by Judith S. Scherff
    p.   cm.
  Includes bibliographical references.
  ISBN 0-8264-0520-7
  1. Environmental protection—Citizen participation. I. Scherff,
Judith S.
TD171.7.M68   1991
363.7'0525—dc20

                                              90-45233
                                                  CIP

The Mother Earth Handbook is dedicated to ALL of God's creatures from microorganisms to elephants; to the Earth itself; to its vegetation; and to all humans who are committed to preserving the integrity of the Earth as it is intended to function for the benefit of ALL life.

---   ---

Let there be no illusions. Taking effective action to halt the massive injury to earth's environment will require a mobilization of political will, international cooperation and sacrifice unknown except in wartime. Yet humanity is in a war right now, and it is not too Draconian to call it a war for survival. It is a war in which all nations must be allies. . . .

"We to not have generations, we only have years in which to attempt to turn things around," warns Lester Brown, president of the Washington-based Worldwatch Institute. Every individual on the planet must be made aware of its vulnerability and of the urgent need to preserve it. No attempt to protect the environment will be successful in the long run unless ordinary people — the California housewife, the Mexican peasant, the Soviet factory worker, the Chinese farmer — are willing to adjust their life styles.

Thomas A. Sancton, "Planet of the Year,"
Time (January 2, 1989)

Editor's Note

Opinions expressed in individual chapters do not necessarily reflect the views of the other authors.

Contents

Foreword

Earth Day, April 1990

Mother Earth. For some it is a living, breathing organism; part of an organic whole. For others, it is simply a place composed of rock, dirt, organic and inorganic materials, and water. Mother Earth has been shaped by the natural forces of wind, water, fire, and the movement of Earth in an ever-changing primordial soup of electromagnetic, biochemical, physical, and gravitational reactions. It once was home to an incredibly diverse plant and animal kingdom. However, uncontrolled growth and material development of the human species have radically altered the face and fate of this planet. Virtually all of Mother Earth's wilderness and natural areas have been significantly altered or destroyed by human action and inaction.

This book brings together numerous perspectives on the environmental and human crisis we are NOT facing. It is a warning, call to action, and a partial field guide to what people all over the world are doing about human degradation and environmental destruction. For those appalled and repulsed by it, action is compulsory, education is mandatory, and changes in attitudes are imperative. People must understand and be angered by the folly of our human arrogance and ignorance. People have to DO something.

This handbook is the product of many of these special people who realize what we are doing to Mother Earth and ourselves. As the project grew and the stories came in from all over, it became obvious that the stories alone were not enough. Suggesting what individuals and groups could do in response to the call to action became ever more important. The result was that a book designed initially to chasten our collective conscience was expanded to include "Taking Action" sections at the end of each chapter.

Sit upon a patch of grass or a rock or pull up a chair. Learn about the sacred and beautiful tropical forests and how to live a more compassionate life-style. Read, too, about our air, water, oceans, animals, wetlands, and forests. Discover how to make environmental economics add up, how to control energy use, and how to work together in communities to multiply the impact of individual action. Come to understand the population explosion, the toxic consequences of pesticide use, the garbage of a consumptive society, and the environmental illnesses of twentieth-century living.

The Mother Earth Handbook is intended as a guide to educate yourself about how to help in the personal and collective efforts needed to take better care of each other and Mother Earth. It is said that we reap what we sow. This guide hopes to cast the seeds of better awareness, giving alternatives and suggestions on where to go and what to do. Its harvest, we hope, will be a healthy, productive, and sustainable future for Mother Earth and ALL of her inhabitants.

Kent Foerster

In Appreciation

I wish to thank all the contributors to this effort, for their dedication to preserving our environment as they labor on a daily basis towards that goal and for their work on the contributions herein.

Thank you to The Venerable Frank N. Cohoon, Diocese of Kansas (Episcopal), and The Reverend William E. Crews, Diocese of Colorado (Episcopal), for their encouragement and for their recognition that organized religion has a responsibility for stewardship of the Creation. Thanks, too, to other clergy who believe that the church has an obligation to be at the front of the parade on both the practical and moral issues of environmental integrity.

My appreciation also to Kent Foerster who helped immensely; to Jerry deNoyelles and Edward Martinko of the Environmental Studies Department at the University of Kansas for their commitment to Earth's integrity. Thank you to Chawcer and special others who, over the years, have added to the reverence I have for the Creation.

J.S.S.

Introduction

Human beings typically "take things for granted." Our health, for example. We do not appreciate the absence of pain. We go along day after day, year after year, paying very little attention to our bodies until a body part fails to function or is broken or injured in some way. Many times we begin to feel bad and while visiting a doctor are startled, distressed, depressed, and sometimes terrified to learn that part of us is not working correctly. Illness is a threat. It is a reminder that we are mortal and that we, too, can be victims of multiple diseases and disorders. We are living organisms and living organisms get sick.

The Earth, too, is a living organism. Beneath its surface, it is moving and alive as is evidenced by earthquakes and volcanoes. Life is confirmed on its surface as seeds are planted and crops grow from its soil; as trees shed leaves in the fall and sprout new growth in the spring; as rivers flow; and as the myriad of species survive on the produce of this amazing planet. Around the Earth, and inexorably a part of what takes place on the surface, is the Earth's atmosphere — which provides rain and the vital air we breathe.

Although a few environmentalists and scientists have been warning us for at least twenty-five years, it seems that suddenly we have discovered what has been happening to the Earth. The Earth is ill and parts of it are very ill indeed. The air is filled with toxic chemicals; very little pure water is left to drink; species are becoming extinct at an unprecedented rate; and the number of humans demanding the Earth's resources is approaching overload. The Earth is in trouble. And if the Earth is in trouble, all life on Earth is in trouble as well.

Many Earth watchers believe that our planet is now suffering from some ills that cannot be reversed and that our way of life will have to change dramatically in order for us to survive. And the cause of all of the ills that have been imposed on the Earth is just one species: the human being. We have inflicted serious injury upon our

13

life-support system, inducing a gradual, creeping, silent destruction that, if continued, will lead to the eventual demise of our own species.

This book is an effort to inform the reader about that life-support system and of what has happened to it. It is also an action manual that offers many suggestions as to what individuals can do to improve situations that are either at a critical stage or getting close to it.

The style for each chapter varies because each one bears the thumbprint of its author. Certain themes are repeated in various articles, even though the articles were written by authors miles apart and without knowledge of the others' work. What might seem to be redundancy is really a testimony to the fact that seemingly distinct environmental issues are interrelated. We cannot point out any better than in this kind of repetition that everything in this universe is interconnected and that includes human beings.

Destruction of the environment, in the thinking of many scientists and interested parties, can do as least as much — if not more — damage as a nuclear holocaust. While we have been transfixed by the possibility of a nuclear blowup, we have been ignoring the disaster that IS taking place, this very day, this very minute.

Since every single malaise from which the Earth is currently suffering was created by human beings, it follows that within the human species lies our hope. If we have caused the problems, we can cure most of them. The three human conditions that have created the basis for the Earth's illnesses are: ignorance, indifference, and greed.

Ignorance is probably the easiest condition to cure. The hope and belief of most environmentalists is that if only individuals really knew what was going on, they would care enough to do something.

Indifference is an attitude for which there is no excuse. It is a thought process based on selfishness and narcissism. However, education also may help the indifferent by forcing them to realize that what they are doing amounts to turning on themselves. Perhaps, they may just wish to change their behavior patterns. Maybe. One can hope.

And greed. The trendy, fashionable, and wholly unjustified condition of the eighties. The immoral collecting of excessive "assets." The new word for stealing. The Earth has been abused more from greed than anything else. This way of life can and must be changed if civilization is to continue with any semblance of a reasonable quality of life. Putting an end to greed will require different methods from putting an end to ignorance and indifference, but it can, very definitely, be accomplished. We may not be able to convince people to be less greedy, but we most assuredly can see to it that their greedy methods are significantly less profitable.

If we do not choose to heal the Earth, it will probably continue on without us. Scientists know that the Earth has a capacity to heal itself if left alone. The scenario, if it continues, will allow just that. The way we are going now, it appears that there will be a time when this life-support system will not function well enough to keep the human race alive. The extinction of thousands of nonhuman species bears this out, for let us remember that the conditions of the nonhuman are a forerunner of what will happen to humans. One hopes the epitaph of the history of human involvement on this Earth will not read, "And on the eighth day, they bulldozed it."

This book is written, also, to remind organized religion that it, more than any other structured body, has an obligation to lead in the process of environmental stewardship. Although there are notable and worthy exceptions, organized religion has failed in the very critical area of teaching and encouraging respect for and preservation of the magnificent gifts the Creator has provided in our life-support system. This may be organized religion's greatest sin of omission. But we, too, can alter our course and accept our moral obligation to be a leading force in environmental restoration and healing — itself a moral issue.

In an article entitled "Church Activism to Stop Toxic Pollution," published in *Christian Ecology*, Les Ann Kirkland stated, "The Church may be the only institution that can save the Earth from destruction, and it needs to wake up to this fact."

Emergency action is the only response adequate to some issues. The remainder will require a variety of restorative and healing measures. We can recover to a large extent because each of us has a choice of whether to continue to desecrate or to begin the healing process. We are ALL responsible for the fate of Earth, whether or not we want to be. Our responsibility to this Earth, including to all other species, is not debatable; it is fact!

J. S. S.

— start by teaching children !

THE BASIC PROBLEM

— 1 —

Population Control:
Necessary but Insufficient

Paul R. Ehrlich and Anne H. Ehrlich

There are getting to be too many of us.... We have begun to strain the limits of the global life support systems — our oceans, farmlands, forests, and wetlands. Ever more of us are consuming ever more of the earth's resources, dooming hundreds of millions of the earth's inhabitants to a life described by philosopher Thomas Hobbes as "poor, nasty, brutish, and short."

Blueprint for the Environment

Civilization's problems would not all be solved if population growth were halted humanely by limiting births. They would not necessarily be solved if the world population were ultimately reduced to a size that was more or less permanently sustainable. Society might still be plagued by racism, sexism, religious prejudice, gross economic inequity, the threat of war, and serious environmental deterioration. But without population control, none of these problems can be solved; halting growth and then moving toward lower numbers simply would give humanity an opportunity to keep on trying to solve them. The old saying still holds: "whatever your cause, it's a lost cause without population control."

Yet in spite of the critical role that population size and growth play in shaping the human condition, overpopulation is rarely explicitly recognized as an issue by public figures. For instance, in the bitterly fought presidential election of 1988, not one of the important population related issues facing civilization entered significantly into policy debates. These neglected issues include:

1. The greenhouse warming of the atmosphere with its potential to cause serious disruption to agriculture (leading to reduced production and less dependable harvests), not to mention rising sea levels and other problems.

2. High rates of soil erosion and the depletion and despoliation of groundwater supplies, both of which also have serious implications for agriculture.

3. The accelerating "extinction crisis" in which the disappearance of populations and species of other organisms threatens the provision of crucial life-support services by ecosystems and exacerbates both global warming and soil erosion.

All of these problems are at least partly caused by overpopulation in rich nations and by overpopulation and continuing rapid population growth in poor nations. Yet to address the demographic situation remained under a strong taboo throughout the 1980s. It was never even hinted at by the Reagan administration or by the candidates in 1988, and thus was effectively removed from the policy arena. During that time, the population connection to other problems was almost never discussed by the press.

How is population connected to these important environmental issues?

The Greenhouse Effect

The role of population in generating greenhouse warming can be seen through a few simple calculations. It is widely recognized that industrialized countries (with about one-quarter of the world's population) bear major responsibility for injecting excess carbon dioxide (CO_2), the leading contributor to global warming, into the atmosphere. Roughly three-quarters of the CO_2 released by burning fossil fuels comes from automobiles, power plants, and other industrial apparatus used mainly by the rich. In terms of carbon dioxide produced per unit of energy generated, coal burning is the worst offender: for every ton of high quality coal burned, roughly *three* tons of CO_2 are released.

Suppose the United States decided to take dramatic steps to cut its contribution to the CO_2 component of global warming. Suppose it did so simply by terminating all burning of coal (which now supplies more than 20 percent of our annual energy consumption). Suppose also that, at the same time, China managed to halt its population growth and in the course of development double its per capita energy use, using its vast supply of coal. China, in moving towards what virtually everyone would agree is a legitimate development goal, would more than compensate for the reduction of CO_2 input produced by

America's unprecedented sacrifice. Thus, even without considering the *growth* of populations of either rich or poor countries, the vast levels of human overpopulation already achieved can magnify small and reasonable per capita changes into gigantic impacts.

If one then considers population growth, the situation looks even worse. If India's per capita energy consumption rose just to about the level of China's today, that combined with India's projected population growth would, a century from now, produce an impact equivalent to that of doubling China's per capita consumption without increasing the Chinese population. So, while poor nations are now relatively minor contributors to the CO_2 load generated by burning fossil fuels, the effects of their legitimate need to develop, multiplied by their population sizes and growth will certainly increase their role in the near future.

Other contributions of population growth to the CO_2 problem are also significant but much harder to quantify. Plants take up carbon dioxide in the process of photosynthesis; when they die and decay or are burned, they release it again. One long-term action that would help mitigate the greenhouse problem therefore is to replant forests, using trees whose wood would be sequestered rather than burned — ideally, high quality tropical hardwoods. But, of course, it is precisely in the tropics that expanding human populations are contributing heavily to the accelerating destruction of forests, although much of that destruction can be traced to overconsumption and overpopulation in rich nations. And the massive cutting and burning of tropical forests is itself a major source of the CO_2 being added to the atmosphere.

In the next century, methane will be making an increasingly important contribution to atmospheric warming. Methane's concentration is rising faster than that of CO_2, and it is many times more effective as a greenhouse gas. The population connection here is very clear, for two leading sources of methane are rice paddies, and the digestive tracts of cattle. Both sources are intimately tied to the task of feeding the burgeoning human population, so substantial reductions in methane releases may be difficult to achieve. Yet these two sources of methane are only a part of a very complex and still poorly understood situation; clearly, efforts to reduce a variety of sources will be required for significant results. Fortunately, methane has a relatively short residence time in the atmosphere, so moderate reductions in key sources may suffice, provided others are not allowed to rise. Similar problems surround nitrous oxide, another powerful greenhouse gas, which is omitted from nitrogen fertilizers. Unfortunately, nitrous oxide is long-lived in the atmosphere and not all of its sources are understood.

A third major set of greenhouse gases is chlorofluorocarbons (CFCs), the same human-made gases that cause depletion of the stratospheric ozone layer. They, too, have been rising rapidly and are highly effective. Like nitrous oxide, some CFCs have very long residence times, and elimination of their release is therefore imperative. Emission sources, fortunately, are relatively few, often nonessential (spray cans, for instance), and largely restricted to the developed nations. The use of CFCs as cheap refrigerants is the main one for which substitutes must be found.

Some progress has been made on an international agreement to ban CFCs and to find and deploy substitutes, but the sooner the better. The greenhouse and ozone-destroying effects of CFCs are worrisome enough, but the resultant increase in ultraviolet radiation reaching Earth's surface could kill or injure tiny photosynthesizing organisms in the oceans, thus reducing the oceans' capacity to take up some of the excess CO_2 from the atmosphere and further accelerating global warming.

Losses of Soil and Groundwater

Humanity is able to support almost five-and-a-half billion people today only by destroying and dispersing a onetime inheritance of "capital" — resources such as fossil fuels and other minerals, deep fertile soils for agriculture, ice-age groundwater, and a rich storehouse of other species of plants, animals, and microorganisms. All these resources are being used up at rates far beyond those at which they can be replenished; they are for practical purposes "nonrenewable." And the most critical of them are not the minerals.

Indeed, one of our severest problems is that fossil fuels are being overused. The problem with energy resources, as physicist John Holdren has often pointed out, is not providing "too little too late" but "too much too soon." Profligate use of energy, especially by rich countries, lies behind many of our most pressing environmental problems including global warming, acid precipitation, and air and water pollution.

Serious though that is, the depletion of soils, groundwater, and biodiversity are much more critical. Soil is irreplaceable on any time scale of interest; centuries to millennia are often required to produce a few inches. Continual losses of soil to erosion in natural ecosystems such as grasslands and forests are negligible and usually compensated by natural processes of soil generation. In agricultural systems, by contrast, losses can be measured in inches per decade or tons per acre per year. While certain tilling and planting methods can dramatically reduce erosion rates, short-term economics commonly works against soil protection. Global soil losses above "tolerance levels" have been estimated at twenty-four billion tons per year. As agricultural economist Lester Brown, president of Worldwatch Institute, has observed, civilization could survive the exhaustion of petroleum reserves, but not the exhaustion of the world's agricultural topsoil.

Groundwater, too, is both essential to the support of the human population and made less available as population growth leads to rising demand for water and huge overdrafts of many aquifers. A good example is the rapid depletion of accessible portions of the Ogallala aquifer underlying the great plains of the United States. The water accumulated over several ice ages; in some places where the Ogallala recharges at a rate of about a half-inch a year, four to six feet of irrigation water are being pumped out annually. A deliberate decision was made to mine the aquifer to economic exhaustion in less than a half-century — the greatest overdraft of groundwater in human history. The rate of withdrawal is roughly equivalent to the flow of the Colorado River.

The overdraft policy was established on the assumption that an infinite number of tappable water resources exists. As one water engineer in New Mexico put it, "We can always decide to build some more water projects." But that assumption is ridiculous, and the exhaustion of accessible portions of the Ogallala aquifer in the next few decades will result in bankruptcy for many farmers in the great plains and a significant loss in production of grain for export. Overdrafts can destroy aquifers permanently. The water-filled cavities in rock formations can collapse once the water is pumped out, or, in coastal areas, be infiltrated by salt water.

Aquifers can also be poisoned by human activities and thus rendered unusable. The growing US population demands more and more products whose manufacture results in the production of toxic wastes. Toxins seeping into the ground from spills and unsealed dumps can more or less permanently pollute aquifers. Sunlight and microorganisms are essential to natural purifying processes, but the former is absent and the latter in short supply hundreds of feet beneath the surface. That same expanding population also keeps demanding more roads and parking lots. Paving over large areas of land often results in rainfall running off directly or through sewers into rivers or the sea rather than percolating into the ground to recharge aquifers.

The Extinction Crisis

Earth's biotic diversity is now threatened with an anthropogenic extinction epidemic that may prove even more severe than the natural episode that ended the reign of dinosaurs at the end of the Cretaceous period some sixty-five million years ago. There are aesthetic and ethical reasons for deep concern about the decimation of humanity's only known living companions, but those arguments carry little weight with most policymakers. They tend to respond most readily to the prospect of other effects on society from a decline in biodiversity, especially direct economic losses.

Humanity already has withdrawn the very basis of its civilization from nature's "genetic library" — including all crops and domestic animals, important industrial materials, and the active ingredients of numerous prescription medicines. Even so, the potential of the library to provide such useful items has barely been tapped; in exterminating genetically distinct populations and species, *Homo sapiens* is foreclosing a myriad of opportunities to improve human health and welfare. Indeed, it is even removing the very raw material that many are counting on to use to improve the human condition. The diminution of genetic diversity also threatens the ability to maintain high-yielding strains of crops which often can be improved by transferring genes from wild relatives. In many parts of the world, close relatives of crop plants are being extirpated.

The most serious impact of extinctions on society, though, is not these direct economic losses, but the consequences of disruption of ecosystem services. These services are dependent on the participation of the plants, animals, and microorganisms that make up working parts of ecosystems. They include control of the gaseous content of the atmosphere (and thus the climate); moderation of the hydrologic cycle (including prevention of droughts and floods); the generation and replenishment of soils, disposal of wastes, and recycling of nutrients; pollination of numerous crops and control of the vast majority of the pests that potentially could attack them; and provision of food and other materials from forests and the sea.

The extinction of populations often causes disruption of ecosystem services well before entire species are seen to be threatened. Human population growth in the Himalayas after World War II was a major factor in the decimation of tree populations there. The ecosystem's control of the hydrologic cycle was impaired as exposed soil, no longer held in place by plant roots or sheltered from the force of downpours, eroded away. Some of that soil has ended up in the joint delta of the Ganges and Brahmaputra rivers — the nation of Bangladesh.

Bangladesh is vastly overpopulated, with its 118 million people crammed into an area the size of Wisconsin. Many Bangladeshis have been forced onto low siltbars ("chars"), composed partly of Himalayan soil, where they are especially vulnerable to the larger and more frequent floods originating in the denuded Himalayas. They also suffer from storm surges caused by cyclones in the Bay of Bengal. In 1970 some 150,000 people perished when such a surge swept over the coastal lowlands. In this, as in other cases, overpopulation leads to international tensions. The Bangladeshis are unhappy over the way in which India operates the Farakka Barrage upstream on the Ganges, claiming that India does not close the gates and absorb enough of the floodwaters behind the dam. In 1988 more than half of Bangladesh was inundated and fifty million people made homeless, while India's flood problems were comparatively minor.

Growing human populations are causing extinctions of organisms in part by competing with populations of other animals for Earth's bounty. The level of our competition was shown in a recent study of the proportion of the net primary productivity (NPP) of terrestrial ecosystems that is being directly used by human beings or channeled through altered and degraded ecosystems. NPP can be thought of as the energy captured from sunlight and bound by plants in the process of photosynthesis, minus the energy that the plants themselves need to grow and reproduce.

Today, our species controls nearly 30 percent of the NPP generated on land worldwide (most of Earth's NPP is produced on land), while having reduced Earth's potential NPP on land by some 13 percent in recent decades. The total terrestrial impact, including the losses, was found to be nearly 40 percent. To ecologists, these are stunning figures, adding to evidence from physical systems (e.g., rates of human mobilization of minerals compared with geological processes, and the rapid rises in atmospheric concentrations of greenhouse gases) that humanity has truly become a global force. The fraction of terrestrial NPP diverted to human systems becomes all the more impressive when one realizes that our species apparently is "planning" to double its population again within the next century!

Overpopulation, Maldistribution, and Faulty Technologies

It is sometimes claimed that there is no global problem of overpopulation, only problems of maldistribution and the use of faulty technologies. While it is undeniable that humanity *does* suffer from serious problems of maldistribution and has deployed numerous ecologically unsound technologies, it is preposterous to claim that there is no significant population component to the human predicament.

The case for maldistribution is often made in terms of diet, the thesis being that if all food were equally distributed and if everyone ate a vegetarian diet, all could be adequately fed. Recent studies show that this is indeed true — at the moment — presuming people were willing to eat grains now fed to livestock or that more palatable grains were planted instead. Consider the global grain harvest of 1985, which was significantly larger than in drought-plagued 1988 and about equal to that of 1989, although the population was smaller in 1985 by some 300 million. It has been estimated that about six billion people could be fed a mainly vegetarian diet with that harvest under ideal conditions of distribution. That is only about 700 million more people than were alive in 1990. But if the quality of the diet were raised to that of the average South American, only about 4 billion could be supported on the food produced in 1985 — more than 1.3 billion *fewer* than the 1990 population. With a North American dietary standard, only about 2.5 billion people could be fed, well under *half* of today's population.

Food production may, of course, be substantially increased in the future, although the trend is less and less in that direction. But the world population is also expanding rapidly, producing some ninety-five million more mouths to feed each year, and will pass six billion by 1998. Even if estimates of how many can be fed are conservatively low, it is clear that humanity would be close to running out of food even if conditions were ideal, distribution were equitable, and human beings were transformed into a vegetarian species.

Of course, there are also absolute limits to potential food production set by physical and biological constraints. Exactly when these limits will be reached is a matter of conjecture. But the numbers cited earlier on the human takeover of global NPP and the increase in global environmental trends that are inimical to agriculture and fisheries (such as depletion of soils and water, rapid climate change, ozone depletion, and acid precipitation) give little reason to believe that anything approaching twice today's food production will be easily extracted from Earth's ecosystems.

That more benign technologies could and should be deployed cannot be disputed. There should be, for example, more mass transport (and less use of automobiles), the substitution of less toxic chemicals for the most dangerous ones in use; and a substantial reduction in petrochemical production (with substitution of natural products in many cases). But even if such changes could be readily accomplished (and they will not be), it is easy to overestimate how benign they would be.

For instance, growing more cotton to replace synthetic fibers would require roughly doubling the cropland dedicated to cotton, at the expense of land now growing food. Because cotton is one of the most pesticide-intensive crops, the change would entail massive increases in the use of pesticides with their unhappy environmental side effects. Similarly, substituting wool for synthetics on a large scale would increase overgrazing and accelerate the already too high rates of desertification.

There is not the slightest question that human society should be striving both to reduce inequities in the distribution of goods and to make the technologies with which it supports itself more environmentally benign. But, of course, *any* progress in these areas can be quickly overwhelmed by population growth — a factor too often overlooked. If humanity succeeded in reducing the environmental effects of all its technologies by 10 percent with no increase in per capita affluence, for instance, world population growth would return the collective impact of *Homo sapiens* to the previous level in about six years.

Unfortunately, people have a great deal of trouble coming to grips with slow-moving but dangerous trends that take place over decades or centuries. In no small part, this is because our evolution has not prepared us to do so. For millions of years of our evolutionary past, it was important for our ancestors to react to immediate dangers. When a bear entered the cave, early humans had to fight or flee instantly. Evolution prepared us well to react to an oncoming car swerving into our lane but not to recognize trends that lead to danger over the decades. In the past, people could do nothing about such trends. Consequently, neither biological nor cultural evolution prepared us to deal with steady changes in demographic statistics, a slow and irregular change in average global temperatures, or the gradual accumulation of deadly nuclear weapons.

Because of this built-in blindness to slow-moving trends, people have been extremely loathe to recognize the consequences of uncontrolled population growth (as well as other dangerous trends). Indeed, many go to remarkable lengths to deny them. But the increasing deterioration of Earth's life-support systems under the impact of our still-expanding population is a clear signal that not only is it essential to end growth as soon as humanely possible but also to decrease considerably the population's long-term size.

Policies for Population Control

How soon could human population growth be humanely halted? Could people then accept the necessity of a slow decline to a population size that is sustainable in the long term? Such a population must be able to support itself predominantly on income (the energy supplied daily by the sun) rather than by consuming its capital (nonrenewable resources). How might this optimum population size be determined, let alone attained?

Because of the momentum for growth inherent in the youthful age composition of exploding populations, stopping population growth on a worldwide basis will take many decades — unless some catastrophe intervenes to raise death rates substantially. Currently, growth rates among nations vary enormously. A dozen European countries have already stopped growing or are very close to it; a few even have begun slow population declines. By contrast, populations in most developing nations are still expanding rapidly — some by more than 3 percent per year, a rate that, if continued, would double them in twenty-three years or less. Many of these countries are projected by demographers to double or even triple their current populations before growth can be ended. Worse yet, the assumption beneath those projections that birthrates will continue to fall in poor nations may well be faulty.

Ironically, the majority of poor countries have more or less explicit population control policies and active family planning programs to help couples limit births, while most of the relatively slow-growing developed nations have no explicit population policies (although most do provide family planning assistance).

What policy options are available today to hasten the process of ending population growth? In the United States, increased public education is obviously needed, for without public understanding and pressure put upon decision makers, no policies are likely to be formulated. The unspoken taboo of the 1980s that prevented most politicians from speaking out on population, even those well informed about it, must be broken.

One obvious source of change is the media. *Time* magazine, for instance, for years neglected the big picture in its environmental coverage and determinedly avoided discussion of the population problem. In 1989, however, *Time* made beleaguered Earth "Planet of the Year" and gave extensive coverage to environmental issues, including population problems. Even before *Time*'s conversion, its competitor *Newsweek* was giving excellent coverage to the connections between population growth and global environmental problems. Both magazines made important contributions in raising public awareness of these issues.

There seem to be many sources of the still pervasive taboo, however. These include religious attitudes, a basic humanistic feeling that "there can't be too many people," and the notion that population growth will enhance economic growth. Whatever the source of the taboo, we believe the chances of breaking it would be greatly enlarged if the scientific community itself were both more knowledgeable about the effects of overpopulation on the environment and more willing to speak out about them.

Ecologists and evolutionary biologists have begun to address the general public on this issue. The "Club of the Earth," a group whose members all belong to both the National Academy of Sciences and the American Academy of Arts and Sciences, released a statement to the press in September 1988, which said in part:

> Arresting global population growth should be second in importance only to avoiding nuclear war on humanity's agenda. Overpopulation and rapid population growth are intimately connected with most aspects of the current human predicament, including rapid depletion of nonrenewable resources, deterioration of the environment (including rapid climate change), and increasing international tensions.

If such statements were released more frequently by scientists in a variety of disciplines, they could help create a social climate of respectability and urgency that would lower the risk for politicians who wish to deal with population related issues. Political leaders could then create a new American population policy, which we believe is an essential prerequisite for gaining effective global action.

What sort of policies should be considered? First, a commission on global population, resources, and the environment might be established to stimulate renewed public debate on the issue. It may appear that past studies have had little impact on policy. In 1972, the letter transmitting the report of the Commission on Population Growth and the American Future to President Nixon and the Congress concluded that "no substantial benefits would result from further growth of the Nation's population, rather . . . the gradual stabilization of our population through voluntary means would contribute significantly to the nation's ability to solve its problems." The Nixon administration ignored it, and the American population has since grown by some forty million.

Almost a decade later, the transmittal letter of *The Global 2000 Report to the President,* initiated by President Carter, was even more explicit. "Our conclusions . . . indicate the potential environmental, resource, and population stresses are intensifying and will increasingly determine the quality of human life on our planet . . . the earth's carrying capacity — the ability of biological systems to provide resources for human needs — is eroding. . . . Changes in public policy are needed around the world before problems worsen and options for effective action are reduced."

Global 2000 was the result of a pathbreaking effort that involved coordinating the analytic capabilities of a dozen government agencies and the World Bank, with advice from people outside government. Its "pessimistic" conclusions undoubtedly were too optimistic. As was recognized in the report, standard problems that plague most narrow examinations of the future could not be entirely avoided in *Global*

2000: "Most of the quantitative projections simply assume that re-source needs in the sector they cover — needs for capital, energy, land, water, minerals — will be met. . . . It is very likely that the same resources have been allocated to more than one sector."

Unfortunately, *Global 2000* came out as Ronald Reagan was coming in. The new administration, in keeping with its anti-environmental stance and broad opposition to family planning and women's rights, did its best to sweep the report under the rug.

The results of these earlier commissioned studies might seem to be minimal, but it is easy to underestimate their influence. A great deal of publicity accompanied each, and all together they provided substantial "authoritative" documentation for scientists and politicians to cite in recommending policy. *Global 2000*, moreover, had substantial impact outside the United States. It was circulated world-wide by the Carter administration through US embassies, and is credited with helping to boost awareness abroad of global environmental problems and interest in accepting aid for family planning. This interest no doubt led to the study by the World Commission on Development and the Environment, culminating in the widely admired 1987 report, *Our Common Future* (also known as the Bruntland Report for the commission's chair, Gro Harlem Bruntland, then Prime Minister of Norway).

Because of these and other studies, people everywhere have become much more aware of the connections between population growth and environmental problems, especially those that contribute to poverty such as desertification and tropical deforestation. And in the United States, the public seems more receptive to the notion that demographic factors will be crucial in shaping the future of civilization.

A new study, perhaps conducted by the National Academy of Sciences, might be a valuable aid in promoting public education about the human predicament. To fill that role, the study must be supervised by scientists from the most critical disciplines — ecology, climatology, toxicology, epidemiology, and so on — not just demography and economics. The dependence of social and economic systems upon the functioning of ecosystems must be made explicit. The role of the social sciences in designing economic and political systems that can function within the constraints set by physical, chemical, and biological systems is extremely important, but not yet clearly appreciated by social scientists. To put it starkly, ecology must take precedence over economics; nonsensical notions about perpetual growth of gross national products must be put to rest once and for all. Indeed, in the rich nations, economic growth is more the disease than the cure.

Some educational initiatives that could be taken in the United States include:

1. *Basic demography and the issue of population control added to all high-school curricula in the context of citizen responsibility.* Every citizen should be at least as familiar with the demographic and environmental status of society as with its economic status.

2. *Revitalization of the White House Council on Environmental Quality with increased staffing to provide a steady flow of information monitoring the environmental status of the nation and the world.* The Council's charge thus should be expanded to monitor global change. Its reports should include: American and world demographic statistics; changes in global climate and in concentrations of greenhouse gases and other atmospheric pollutants; acidification of lakes, streams, forests, and agricultural areas; rates of soil erosion, groundwater pumping and recharge; yields and compositions of fish harvests; changes in energy use and efficiency in various sectors of the economy; and preservation or loss of biodiversity. This kind of information should be generated and reported regularly, just as the Dow Jones stock index, the prime rate, the trade deficit, leading economic indicators, and the value of the dollar are now.

3. *Coverage of demographic, ecological, and climatic trends and indicators in public media at the same level of attention as is now provided for economic issues.* Ecological commentators should be as omnipresent as economic commentators are today (their predictions can hardly help being more accurate).

Heightened public awareness of population related issues would open the way for instituting more substantive policies to deal with American and global population problems. This would make possible a governmental campaign to lower the US birthrate a little further ("patriotic Americans stop at two") and hasten the day when a gradual population *decline* could be initiated.

Such a campaign should include efforts to increase public knowledge and practice of birth control, especially among young people, with an emphasis on the responsibilities of parenthood. Support for research and development of improved contraceptive methods and materials is also needed as well as better access to those now available. Wider public education on the proper use of condoms is essential, both for family planning and to help stop the spread of AIDS and other sexually transmitted diseases. If successful, this campaign would have three salient benefits: it would help lower the birthrate, limit the spread of AIDS, and greatly alleviate the vexing problem of abortion.

In conjunction with improving the nation's policies on family planning, a review of its immigration policy should be instituted, this time addressing the question of the future population size of the United States as a major factor. Few areas of public policy involve more, or more difficult, ethical choices. Our population growth is unlikely to cease in the foreseeable future unless our policies address the imbalance between immigration and emigration. A part of this reevaluation, the role of US foreign policies (including trade and investment policies) in generating immigration from poorer countries must be considered.

Finally, helping other nations control the growth of their populations should return to a prominent place on the American foreign policy agenda. The United States until 1981 was a leader in this area; the recent resurgence of population growth in the developing world is at least partly traceable to the Reagan and Bush administrations' abdication of leadership in population assistance. This leadership should be reasserted and augmented by new leadership in addressing global environmental problems.

The time could hardly be more propitious. With the Soviet Union's dramatically changed policies toward its former enemies and withdrawal from domination of its former satellites, it now seems possible for the world's military superpowers to put aside the East-West confrontation, enlist the help of other economic superpowers (Japan and the European Economic Community), and begin to tackle together the most crucial issue of the twenty-first century: controlling human numbers and keeping Earth habitable.

P. R. E.
A. H. E.

* * *

TAKING ACTION

1. Support organizations that provide funding for family planning, such as the U.N. Fund for Population Activities and the International Planned Parenthood Federation. According to these organizations, women who are educated to the eighth-grade level have half as many pregnancies as women who have no more than a first-grade education. Support programs that educate women.

2. Help introduce population-educational materials into your school district. Obtain the Teacher's PET Project materials from Zero Population Growth, 1400 16th Street NW, Suite 320, Washington, DC 20036, and make educators aware of their existence and content.

3. Lobby. Support the recommendations offered here. As population issues come before Congress, be certain your representatives are aware of the connection between overpopulation and many environmental problems.

4. Let your national representatives know that you favor foreign aid for development of employment opportunities for women in the third world. Give women options other than the annual pregnancy cycle.

5. Support measures to control local growth and development; work to preserve open spaces. Work to protect local wetlands and other important biologically-rich habitats. (Source: *Zero Population Growth*)

OUR OVERINDULGENCE

—— 2 ——

The Greenhouse Effect:
Creation Waits

The Reverend Warren G. Hansen, Ph.D.

Every time you turn on the lights, every time we produce or use energy, the power plant is giving you electricity that it had to produce usually — but not always — by burning coal or oil. Every time you start your car you contribute to the greenhouse effect. A a car, a typical car, weighs a ton or two, and it contributes about that amount of carbon dioxide to the atmosphere every year.

The summer of 1988 in many ways telescopes a lot of the changes that we're going to see in the future if we don't get the greenhouse gases under control.

Dr. Michael Oppenheimer

It is written that in the beginning human beings were settled in a beautiful, harmonious garden by God, and given dominion over the Creation and the responsibility of caring for the garden — tilling it, co-creating with their Creator. But they, ambitious to be like God, answerable only to themselves, were tempted into disbelieving and ignoring the warning that God had given them.

God created a cycle that works well when undisturbed. God called it good! But as is true in all situations where humankind seriously disturbs the balance in nature, disaster can follow. We, the human species, never quite learn this very basic lesson because we are too busy satisfying our needs, wants, greed, and self-centered goals to pause, to look, to be still, to listen. The signs are there to be seen and heard, if we will only look — and listen. Until recently, we really haven't been aware of the problem we have been and are creating.

During the summer of 1988, Yellowstone National Park experienced the most devastating forest fires ever, caused mostly by lightning unaccompanied by rain and sustained by the hot, dry summer. Disastrous to everyone except a few who saw them as a opportunity to study the role of fire in the self-regulation of western forests, the naturally caused fires were not controlled early in the season. By early fall they grew to monstrous proportions, and things became too far-gone for fire fighters to be effective until finally their efforts were assisted by the cold and snowfall of approaching winter.

The "let burn" policy of the National Park Service contributed immensely to the destruction of hundreds of thousands of trees. These trees had been effective removers of carbon dioxide from the atmosphere. The fires converted much of the woody substance of the trees back to carbon dioxide, adding to the burden in the atmosphere and making the blanket more efficient. The left hand of ecology was ignorant of the right hand's concerns. The value of studying the ecology of fire in western forests can legitimately be debated. However, the debacle of adding unnecessary tons and tons and tons of carbon dioxide to the atmosphere at this time is not debatable! The blackened snags stand as a monument to the "let burn" folly.

Skepticism, ignorance, indifference, conflicting views, and apathy notwithstanding, the warming of the Earth is inevitable. The results do promise to be catastrophic. The time is short.

Academic pride or simply professional caution in the interpretation of data may contribute to debate over whether or not the recent warmest years since measurements began are in fact the earliest detection of that inevitable warming. This debate contributes only obscurity to ordinary people while providing excuses for doing nothing, and causes delay in dealing with the inevitable warming that will be experienced by all living things on Earth. We, the human species, must look at our options with a combination of great care and great urgency! We must sort out things that will help, from things that won't help; things that are possible from things that are not; things that people will do voluntarily from those that they won't do unless forced.

To deal creatively with the challenge that confronts us requires returning the carbon cycle to a state of balance or equilibrium. We must look for ways of accelerating the removal of carbon dioxide from the atmosphere and ways of slowing down the rate at which the gas is injected into the atmosphere.

To move into a state of carbon equilibrium from the present

grossly unbalanced situation in which more and more carbon dioxide is spewed into the atmosphere while less and less is removed from it, requires that we, the human species, on a worldwide level, take seriously the threat that this imbalance poses to our habitat and resolve to do what can be done to modify that threat. It requires boldness, ingenuity, real altruism, faith in ourselves, and faith in the enabling aid of Divine Providence. This observer believes that these efforts will need a deep and pervasive spiritual dimension if they are to succeed.

If we recognize that the Deity is the Creator and Sustainer of all things, we then also recognize that in a very true and real sense the natural laws and forces that maintain balance in nature are in fact the Creator's laws. Human disruption of these laws carries with it very serious moral consequences. The warming of the Earth is the moral responsibility of all peoples on Earth, not just those in the western consumer societies, but the more hungry third-world people as well, for they, too, are very much a part of the problem.

Ambassadors of God's Grace are being urgently recruited! The call extends to every human being on Earth; every human being on Earth can, in some measure, answer the call and become involved. With such an effort, catastrophe will be greatly moderated, perhaps even be set aside! We can be God's instruments of Salvation! There is hope!

We can begin with REFORESTATION! Trees take carbon dioxide out of the atmosphere to make wood and fiber as they grow. Let's plant trees. Let's conserve trees where they already exist. Let us add trees by the millions everywhere to sponge the carbon dioxide out of the air and to create beautiful landscapes, shade, cool and, yes, human resources, as well.

Trees do many things. In the bygone days of the dust bowl, trees were planted along fence rows and boundaries on the prairies of Kansas and Colorado as shelter belts. They tamed the ferocity of the surface winds; helped retain soil and water; provided mini-woods for wildlife habitat; and made a relatively cool and shady place to relax and rest from midday heat of the summer. Trees are carbon dioxide sponges!

Let us plant trees wherever vacant land is not being used for agriculture, even in areas where there aren't naturally many trees as in the prairies of Kansas and Colorado. Where land has been farmed and then abandoned, let us plant trees! Where the climate is hot and dry, let us plant hardy trees: Russian olive, hedge, red cedar, juniper, even ponderosa pine. Where climate permits, let us plant rapidly growing lush trees. Where land is farmed, everywhere, let us plant hedgerows and shelter belts of trees around them. And let us not forget to plant the rare and endangered species of trees to not only insure that they remain but to contribute to the critically important biodiversity of the planet.

Where existing woods and forests are being ravished by bulldozers and made into giant open-air bonfires, let us do whatever is possible to stop such waste! We do not need more pasture or grazing land. We need forests and woods! Let us encourage those who own wooded land to be part of the solution rather than to contribute to the problem. Let us encourage management of the woods we create, so that they grow as rapidly and gracefully as possible.

Help save the Earth by creating woods. We can all do that. You and I, most of us. We can plant a tree or two in our own yard. We can encourage our small towns to plant trees, especially where old trees are dying (as many elms are of Dutch elm disease).

We can encourage planting of green belts around our cities not only to sponge up the carbon dioxide generated by urban activity but to help remove other pollutants as well.

We can encourage developers to leave existing trees — to build around them. Where no trees exist, they should be planted in conjunction with the developments.

We can create English gardens that feature trees in church, civic and commercial courtyards.

Were the land is available, we can encourage wooded public parks within our cities.

Attention: developers, landowners, captains of industry, labor unions, entrepreneurs, planners, political leaders, parents, children, ranchers, farmers, factory workers, office dwellers — think trees! Let's create woods and forests.

There will be a discernible social benefit from all of this as it matures. The human species developed on the forest edge, and the need for trees in the environment, as well as open grass, lies deep within human nature. For those rushing, bustling, frantic people of contemporary urban centers, leafy green shade, grass, and flowers fill a basic inner human need and offer relief from the stress of city living at any level! The human benefits of nature's green can be enormous!

For tree planting to be truly effective, it must be worldwide! In various places around the world, local residents are realizing just this fact and they are beginning to respond. For example, much of the forest cover was stripped for fuel from the Himalayan Mountains in Nepal. A negative result not directly related to the greenhouse effect is the rapid runoff of water not held back by forest floor during the rainy season with consequent disastrous floods in Bangladesh. Now, children are planting trees in an effort to reforest the magnificent Himalayan Mountains. Let us encourage, through membership and activity in conservation organizations, efforts like this everywhere on Earth!

Reforestation alone will move our world back in the direction of carbon equilibrium and will significantly help, but will not, by itself, do the entire job. The ever-increasing injection of carbon dioxide into the atmosphere must be turned back radically! Cutting down drastically the consumption of fossil fuel is the only way that injection of carbon dioxide into the atmosphere will be reduced.

We will be forced to do this some time in the future, for the supplies of fossil fuel are finite and eventually will run out. A few years ago, we started to explore alternatives when the Arab oil embargo strangled our gasoline supplies. But the embargo ended, and it was simply easier and economically more profitable to set research and development of alternative fuels aside. Human nature and corporate profits may dictate that we delay the development of alternative fuels until petroleum supplies actually do run short and all of the delicate ecosystems overlying oil deposits have been disrupted or despoiled. Let us pray and hope otherwise! Let the alarming impending disaster of a warming Earth move our giant corporations to form radical new goals, spur our ingenuity, and inspire us to develop fuels that will maintain carbon balance.

This also would spur the research and development of new engines and carburetors and fuel tanks to utilize the new fuels. Racing cars such as those that speed around the Indy 500 do not burn gasoline but pure alcohol. Not much research and development would be required to create an attractive family car that burned alcohol. If legal steps mandated that the alcohol fuel be derived only from annually replenishable biological sources and not from petroleum, the carbon cycle for motor fuel would soon be in balance.

Engineers! Sharpen your pencils!

Ford, Chrysler, Honda, General Motors — get busy with this!

Electricity is generated from burning coal, vast quantities of coal. Great trainloads of coal empty themselves at generating plants daily. Pressure from dwindling supplies does not yet exist. But perhaps the hundreds of thousands of tons of carbon dioxide released from burning coal, which continues to make the blanket more efficient and does a progressively better job of warming our planet, will nudge the utilities into looking elsewhere. They, too, will eventually suffer from the greenhouse effect. As long ago as the mid-1960s, the combustion of trash as a fuel for power generation was tried experimentally. There are problems with it that have not been thoroughly worked out. But why should they be? Coal is available, and the coal-fired generating plants exist and the delivery system is usually efficient.

But organic solid waste is mostly of biological origin — including paper, cardboard, and derivatives of them — and burning this to generate electricity would move us in the direction of carbon balance and contribute significantly to solving landfill problems for cities as well. Enough early success was had with it to tell us that an inspired ingenuity could work out the remaining "bugs."

Engineers: take another look at this!

Owners and Boards of Utilities: encourage your designing engineers in this direction!

Our society burns vast quantities of natural methane gas to heat homes and public buildings. Eventually, those resources will run out. We have the scientific knowledge, and surely can develop the technology, to generate large quantities of methane gas from biological sources. In turn, we could cap off fossil underground stores of gas, reserving the latter for special needs or emergencies.

The process by which methane is created from organic matter is the same as occurs naturally in swamps by anaerobic (without oxygen) fermentation. For a time, it was popular for farmers who had manure to dispose of to set up a home system of methane generation and storage. This was often sufficient to eliminate dependence on a propane supplier. It is not impossible that cities, even large cities such as Chicago, could convert sewage disposal plants from aerobic to anaerobic digestion and sell the methane to consumers. Although there are initial economic and commercial barriers, they can be overcome.

Bio-engineers and city managers — get creative!

A fuel whose potential ought urgently to be explored is liquid hydrogen. The raw material is water, which is virtually inexhaustible, since the combustion of the hydrogen fuel would return the water, as vapor, to the environment. A perfectly balanced cycle could be maintained indefinitely. The suggestion would be that production of hydrogen take place along the seashore in places where full sunshine occurs most days of the year. The abundant solar energy would be converted to electrical energy that would, in turn, be used for electrolysis of the water to produce hydrogen. The engineering problems for creating such an industry on a large scale are formidable; yet the creativity of our bright engineering minds, encouraged by the leaders of the industries that retain their services, would find practical solutions to these problems. The need is urgent!

Oil companies: petroleum supplies will soon run out. Turn your expertise in this direction NOW! Don't wait until it's TOO LATE!

Are these changes possible? Absolutely! Engineering and technology can be developed to make them industrially and commercially practical. Human ingenuity has overcome much greater technological hurdles than appear to be offered by these suggestions.

The greatest limiting factor in today's society would appear to be economic — *corporate profits!*

These changes will cost money before they make money although they should make money eventually. How much is it worth for the Mississippi River Delta to remain near New Orleans rather than to be at or near Memphis or even St. Louis? *The warming is inevitable; the results promise to be disastrous.* But the severity of the warming can be lessened by the extent to which carbon balance can be restored. Is that worth something? These and similar efforts at using renewable biomass for energy are well worth exploring.

These suggestions show only the tip of the iceberg of the possibilities that might come to inspired bright minds with expertise in these fields. Consider this: many aspects of agribusiness and energy business have suffered severe economic setbacks in recent years. Even the word "depression" gets whispered by those involved. What would be the economic consequences if agribusiness and energy business worked together to produce rapidly growing, renewable high volume crops that would be converted industrially into fuels for automobiles, trains, aircraft, and for heating dwellings?

Agricultural engineers, chemical engineers, industrial giants: get your pencils busy and your computers humming.

On the long haul, this should not only solve some bothersome economic problems, but also should surely generate economic health. It would contribute immensely to a healthy, sustainable Earth. To repeat, lest this point be missed: the time is approaching when things such as this will have to be done, because fossil fuels will eventually be exhausted.

If we wait until that time, we — the human species — may not have to bother, for as the increased warming of the Earth sets in upon us and causes drastic reorientation of climate, rainfall, and sea levels, our struggle will be to survive if we can.

Let's do what we can — NOW! Let's move out of the inertia that puts things off until the emergency crashes down around us. THE FUTURE IS OURS TO SAVE!

Industrial giants, leaders of international industries: you are urgently invited to become involved in dealing with the warming Earth, for the success of our efforts desperately needs your involvement. Token support won't help; nor will throwing up a smoke screen of conflicting scientific opinions and conflicting interpretations of presently available data. You industrial giants have the resources to throw up such smoke screens for years to come and to use them to defer any direct involvement for years and years.

You industrial giants also have the resources to contribute immensely and creatively toward minimizing the inevitable warming and creating a sustainable, liveable, habitat for all human beings, as well as other life on Earth. Which will you do?

Corporate America, you do, indeed, bear a significant share of moral responsibility for the warming that is happening. How will you handle that? The all-encompassing consideration of corporate profits — will they persuade you to ignore your moral responsibility? Will you play a waiting game — at expense of the Earth and all who live on our planet — to see who gets on the bandwagon first?

You individual board members of giant industries: if your thinking leads to negative decisions, what will you say to a grandchild who asks during a cool spell of 110 degrees in the shade, "What was winter like when you were my age, Grandpa?" Industrial giants, *bear your responsibility*. Get on board! Nothing less than the future of the world is at stake. *Warming is inevitable.*

If we make the effort to do these and other things that will help to alleviate the greenhouse effect, we will be responding in a way similar to how the ancient Jewish people responded to the call of the prophet Joel. With our bodies, our ingenuity, our farms, our political systems, and the massive economic and technological power of our global industrial establishment, we will be doing a very positive kind of repentance for the problem we have caused and for which we are morally responsible. But our efforts will far transcend mere repentance. In these efforts, we will appear transfigured as the Sons and Daughters of God, for whom the Creation has been waiting and groaning. We will help to recreate the Earth, making it sustainable; we will be doing the work of Jesus; we will be ambassadors of His Grace! Our human creativity will enter its finest hour — participating with God in creativity! *Creation's long wait will be ended!*

> *Almighty God, in giving us dominion over things on earth, you made us fellow workers in your creation: Give us wisdom and reverence so to use the resources of nature, that no one may suffer from our abuse of them, and that generations yet to come may continue to praise you for your bounty; through Jesus Christ our Lord. Amen.*[1]

W. G. H.

* * *

TAKING ACTION

1. Save energy! In addition to turning off lights not in use, select energy-efficient windows for your house, insulate properly, and practice a multitude of seemingly minor but very important measures

for reducing energy in your home. Consider, for example, planting short, dense shrubs close to your home's foundation in order
to help insulate. (Source: North American Conference on Religion
and Ecology.)

2. Organize your travel. Plan your activities so that you need not
backtrack and drive unnecessary miles. Saving on gasoline is an
important measure in limiting fossil fuels.

3. Discipline yourself. Many gadgets are available on the market and
promoted on television ads. They are not really necessary and only
serve to consume yet more energy. They're fun, they're trendy, but
they're costly in terms of our environment. Make the distinction
between what you really need and what you are told you want.

4. Amory Lovins, one of the nation's leading energy experts, states
that the average American home has one square yard of holes in it.
(Source: *Garbage*, November–December 1989) When purchasing a
home, check for its energy efficiency. When building a home, learn
which builders are concerned with providing a well insulated home
as opposed to building subdivisions in order to meet deadlines. Don't
ask the builders. Ask the people who live in homes constructed by
the builders.

5. Keep your refrigerator and freezer at moderate temperatures.
Insulate your water heater with an insulation blanket and turn it
down to 120 degrees. (Source: *Utne Reader*, November–December
1989)

6. Plant deciduous shade trees to protect west windows from summer
sun. Plant trees, including fruit and nut trees as well as rare species
of trees in order to insure the species. Donate trees to your city
or county parks if you have no room in your yard. Give trees for
memorials.

7. Use the solar dryer. It's not always available (depending on your
climate) but it is absolutely free, does not require any energy, and
adds nothing to your monthly utility bill. And when you use an
electric dryer, keep the lint screen clean.

8. If you are healthy and do not have circulatory or other problems,
keep your thermostat at sixty-eight degrees in the winter time and
put on a sweater. If you are over sixty-five years of age, be cautious
about turning down your thermostat. You need your home a little
warmer; just be sure it's well insulated.

9. Demand that corporations produce energy-efficient products. The automobile industry reportedly already has designs and knows what to do. Their excuse is that the public doesn't care. Show them you do care. As the Earth heats up, as the climate changes, as we experience more and more "natural" disasters, we are going to have to make changes in favor of energy efficiency everywhere we can.

TREES:
OUR *LIVE* SUPPORT SYSTEM

— 3 —

Tropical Forests

Douglas B. Trent

Less than 10 percent of the Brazilian coastal forest that Darwin admired remains today. Barely 2 percent of the tropical dry forest that once cloaked the Pacific Coast from Central America to the Gulf of California still stands.

Edward C. Wolf

Our planet's biological treasurehouses, the tropical forests, are being pillaged. The consequences will forever impoverish mankind — and all life in the future.... The impact of tropical deforestation has been linked to the effects of Nuclear War.

Craig Van Note

Preface

As a nature tour operator in Brazil, I have the good fortune to visit a number of tropical forests regularly. The incredible diversity of plants, birds, insects, and mammals still holds me in wonder. The roar of the jaguar, the metallic-blue Morpho butterflies, the myriad of orchids and bromeliads, and the colorful toucans, trogons, hummingbirds, and tanagers leave the visitor with a sense of blissful stability. Time stands still. The forest has more life than we have been able to classify and name. We're much further still from understanding the intricacies that allow tropical forests to exist.

The peace we find in the forest, however, is misleading. Most tropical forests I visit require me to travel through what used to be tropical forests, now reduced to vast stretches of brown hillsides,

sandy wastelands, and cattle ranches. The smell of smoke is not unusual in the forest, no matter how far in you are. Airports were shut
down for days on end because of smoke this year. And last year.
And the year before. Places where I have watched Marsh Deer feed,
play, and mate are now charred stubble. I've camped in the rain forest next to crystal clear rivers above great falls. Now the rivers are
brown with about half the previous volume of water, and the rain
forest is pushed back to the horizon. The Kayapo, Yanonami, Zingu,
and a hundred other Indian tribes are suffering from introduced diseases, the destruction of the homelands, and invasion of their land.
Where has the jaguar gone? The anteater? The monkeys?

Perhaps it is too easy to dismiss this destruction when you don't
see it happening. Perhaps Latin America, Southeast Asia, Africa, and
even Hawaii are too far and foreign to be concerned with. Still, I'm
willing to bet the complacency in some of us comes from a different
source.

The rain forest is Earth's richest resource. It is imperative that
we all learn about it. Throughout history, we have united our voices
and resources to help others when we became aware of the need.

What Is a Rain Forest?

Rain forest is a loosely applied term used to cover all types of tropical
moist forests. Tropical forests are defined by a number of factors,
usually rainfall and temperature. The tropics, that area between the
Tropic of Cancer and the Tropic of Capricorn, contain most of the
tropical moist forests. Vegetation in tropical areas that receive less
than twenty inches of rainfall per year consists of scrub brush and
thorn woodlands. Broad-leaved deciduous forests (sometimes called
"moist forests") occur when rainfall reaches 39–157 inches a year.
Rain forests receive between 157 and 393 inches per year, and the
temperatures are higher, averaging eighty-one degrees Fahrenheit.

Most significantly, rain forests host a much more diverse flora and
fauna. A typical moist forest will have only half as many species as
a rain forest, and a typical dry forest will have only a third as many
species as a moist forest.

It is not as important that the average person be able to define the
various kinds of tropical forests as it is to be aware that technical differences exist. Let me show you why. Last year I, along with several
thousand other concerned citizens, wrote Coca-Cola asking them to
reconsider their plans to deforest a huge portion of Belize. I pointed
out the importance of the rain forest ecosystem. The response I received stated that Coca-Cola had no plans to destroy any rain forest
in Belize. What they didn't say was that the 196,000 acres they were

planning to deforest was not *rain forest,* but technically another type of tropical moist forest. Don't be fooled by this technical jargon.

Other necessary distinctions are made between primary, secondary, and degraded forests. A primary forest has reached a state of maturity and equilibrium. It has worked its way through different states of development to the state of ultimate diversity and complexity. Primary forests are sometimes known as climax forests and virgin forests.

If a patch of primary forest is cleared and left alone, it will begin to regenerate. Grasses and other weedy ground cover will invade almost immediately, followed by taller, woody plants that will sprout up shortly thereafter. As new plant species appear, more insects, birds, and animals begin to use the land. They contribute to this secondary growth by bringing seeds from other areas, and in so doing, new plants are introduced. In about twenty years time, the amount of forest biomass will peak. This, then, is a secondary forest.

After about seventy-five years, this secondary forest will appear to the untrained eye to be just like the original primary forest. In fact, it will harbor only about a fourth of the plant and animal species of a primary forest. The trees will not be as long-lived. More energy will be put into seeds that are dispersed by wind rather than animals. As similar appearing as a secondary forest can be, it is in fact, only remotely similar to the primary forest. It will take four to six hundred years for that secondary forest to evolve back into a primary forest. Some scientists have good evidence that the forest evolution can take over a thousand years.

A degraded forest has been interfered with to the point that it is no longer able to regenerate itself. Fifty million acres of tropical forests in Indonesia have been degraded to alang-alang grasslands through overuse.

A primary forest, therefore, is by far the most valuable in bioecological and economic terms. Although tropical forests cover only about 6 percent of Earth's land surface and comprise just under one-third of all the world's forests, they contain over four-fifths (80 percent) of the Earth's vegetation.

At one time, primary forests covered sixteen million square kilometers of the Earth's surface. Today, nine million square kilometers of that remain, at best. Roughly five million square kilometers are in Latin America with Brazil alone accounting for a third of the world's total. Some two million square kilometers are in Asia, mostly Southeast Asia. Indonesia had 10 percent of the world's total. The remaining part is found on a few Indian ocean and Pacific ocean islands. Of the original forest cover, Latin America and Asia have lost about 40 percent. Africa is over 50 percent deforested.

SOIL AND NUTRIENTS

In spite of the fact that tropical moist forests, especially rain forests, are so lush, the vast majority of their soil types are extremely poor. This misunderstood fact — how can soil that produces that much growth be poor? — has been responsible for much of the destruction. The answer lies in the highly complex systems for recycling forest nutrients that have evolved.

Rainfall is the major source of nutrients. In the Brazilian Amazon, rainfall can deliver 6.6 pounds of phosphorous, 4.4 pounds of iron, and 22 pounds of nitrogen per hectare (2.471 acres) each year. These nutrients are then filtered out by the several layers of leaves that the rain passes through on its way to the ground. I've been in torrential tropical downpours in Amazonia where only a light mist made it down to the rain forest floor.

The ground below the canopy is a tangle of roots. Some roots follow the surface for three hundred yards, while others climb up neighboring trees. With the soil being so poor, the roots get more nutrients on the surface. This tangled root mat is incredibly efficient at absorbing the nutrients from rotting vegetation on the surface and the little rainfall that makes it down this far.

The rain forest is structured in layers. The principal canopy is between 100 to 120 feet above the root mat. Taller trees will protrude above the canopy, reaching heights of at least 200 feet. Below the main canopy, there is a canopy of trees 50 to 80 feet tall. The main canopy receives more rain, sun, and wind than the lower areas which are darker, stiller, and more humid.

Diversity

Diversity (also referred to as biodiversity) has emerged as one of the most important concepts in the world today. The greater the number of plant and animal species in any given ecosystem the greater its chance for survival. A typical two-acre primary forest in the northern United States will most likely have no more than five species of trees on it, but several of each species. If it loses three of those to disease, it loses 60 percent of its total. The same sized plot of primary tropical forest is likely to have between fifty and two hundred species. Where there is greater diversity, there is less room for each species to have as many individuals. In an undisturbed forest, this is an advantage. More tree species provide more types of fruits, habitats, and resistance to disease.

The United States and Canada together have around 700 bird species. The city of Rio de Janeiro, alone, has 410, while Brazil has around 3,000. Thirty percent of all bird species are found in tropical forest habitats. About half of all the life species in the world are found in the 7 percent of land mass that supports tropical forests.

The majority of Brazil's 20,000 known plant species are in her three million square kilometers of forests. The US has roughly the same number of plant species over her nine million square kilometers. Costa Rica, with just fifty-two thousand square kilometers, supports 8,000 plant species. Great Britain, with nearly five times as much area, possesses only 1,443.

How does the destruction of tropical forests affect us? More than one might think. As Dr. Norman Myers points out in his book *The Primary Source,* one of the plants found there is related to the avocado. It could offer rot-resistant root stock to commercial growers in the tropics and sub-tropics, and to avocado consumers. A species related to the cacao is reputed to yield a tastier form of chocolate, which could contribute to the lives of locals and chocolate lovers everywhere. A number of species could be brought into commercial production.

The animals in the tropics are some of the most varied, bizarre, and developed on Earth. Species in the rain forest tend to be giants. Bamboos are grasses, but grow to be sixty feet high and thick enough to stop a herd of stampeding elephants, another tropical giant. Poinsettias are trees.

Insects make up 75 percent of all species on Earth. A few hundred butterfly species can be seen in an hour in some parts of eastern Amazonia. A sloth typically has twelve insect species living in its fur. Some are found only there. Researchers studying insect life in the forest canopy are reshaping our ideas about how many insect species exist. It is now thought to be very possible that thirty million arthropods (insects, spiders, millipedes, etc., with a hard-joined external skeleton) exist. The number could be ten times that. We simply don't have enough qualified researchers in the field. In the meantime, Brazil alone is losing ten thousand acres of primary forest each day.

A danger in being part of such a highly specialized scheme is that those life forms involved — insects, plants, and animals — are more likely to become extinct if their environment is disrupted. In the meantime, humankind goes headfirst into destroying the forests and the critical links between these species — this biodiversity — with almost no idea of what it is doing.

The Roots of Destruction

By far the biggest cause of tropical forest destruction is slash-and-burn agriculture. Around one person in twenty on Earth is a slash-

and-burn farmer. Around the world, the tropics are assaulted by poor people trying to scratch a living out of the forest.

Shifting cultivation has been practiced in a self-sustaining manner for thousands of years. Peasant farmers and Indians would clear a patch of forest and farm it for a few years until it lost its fertility. They would then leave the plot to regenerate, returning decades later. The problem now is not overpopulation of the original forest inhabitants, but rather massive programs to settle the tropical forests when overpopulation became a problem in the cities.

It is this urban overpopulation that led governments to promote settlement of their "wastelands," the forests. Throughout the world the same pattern occurs. The forest is cut into piles of brush and allowed to dry before being set ablaze. The thick ash is loaded with the nutrients of the destroyed vegetation, and the first year of crops is good. The second year's crop is often less than half of the first. The forest floor, by this time, has been baked by the tropical sun, leached by the downpours, and is unable to regenerate. The farmer cannot grow crops, and turns to another patch of forest to begin again. The Earth's oldest, most complex ecosystems are thus exterminated. *One hundred million years or more of continuous, uninterrupted growth is sacrificed for a couple of years of unsustainable farming.*

The problems, then, are caused by people who practice shifting cultivation but do not rotate their land. They lack the knowledge of the traditional forest dwellers and often scoff at their advice. Before leaving their original plot, they manage to permanently harm the land, leaving it useless for agriculture of forestry.

In Nigeria and the Ivory Coast, the deforestation rate is about 10 percent a year. Agricultural clearing of primary forests has, according to a 1981 FAO report, "significantly jeopardized the future of forestry in these countries and wasted a considerable potential wealth, much higher than that of the logs extracted before clearing." West African farmers are clearing forty-seven hundred acres of productive primary forest each day. In Latin America, two-thirds of the deforestation is for permanent use and not allowed to return to sustainable forest.

Many tropical forests have been deforested through government-sponsored colonization programs. In Brazil, thousands of temperate-zone farmers from the south were forced off their land. It was then used to plant soy and other export crops to help service Brazil's monstrous debt. The peasant farmers were provided transportation to the Amazon, where they tried to use their previous farming practices. Only a few farms located on rare, fertile soils are successful, and the people have no way or place to return to. The peasants are plagued by malaria, yellow fever, and a host of other tropical diseases. There are frequent conflicts with the Indians whose lands the colonists are invading. Promised agriculture support is nonexistent or too expensive to take advantage of. The only option in these crowded areas is to burn more forest.

The burning and destruction is so vast in Brazil that scientists believe it accounts for 10 percent of the global output of human-made carbon dioxide, one of the causes of the Earth's warming through the greenhouse effect.

Brazilian scientists estimated that in 1987, the fires in just the Brazilian portion of the Amazon destroyed seventy-seven thousand square miles, an area one-and-a-half times the size of New York State. Thirty thousand square miles of this was virgin forest.

Dr. Alberto Setzer of the Brazilian Space Research Center reports that smoke from the Amazon fires often rises to twelve thousand feet. The gases and particles are then lifted into jet streams and blown in the direction of Antarctica. Although we have no proof that the material is interacting with the ozone shield, the smoke contains gases such as methane and nitrogen oxides that are known to deplete ozone.

Dr. Setzer contends that even without the ozone question, the emissions present a serious problem. "They are large enough to cause significant changes in the chemical balance of the atmosphere and influence the global weather." Standing forests absorb carbon dioxide, thus reducing the amount of ozone-destructive gases. A burning forest releases it all at once. The tropical forests are, in fact, the greatest storehouse of land-based carbon dioxide. On just one day in September, 1987, satellite photos showed 7,603 different fires in just the Brazilian Amazon. Conservative estimates put the yearly total at 170,000. NASA satellite photos show that fires in Bolivia and Peru are increasing as well.

LOGGING

After slash-and-burn agriculture, logging is the next major cause of destruction. Some four billion cubic yards of wood were harvested in 1980. Over half of that was used to produce heat and power. The rest was "industrial wood," destined for construction or converted into paper, cardboard boxes, etc. In 1979, 75 percent of all log exports and 58 percent of the world production of hardwood logs came from Malaysia and Indonesia. Developed countries produce and use over 80 percent of the world's industrial wood. Japan accounts for over half and Europe imports more than 25 percent of all wood exports.

Tropical forests are increasingly annihilated as more people, especially citizens of developed countries, want more tropical hardwoods. An average American uses about one-and-a-half tons of wood each year. Wood is economically competitive compared to aluminum, steel, cement, and plastics, which require more energy in their production. American industries now consume over 1,500 million cubic meters of industrial wood, exceeding the weight of our steel and plastics consumption combined.

Your home may well contain products from the forests of Southeast Asia or Amazonia, perhaps the veneer on your dining room table, stereo speakers, windows, bedroom furniture, desk, salad bowls, cheeseboards, serving trays, window frames, decks, and siding. Over 250,000 mobile homes using tropical hardwoods are constructed each year in the United States. House remodeling is a larger industry than new construction. Remodeling typically uses far more tropical hardwoods than building the original structure.

Current methods of hardwood timbering practiced throughout the tropics are particularly damaging. The favored trees are the emergents — those towering high above the upper canopy. They, and to a much greater degree the trees below, are connected to each other by epiphytic vines, extravagant hanging roots, and interlocking branches. Each tree that falls takes down or fatally damages another fifty or so. Of the over one thousand tree species known in the Amazon, only around twenty are harvested. With the scattered nature of tropical forests, this means that the logger must travel a good distance between each tree he wants to harvest. Bulldozers push the trees over easily as their roots don't reach far into the soil. In doing this, they pack the soil so that rainfall cannot penetrate into it. Many roads are made into each area, and during the rainy season each road is used only once. A fallen tree is dragged through the mud, destroying the trail for the next. Perhaps the biggest negative effect of logging, however, is that once the logging crew abandons a forest the roads left behind open the way for a surge of colonists.

Japan is the largest importer of tropical hardwoods, even though two-thirds of that country is forested — a greater proportion than any other developed nation. Their own hardwood forests are increasingly off-limits to loggers as they import on the grounds that supplies are "cheap and abundant." After Japan, comes the United States. Demand in the US has grown faster than the growth rate of the GNP. Still, temperate hardwood forests in the US produce 50 percent more wood than the country uses, and a growing number of foresters point out that this could be doubled or even tripled within fifty years. Why are we not using our own supply of hardwoods? Because timber, plywood, and paneling materials can be imported for less (much the same as beef).

We could switch most of our logging practices to the two to three million square miles of secondary forests. When left to regenerate, the trees grow much faster than they do in a primary forest. Many of these have commercial value, especially for paper pulp, thin-slice plywood, some types of veneer, particleboard, chipboard, fiberboard, and laminated-wood products. All of these final products are in the leading sector of the timber trade. Secondary forests are usually close to settled areas, do not require new, expensive road systems, and are closer to markets. By planting secondary forests with desirable species and selectively taking out unwanted ones, we could produce most, if not all, of the industrial wood needed up to the year 2000.

WOOD FOR FUEL

Throughout much of the undeveloped world, the major heating and cooking fuel is wood. There has been an energy crisis created by the lack of fuelwood in the third world long before OPEC was formed.

Shortages in fuelwood cause problems not just for cooking but also in raising food to cook. As fuelwood supplies are depleted, people look for substitutes. In many countries, the preferred option is cattle dung. Over 400 million tons of dung are reported to be burnt each year in Asia and Africa. Each ton burnt can no longer be used as fertilizer. One ton of dung can enable land to produce 110 pounds of grain, representing a potential loss of 20 million tons of grain each year. That is enough to feed 100 million people a year. The market value of that grain is around $4 billion.

To take the pressure off of forests, there are a number of practical steps that could be taken. For example, in Java, the average stove is 6 percent efficient. An American gas stove is nearly 70 percent efficient. Simple, inexpensive improvements in stove design together with cooking pot improvements could save millions of tons of fuelwood each year.

We need approximately six hundred thousand hectares, an area the size of Texas, of fuelwood plantations to meet total third world needs. Many plantations have already been started, but the planting rate needs to be increased 500 percent immediately. Emergency areas such as West Africa need to step up planting to between fifteen and fifty times the current rate.

CATTLE IN THE FOREST

As landless peasants follow loggers into the forests, cattle ranchers follow the peasants. Cattle raising is the number one cause of tropical forest destruction in Latin America. If you've ever eaten a TV dinner, fast-food hamburger, or canned soup, chances are very good you've eaten some rain forest beef.

It is the large-scale cattle rancher that eliminates most forests in

Central America and Brazilian and Colombian Amazonia. Ranching activities account for twenty thousand square kilometers of forest loss in this area. This is much less than the amount deforested by loggers and forest farmers in Asia and Africa, but the rancher's impact is growing fast. Why? In response to international demand for beef. The United States accounts for most of this. Like logging, this is another area where our actions are responsible for the elimination of Earth's richest resource.

Why is this demand so great? It is partially due to Americans' seemingly insatiable appetite for beef. The US, with 5 percent of the world's population, is the largest beef producer, consumer, and importer. In 1940, the average US citizen consumed less than 80 pounds of beef each year. By 1976, that rose to over 140 pounds. The number has now dropped, but because of population growth, the overall total continues to increase.

US beef continues to be about twice as expensive as beef imported from Central America. The Meat Importers Council informs us that the vast majority of Central American meat is used to produce hamburgers, hotdogs, chili, stew, frozen dinners, baby foods, luncheon meat, salami, and other processed meat for humans. It also is used in dog food. Hamburgers alone account for over 35 percent of this. And the demand for cheap beef is not likely to let up.

Government estimates show that rain forest beef imports reduce the cost of a fast-food hamburger by five cents. Some fast-food chains admit that they use rain forest beef and others deny it. It is difficult to tell just who does because once beef is imported into the US, it is categorized as domestic beef. When a chain asserts it uses only domestic beef, it may not be aware of the beef's origins.

Japanese beef imports jumped 500 percent between 1960 and 1980. They eventually expect to import 125,000 tons, equal to what the US is currently importing from Central America. In the same time period, Western Europe beef imports jumped 45 percent. The governments of tropical rain forest countries are rapidly increasing their willingness to sacrifice the forests in order to raise cattle.

In 1950, about 12 percent of Costa Rican land had been converted to cattle pasture. Today, it is over 35 percent. In 1960, there were nine hundred thousand head of cattle; by 1980, there were 2.2 million. Clearing tropical forests this way is certainly one of the worst forms of destruction. Herbicides such as Agent Orange are used to kill the vegetation before it is burnt. The first year, a two-and-a-half acre plot can sustain one cow. This falls to one head of cattle on every eleven to fifteen acres in five years. The average beef yield is less than nine pounds per acre per year!

A number of US and other foreign corporations own or have a

part in ranching operations in Amazonia. The US consortium of Brescan-Swift-Armour-King Ranch has a $10 million, 720 square kilometer holding in eastern Amazonia. Other US companies with at least part shares include: Twin Agricultural and Industrial Developers, Caterpillar International, Beltec International, Dow Chemical, International Foods, Massey Ferguson, W. R. Grace, United Brands, Hublein and Sifco Industries, Anderson Clayton, Gulf and Western, and Goodyear. Ask them about it.

RAIN FOREST ROADS

Without roads, which are usually funded by international lending institutions such as the World Bank, the forest would be destroyed at a much slower rate. The Transamazonian Highway in Brazil, connecting Belem with Brasilia, was completed in 1959. It attracted 2.5 million settlers by 1978. In 1969, the Cuiaba-Porto Velho highway through Rondonia was completed. Rondonia experienced a growth rate of 21.3 percent annually until the road was paved in 1986. Over a quarter of all Amazonian deforestation in Brazil from 1966 to 1975 was caused by highway construction.

MINING

Although mining itself is a minor cause of deforestation, associated activities such as road building, toxic affluents dumped in rivers, and siltation of rivers and lakes increase its impact considerably. Many tropical forest countries are rich in mineral reserves. Peru and Ecuador have oil, and it has also recently been discovered in the Brazilian Amazon.

Many mineral deposit areas are also areas with a high number of endemic plants and animals. For this reason, the small area of deforestation can have a disproportionately destructive effect.

HYDROELECTRIC PROJECTS

Dams are other projects usually funded all or in part by multilateral lending institutions. While small, decentralized hydroelectric dams can be economical and appropriate, large dams rarely are. This is especially true in the regions with tropical forests.

Siltation is another problem. Fast-flowing rivers carry more of a load than slower ones. Deforestation of the river's watershed has been one of the biggest problems. Settlers attracted by the dam often settle above it, taking out the forest that maintains the flow of clean water. The hard, tropical downpours take much of the barren soil straight into the river, where it is deposited into the reservoir. As the lake fills, the amount of water available for electrical generation steadily declines.

FOREST DWELLERS

The traditional forest dwellers are the only people who can live and survive in a rain forest without damaging it. They don't drive animals to extinction with their hunting practices. They grow food on infertile soil. They know and use more medicinal, edible, and poisonous plants than our "educated" botanists can distinguish. They limit their own populations to what their environment can support more effectively than any society in the modern world.

As in our own country, the arrival of outsiders has meant death to the Indians. In the name of progress, Brazil's indigenous population fell from an estimated six to nine million in 1500, to just over two hundred thousand today. Indians have been shot, bombed, poisoned, infected with diseases, and forced off their lands.

Examples of the mistreatment of Indians abound. In many countries, they are not considered citizens. They are wards of the state, and the state is usually not too benevolent. Indian nations are often perceived as standing in the way of dams, mines, roads, and other assaults on their homelands.

The question is not whether Indians can adapt to mainstream cultures, but whether or not they will be given a chance to. When first encountering the dominant culture they need medicine and education to help them from being overwhelmed both physically and culturally. They should be made aware of the problems other tribes have faced. Likewise, they should be made aware of the negative side of the western life-style. Indians must understand how new products can affect various aspects of their life. Too often, tribes that hunted with bow and arrow for centuries have wiped out their wildlife with new firearms.

Governments might not be so willing to force them to conform or perish if they realized the value of Indian skills and knowledge. A World Bank report states, "Tribal knowledge encompasses the ecosystem in its entirety, of the interdependence of floral and faunal species, of the specificities of micro-zones and their interfaces, of seasonal and longer term variations in plant and animal life, reproduction, growth, movement and productivity: these aspects of tribal knowledge are almost always ignored or disregarded."

Some forest people are helping themselves. Brazil's Xavante Indians have joined together with other tribes and pro-Indian groups. They have brought pressure on the Brazilian government to better its treatment of Indians and demarcate Indian lands. The Xavantes lobby in the capital and give interviews to publicize their claims.

One Xavante leader was denied entrance into a government office for not wearing a suit and tie. On returning to his tribe, the Xavante passed a law prohibiting the visit of any Brazilian official who was not wearing a penis sheath, feathers, and body paint.

THE MDB CONNECTION —
ARE YOU FINANCING RAIN FOREST DESTRUCTION?

Multilateral development banks (MDBs) began after World War II. They were created to bankroll reconstruction and development in the third world. They are financed by governments in the developed countries and borrowed funds.

The four MDBs are: the World Bank, the Inter-American Development Bank, the Asian Development Bank, and the African Development Bank. Their purpose is to provide technical assistance and loans to underdeveloped countries. The US government is the largest contributor to the MDBs and thereby has the most influence over their policies.

The MDBs' cofinancing approach (private investors often match the loan at a three-to-one ratio) regularly ignores projects that are socially necessary but unprofitable. The World Bank and the other three MDBs lend over $22 billion to tropical forest countries each year. This generates another $66 billion per year from private investors.

The World Bank is notorious for funding ecologically devastating projects that destroy native cultures and destabilize local economies. Many projects are financed for political rather than economic reasons. Labor-intensive and small-scale projects are normally set aside in favor of grandiose "pork-barrel" projects that often turn handsome profits for a few wealthy investors. Anastasio Somoza and Ferdinand Marcos have done quite well with World Bank projects.

The World Bank is the principal financier of the cattle ranching, road building, transmigration, and other colonizing schemes previously mentioned. Through these and other projects, the World Bank plays a major role in tropical forest destruction.

As American taxpayers, we are responsible for at least 19 percent of the funding of these destructive projects. It comes out of our pockets. We are responsible for even more given the leverage of the United States in deciding which projects will be financed. A good portion of the three-to-one funding by private investors also falls on our shoulders.

The World Bank and other MDBs are responsible for much of the destruction of tropical forests. Directed in an appropriate and self-sustaining manner, they could provide the answer to many, if not most, of the problems threatening tropical forests.

Tropical Forests — Can We Live without Them?

If some spider or bird or monkey you've never heard of becomes extinct, what does it matter? Unfortunately, we may never know. But consider that between 25 percent and 40 percent of all products in your local pharmacy come from tropical forests. Brazil, with a third of the remaining forests in the world, has only identified about 10 percent of its forest plants. Only about 2 percent of these have even been looked at to see what value they might hold. And yet, estimates put the rate of extinction in Brazil alone, at between two and fifty species a day.

A number of products we use and consume every day come from, came from, or owe their continued existence to tropical forests. These include coffee, bananas, papayas, avocados, chocolate, mangoes, rubber, antibiotics, tranquilizers, analgesics, cosmetics, bread, rice, many vegetables, spices, doors, floors, furniture, plastics, waxes, resins, dyes, and many, many other household substances.

In the 1920s, the US sugarcane crop crashed from producing over 180,000 tons per year to a mere 43,000 tons. Aphids were transmitting a mosaic virus, and the industry was in serious trouble. Research in Java found some mosaic tolerant varieties growing wild, and the appropriate genes were introduced, saving the US sugarcane industry from bankruptcy.

In 1970, a rust disease appeared in southern Brazil. At least thirty varieties spread to coffee plantations all the way north to Central America, threatening the $4 billion per year crop and major source of foreign exchange. Fungicides were too expensive for most farmers to use. Crop geneticists then found a rust-resistant strain from the forests of Ethiopia, where coffee originated. Eighty percent of Ethiopia's forests were gone by then, but the geneticist got there in time. That forest is now gone.

Twenty plant species provide nearly 95 percent of all food consumed by humankind. Four of those provide 80 percent, which means they support the majority of the human species. Even as you read this, the genes necessary to maintain these may pass into extinction. Is this not an extremely precarious situation?

When we consider that the average American consumes one hundred pounds of sugar each year, we realize the potential success of a natural sweetening agent that doesn't add unneeded calories to our diet or threaten us with cancer. Sugar is a key factor in problems associated with being overweight and is also associated with problems such as heart disorders and tooth decay. Tropical forest plants provide many such substitutes. Consider West Africa's serendipity berry. It has a sweetener three thousand times greater than that of sucrose.

Considered to be a miracle fruit, West Africa's *Synsepalum dulcificum* berry is so sweet it can be eaten with lemons and limes. The katemfe *Thaumatococus danielli,* from the same country, is sixteen hundred times sweeter than sucrose. It is now being widely marketed in England under the trade name Talin. It is strongly established in Japan and may soon be seen on American tables.

Tropical forests are the source of many natural pesticides. Insect pests consume 40 percent of the world's annual food crops. Plants in the forest cannot run away from those that would eat them and have developed biodegradable toxins specific to their insect predators. In fact, many tropical plants that are toxic to one insect are inhabited by another. Some of the defenses make the insect pest sick, while others cause it to molt at the wrong phase of the life cycle. This leaves the insect in a perpetual but harmless juvenile state. Other defenses inhibit the reproductive mechanism of the insects.

Lonchocarpus, a fish species from the Brazilian Amazon, provides a perfect example of animal contributions to natural pesticide production. It produces a poison that is the principal source of rotenone, a commercially important, biodegradable pesticide.

Tropical forests can also provide natural enemies against weeds. The alligator weed in the US created several problems in rivers, lakes, irrigation canals, boating waterways, etc. No herbicide used against it was effective. A flea beetle brought in from South American forests, however, provided a solution. The alligator weed is its preferred host.

The economics of natural pesticides are highly favorable. There is a 4:1 benefit-to-cost ratio for chemical pesticides, while there is a 30:1 benefit-to-cost ratio for importing beneficial organisms. Several natural enemies have been brought in from the tropical forests to date. If we can keep our forest resources from being eliminated the best times still lie ahead for natural pesticide control.

Tropical forests are virtual pharmaceutical factories. Tribal people have long used the plants of the forests to provide their medicinal needs. Some thirteen hundred plant species are used as medicines and for related purposes in northwestern Amazonia alone. Traditional healers in Southeast Asia use around sixty-five hundred plants in treating malaria, stomach ulcers, syphilis, and other disorders. Our pharmaceutical products that owe their existence to tropical forest origins have a worldwide commercial value of $20 billion annually. Medicinal laboratories in the developed countries are screening a good number of other tropical plants to see what they might hold.

The alkaloid drugs vincristine and vinblastine are derived from the Madagascar forest plant commonly known as the rosy periwinkle.

Used by traditional healers for centuries, these alkaloids have increased the chances for survival of a child suffering from leukemia from 20 percent to 80 percent.

There are an estimated fourteen hundred plants that may contain anti-cancer products. Seventy percent of our current anti-cancer products came from tropical forests. The taheebo tree of central South America has been used by the Callaways, descendants of the Incas. Many parts of the tree are used by them against cancer and a number of other diseases recognized as "incurable" by western doctors. Recently however, bark extracts have been successfully used to cure leukemia. Taheebo has also been used to treat debilitating diseases such as lupus, Parkinson's disease, Hodgkin's disease, and others.

Curare was introduced to us by the Rayas Indians of the Amazon. It is derived from the bark of a rain forest tree and is used to relax skeletal muscles. The Rayas use curare to tip their arrows to paralyze their prey. In the 1800s it began to be tested, and today, a product derived from it is essential to eye and abdominal surgery, tonsillectomies, and a number of other surgical procedures. Curare cannot be chemically synthesized in the laboratory. It must be gathered from a healthy rain forest.

These are just a few of the thousands of forest substances that have been and can be developed. Yet tropical forest plants are still so unknown to scientists that only 1 percent of the plants have undergone intensive screening. Plants that hold promise are quickly disappearing.

The babassu palm grows wild in the forests of Brazil. The babassu nut is 72 percent oil, a higher proportion than the coconut. A single tree can produce up to a ton of nuts per year. The oil is suitable for making margarine, shortening, toilet soaps, fatty acids, and detergents among other things. It serves industrial purposes in manufacturing plastic. During World War II, babassu oil was converted into a liquid fuel which burned cleanly and effectively in both internal and external combustion engines. The seedcake (what remains in the nut once the oil is extracted) is 27 percent protein and makes an excellent animal feed. The leaves yield high-value waxes. A one-hectare stand of five hundred trees is capable of producing 125 barrels of oil a year. The remaining seedcake could produce nearly six tons of edible protein and 250 barrels of ethanol as a by-product. Shell Oil's chemical division is studying babassu, but not for its oil. The babassu possesses an ambergris substitute. Ambergris is found in the intestines and nosebone of sperm whales. Because of its extremely high surface area, it releases aromas slowly and is used to make perfumes. Now that whales are finally beginning to be protected, babassu may begin to play a bigger role in the world economy.

A number of tropical forest plants, like the babassu, can provide gasoline substitutes and other energy forms. Already biomass energy accounts for one-seventh of the world's energy production, mostly in the form of fuelwood. Fuel plantations, however, are so promising that the Volkswagen Corporation has estimated that by the year 2000, one car in three will be fueled by such a plantation. Brazil is in the foreground with alcohol-burning cars. Produced from sugarcane, "alcool" is around 60 percent efficient. One stick of sugarcane moves a car one kilometer. Corn, cassave, sugar beet, elephant grass, Bermuda grass, sudan grass, and certain swamp reeds can be turned into biomass. Still, it is safe to assume we have not yet discovered the most promising species.

VITAL ENVIRONMENTAL INTERRELATIONSHIPS

As a result of the loss of tropical rain forests, disastrous floods in India have caused immeasurable suffering and financial costs of one billion dollars. The loss of tropical rain forests in Indonesia has caused extended droughts and the erosion of 20 percent of its land surface.

Tropical forests harness rain's productive capacity while, at the same time, minimizing its destructive potential. Tropical forests cover one-sixteenth of the world's land surface, yet receive a full one-half of its rainfall. They absorb 75 percent of the rain, while the other 25 percent is transpired and evaporated back into the atmosphere. The forest then releases the water, slowly and evenly throughout the year, into the watercourses. Tropical forests moderate extremes. When the forests are cleared, the water is released all at once, causing massive erosion, floods, and severe droughts in the dry season. A single storm in the humid tropics can wash over seventy tons of soil per acre into a river.

Deforestation in many tropical countries is causing landslides, rockfalls, and increased damage from earthquakes. Rain falling on denuded hillsides has caused landslides that have swept away roads and even villages. Terraced croplands have been washed away after the forest above them was cut for fuelwood. Forested lands are much more able to withstand earthquakes as the land is secured by the trees.

Much of the world is heavily dependent on irrigation to raise food. Forest destruction destabilizes the continuous flow of water, threatening the crops irrigated. Some 15 percent of all arable land is irrigated, producing about 30 percent of the world's foods.

Deforestation increases erosion, which is already a major problem throughout the world. Ten percent of the country of Ethiopia was covered with tropical forest thirty years ago. That has been reduced by over 60 percent, causing incredible amounts of topsoil to erode into the Blue Nile. This erosion has played a big part in silting up the Roseires Dam hundreds of miles downstream in Sudan. Ethiopia, in the meantime, is suffering from massive starvation.

The Panama Canal is threatened by siltation. In the 1950s, 85 percent of the watershed was covered with rain forests. By 1970, a third of that had been deforested for cattle ranching and crop growing. If the current trends continue, virtually all of the watershed will be deforested in the next twelve years. The problems are already starting to affect the operation of the canal.

In the Caribbean, many islands have lost all or most of their forests. Forests act as a buffer against cyclones and other freak weather phenomenon. Damage worldwide from cyclones now tops four billion dollars annually. This represents a sixfold increase in twenty years. Part of this increase is due to increased coastal population, but the largest part is due to deforestation.

The virtues of tropical forests are too often not realized until damage to them is irreversible. They rarely enter into developer's cost-to-benefit ratios. It is hard to put a dollar tag on the benefit of a standing forest, but it is painfully easy to put one on the damages that result when an area is deforested.

TROPICAL FORESTS AND CLIMATE

The connection between tropical forests and the climate is not fully understood, but we do know it to be a close one.

Tropical forests represent the largest mass of landlocked carbon. Burning the forest releases this carbon into the upper atmosphere, adding to the greenhouse effect we have been made aware of recently.

When the sun's light meets the Earth's atmosphere, 24 percent of that light makes it through to the surface. Tropical forests absorb light, using it for photosynthesis. When a large amount of forest cover is removed, the ground reflects rather than absorbs the light. That changes the overall heat balance, disrupting mass air circulation and causing shifts in rainfall. If too much forest is removed, and we do not know what too much is, meteorologists expect that there will be an increase in rainfall in the arid zones immediately above the equator, coupled with a rainfall reduction in the major cereal-growing regions of the world.

The carbon released into the air by burning absorbs solar radiation, warming the air through the greenhouse effect. Although most of the current carbon buildup is attributed to automobile exhaust, deforestation contributes to the process. In addition, tropical forest burnings are on the increase.

A temperature rise will cause the poles to melt, at least partially. According to the National Science Foundation, ocean levels have already started to rise. Thirty-five percent of the world population lives within thirty-five miles of the coast, and many of our major cities may have to be relocated.

The bulk of Earth's 40,000 billion tons of carbon is locked away on the ocean bottoms. Large scale atmospheric warming may cause a planetary feedback effect, causing the oceans, in turn, to release this carbon, warming the atmosphere even more. Many scientists believe that this is what happened between the Mesozoic and Cainozoic periods (225 million to 70 million years ago). The shift in climate at that time resulted in the extinction of 75 percent of the Earth's species. Unfortunately, the climatic changes we are beginning to experience are coming on much faster now than then.

As the water warms, the chances of hurricanes become greater. The likelihood is that hurricanes will occur more often and will be considerably more devastating.

There is evidence that leads some scientists to point out that human-made climatic changes may come all at once or in great bounds rather than little by little. We are ill-prepared to deal with changes on this scale.

We must pay attention to the trends because by the time we could prove beyond a doubt that these or other processes are occurring, an irreversible chain reaction would have long since been set in motion. We have many other options for using both the forests and fossil fuels. Will we choose instead to do nothing and continue with our lemming-like stupidity, pursuing our present course?

Conservation is not the art of keeping pretty birds and flowers alive; it is the art of keeping our options open for the future. This is a time to embrace challenge. Never has humankind been offered the opportunity to do so much for ourselves and future generations. Never have the consequences of not meeting the challenge been so severe.

D. B. T.

* * *

TAKING ACTION

1. Join and support conservation organizations. Join a conservation organization that is seriously working on the problems of deforestation. Several organizations focusing on tropical forest destruction are: Rainforest Action Network, World Wildlife Fund, Nature Conservancy. (Addresses are in the appendix.)

2. Write letters. Put pressure on the World Bank (its address is 1818 H St., NW, Washington, DC 20433), timber companies, companies involved in deforesting practices, our government, and others. For a current list of those involved in deforestation, contact the Rainforest Action Network. They also send out monthly "Alert" notices that are excellent for both keeping you informed and concentrating pressure where it is needed most.

3. Educate yourself. We can help relieve the pressures on Earth's richest resource by educating ourselves. The material presented in this chapter is but an introduction to the tropical forest situation. You don't need to become an expert, but you will need to be able to explain the story to others if we are going to be able to work together. Recommended are Catherine Caufield's *In the Rainforest: Report from a Strange, Beautiful, Imperiled World* and *Tropical Moist Forest: The Resource, The People, The Threat*; Norman Myers' *The Primary Source: Tropical Forests and Our Future*; Charles Secrett's *Rainforest: Protecting the Planet's Richest Resource.*

4. Remember your role in deforestation. Think of how you personally are involved in the deforestation process and what you can do to change it.

   A. Buy products (salad bowls, furniture, lumber for remodeling) made from wood other than from rain forest trees. Be sure you know where your wood products come from.

   B. Boycott fast-food producers that use tropical forest beef, letting them know it and why. Most of these companies spend millions of dollars on "image" advertising and are very sensitive about negative publicity. Keep track of which fast-food chains are still using rain forest beef from organizations such as the Rainforest Action Network.

   C. Boycott companies (both American and foreign) who continue to deforest. Keep in touch with the Rainforest Action Network and *Catalyst* (64 Main Street, 2nd Floor, Montpelier, VT 05602) to see who is involved in deforestation and if the players change.

5. Help put out fires! The World Bank-financed Cuiaba-Porto Velho highway opened up fragile Amazon rain forests to ranchers and timber barons who clear rain forest by burning. The province of Rondonia, one of the richest ecosystems in the world, has lost nearly 20 percent of its rain forest. Send a letter to the General Secretary of the United Nations Environmental Programme asking for global action to put out the Amazon fires. Write: Mostafa Kamal Tolba, Executive Director, United Nations Environment Programme, P.O. Box 30552, Nairobi, Kenya. (Source: Rainforest Action Network)

6. Trace the source of beef. Because beef is not labeled with its country of origin upon entering the US, there is no way to ascertain its source. Until there is such a law, don't eat fast-food hamburgers or processed beef products. Write to the secretary of agriculture, currently Clayton Yeutter, and let him know you want a beef-labeling law to specify the country of origin. His address is 14th St. and Independence Ave., SW, Washington, DC 20250. (Source: Rainforest Action Network)

— 4 —

The Deforestation of America

T. H. Watkins and Staff, the Wilderness Society

> Any fool can destroy trees. They cannot run away; and if they
> could, they would still be destroyed — chased and hunted down
> as long as fun or a dollar could be got out of their bark hides.
>
> John Muir

No other nation has attempted to preserve and protect so much of its
forest landscape for public use and enjoyment as the United States.
Our national forests — which belong to all Americans — encom-
pass 191 million acres, an area equal to Illinois, Iowa, Michigan,
Minnesota, and Wisconsin combined.

These forests contain some of the most striking natural beauty
on Earth: from the rich, green rain forests to the Pacific Northwest to the multicolored groves of the southern Appalachians; from
the fjords and misty isles of southeast Alaska to the bogs and piney
mysteries of the old North Woods country around our Great Lakes.

Throughout the mountains of western Washington and Oregon,
and northern California stand the last remnants of some of the
world's most magnificent forests. These ancient forests of the Pacific Northwest harbor some of the world's oldest and largest trees:
cedar, Douglas fir, western hemlock, and Sitka spruce. Some were
seedlings when the Magna Carta was signed more than seven hundred years ago, and now tower as much as 250 feet above the forest
floor. They are ecological history books whose growth parallels the
rise of the modern world.

The ancient forests of the Pacific Northwest are found primarily in twelve national forests in a band running from north-central

Washington to northwestern California. Much of the land in this region, once cloaked in bountiful coniferous forests, is now pock-marked from decades of clear-cut logging. What is left in many instances are mere fragments of the ancient forests, which are precious for their very scarcity and prized for their biological diversity, recreation opportunities, and scenic beauty.

But every day these forests grow smaller. Thread by thread, the intricately woven tapestry that is the ancient forest ecosystem is being destroyed. These forests have been cut at a furious rate for decades and the US Forest Service proposes to continue heavy logging there. It says there is plenty of old growth left. But there is not, and the fight to save the forests is at a critical stage.

In addition to valuable resources such as timber and minerals, the national forests also harbor an immense treasure that cannot as easily be measured in dollars and cents: wildlife habitat, pristine water sheds, recreation opportunities, wilderness, and a wealth of untapped scientific information.

The forest floor and canopy are home to an exceptional variety of unique, and in some cases rare, plants and animals. More than two hundred wildlife species have been counted in the ancient forests from the endangered northern spotted owl to more common game animals such as black-tailed deer, elk, and black bears. A single ancient tree is home to one hundred separate plant species. More than fifteen hundred species of invertebrates can inhabit the canopy of an old-growth stand.

Biological diversity is the essential resource that helps provide humankind with new foods and medicines, clean air and water, energy, and building materials. Researchers have found that the bark of the Pacific yew tree, for example, contains a chemical that fights cancerous tumors in mice and may have application in cancer treatments for humans.

Our national forests are also important for their recreational opportunities — their thousands of campgrounds and other recreational facilities and their ninety-nine thousand miles of trails. Indeed, there are more recreational visits to our national forests than there are to our national parks. Our national forests also provide clean drinking water for hundreds of communities, support three thousand species of wildlife and fish, and sustain important commercial fisheries.

The United States Forest Service was created more than eighty years ago to conserve these lands and manage them wisely for today and for future generations. Most Americans consequently think of the forestlands as a national treasure strongly protected by federal law.

Yet today these forests are being slashed with the most expensive dirt roads in the world, bulldozed, chainsawed, and cut clear of vast expanses of timber at a frightening pace — all under the direction and leadership of the very agency created to protect them: the US Forest Service.

Our ancient forests are now being liquidated at the rate of forty-two thousand acres per year. Roughly 85 percent of the original endowment of approximately nineteen million acres of ecologically-significant old growth has been lost to logging. Most of the old growth will be gone within fifteen years if logging continues at the present pace.

For years the Forest Service has overstated the size of the remaining ancient forests. The fact is that the ancient forests are scarcer than the Forest Service has previously acknowledged. A study by the Wilderness Society found that there was, at a minimum, 50 to 60 percent less ecologically-significant old growth left on the twelve westside forests as the Forest Service claimed. Additionally, even these remaining forests are being highly fragmented, destroying their ecological integrity.

A bitter irony is that American taxpayers are subsidizing the destruction of their own national forest system — at an annual cost of more than $400 million.

The Bankruptcy Factor

By law, Congress has directed the Forest Service to administer the national forests for all of their multiple uses in a carefully balanced manner — for outdoor recreation, clean water, and protection of fish and wildlife habitat as well as timber and range. Yet during the past quarter century the Forest Service has ignored this mandate and concentrated almost solely on logging and road construction.

Today, the national forests account for 17 percent of the nation's timber harvest. But in running this vast logging empire, the Forest Service is doing something no private company could ever do without going into bankruptcy: selling its stock in trade far below the cost of production.

In fact, according to the President's Office of Management and Budget, during fiscal year 1985, the Forest Service spent over $600 million more to administer its timber sales program and build logging roads than it received from sales of trees.

Over the past five years, nearly two-thirds of our national forests lost money selling timber.

Nowhere is the below-cost timber disaster demonstrated more dramatically than in southeast Alaska. Stretching over nearly seventeen million acres, an area larger than the state of West Virginia, the Tongass National Forest contains one of the few remaining largely intact rain forests in the Earth's temperate zone. Its eight-hundred-year-old Sitka spruce and hemlock stands are home for the largest concentrations of grizzly bears and bald eagles in the world. Since 1980, the Forest Service has spent more than $50 million per year to subsidize large-scale clear-cutting and road building on the Tongass, destroying an ecosystem of incalculable value — all in a futile attempt to preserve jobs that inevitably will be lost to a declining demand for Alaskan timber.

The principal beneficiaries of this subsidy are two large corporations, one Japanese-owned, that ship virtually all of the subsidized wood products to Pacific Rim countries. The public is charged one dollar for Forest Service maps of the Tongass; for the same price a timber company can buy a western hemlock tree, one hundred feet tall.

The costs of this wasteful policy are staggering. In 1985 and 1986, the Forest Service recovered less than one cent in timber payments for every dollar it spent on timber sales and road construction. Between 1977 and 1986, total losses in the Tongass were more than one-third of a billion dollars.

Private companies that behave this way are called bankrupt. They are driven out of the free-market economy. But the Forest Service has an advantage. It has access to the pockets of the taxpayers.

Roads to the Moon and Back?

The Forest Service now is in the process of completing fifty-year management plans for each of our national forests as ordered by the National Forest Management Act of 1976. Virtually all of its plans indicate that the Service intends to extend into the future the ruinous policy of favoring timber cutting and road building over all other uses.

More than 360,000 miles of logging roads — eight times the mileage of the entire Interstate Highway System — now crisscross our national forests. Ironically, these expensive and environmentally damaging roads serve in large part only to expedite access to more and more uneconomic timberland.

In Colorado's San Juan National Forest, a land of jutting peaks and alpine meadows, where timber sales lose seventy-nine cents for every taxpayer dollar invested, the Forest Service has already built 2,905 miles of logging roads. The agency plans to add 2,699 miles more.

In the Cherokee National Forest, which surrounds the Great

Smoky Mountains National Park and which contains one of the nation's most diverse wildlife habitats with over four hundred species, the Forest Service plans to add 1,400 miles of logging roads to the 1,540 miles already there. According to agency plans, these roads will enable the timber harvest to double, even though current harvests return only sixty-two cents for every taxpayer dollar spent growing and felling trees.

All seven national forests surrounding Yellowstone National Park lost money with four of them returning to the federal Treasury less than forty cents for every dollar spent on the timber program. Yet the Forest Service is planning to build nearly one thousand miles of new logging roads to access even more uneconomic timber.

These are but a few examples. In all, the Forest Service plans to build or rebuild 580,000 miles of forest roads over the next fifty years — more than enough to reach the moon and back.

These roads are built for the almost exclusive use of the timber industry. The out-of-pocket cost to American taxpayers for this roadbuilding frenzy is $200 million each year. But this is only a small part of the total price we pay, for the environmental damage done is far greater.

The Future of the Ancient Forests

Over the past ten years, the total timber harvest of the twelve westside national forests averaged 3.2 billion board feet per year, rising to record levels in 1987–1988. Mill productivity also rose during the early 1980s. Between 1980 and 1985, lumber production in the Pacific Northwest rose nearly 18 percent and plywood production increased 15 percent. Despite the high harvest levels, approximately ten thousand workers lost their jobs by 1985, a decline of 10 percent from a decade earlier. A major reason for those job losses is the increased productivity of mills in the region. The Oregon Economic Development Commission estimates that further productivity improvements will result in job losses four times greater than losses from timber supply problems. Overall, as many as thirty-five thousand timber jobs could be lost in the next forty-five years.

The Forest Service says it has an answer to this problem. Its plans call for an increase in logging to an average of 3.6 billion board feet annually. But state and local officials, resource planners, and economic development experts question whether increased logging of ancient forests will produce more jobs. Certainly, this approach will degrade the unique quality of life the ancient forests provide in the Pacific Northwest and could slow economic growth. The Forest Service's approach could prove damaging over the long run if industries seeking new homes or plant sites perceive that the quality of life has been diminished by extensive logging in the region.

If logging continues unchecked, the future of the ancient forests is bleak. Consider this picture of the Pacific Northwest in the twenty-first century if the Forest Service plans are fully implemented:

1. More than two million acres of ancient forest lost due to extensive logging, leaving fragmented forests with limited ecological value. The loss of biological diversity will deprive society of opportunities to advance its knowledge in such fields as medicine, ecology, and forestry. The ability of ancient forests to purify water supplies, used for drinking water in Pacific Northwest cities, will decline as streams become more vulnerable to erosion and sedimentation. Sport and commercial fisheries will face severe economic losses as well.

2. Loss of up to 50 percent of the critical habitat for the imperiled northern spotted owl due to logging of ancient forests. The vitality of the spotted owl's habitat, which takes centuries to develop, is essential because the spotted owl acts as an indicator of health of other species within the ancient forest ecosystem. Similar declines in habitat are expected for the pileated woodpecker, the Roosevelt elk, and the Columbian black-tailed deer.

3. More than 1.2 million acres of roadless areas opened up to development within fifteen years, resulting in a 50 percent reduction in roadless acreage. On just eight of the twelve westside forests, the Forest Service proposes to build an additional two thousand miles of new logging roads into virgin forests.

4. Recreation opportunities will be diminished and scenic beauty marred by clear-cutting of old-growth stands. Demand for roadless recreation will be nearly five times greater than anticipated capacity of five of the westside forests as a result of the destruction of ancient forests. Currently the national forests comprise the single largest supplier of outdoor recreation in the country — 237 million visitor days in 1987 alone.

Yet nearly all of the Forest Service's fifty-year plans released to date call for huge increases in the amount of timber offered for sale, the number of roads built, and the number of acres clear-cut. And powerful voices in the logging industry are pushing for yet more development — all of it courtesy of the American taxpayers, and much of it leading to the permanent destruction of all other values.

The Wilderness Society's Forest Management Goals

The National Forest System should be reoriented in order to restore a balance of uses. Our *public* forestland should be managed primarily not for the production of timber but for those *public* resources and benefits that private forestland cannot provide in a market economy — recreation, clean water, wildlife habitat, scenic beauty, biological diversity, wilderness, and scientific values. Once Congress and the public fully appreciate how flagrantly the Forest Service has distorted the congressional mandate assigned to it, they will require fundamental reforms and more strict accountability.

Specifically, the Wilderness Society has five immediate goals:

1. Adoption of a moratorium on Forest Service road construction, requiring the agency to retire its backlog of previously constructed roads and restore accountability to the program.

2. Repeal of the permanent federal appropriation to the Tongass National Forest timber program that costs the taxpayer $50 million per year.

3. Establishment of an orderly process for phasing out subsidized, below-cost timber sales.

4. Abolition of the obsolete timber pricing system that guarantees the timber buyer a profit but ignores the taxpayer costs for putting the timber up for sale.

5. Adoption of policies to preserve rare old-growth forest ecosystems.

These are ambitious objectives. They will require a complete overhaul of Forest Service policy. But they are realistic and achievable. They will allow our national forests to make the greatest possible contribution to the future well-being of our country.

Citizens will have an important role to play in deciding how their national forests will be used, and Congress and the Forest Service are responsive to public opinion. In particular, we must insist that the Forest Service abide by the National Forest Management Act of 1976 and adopt a more balanced approach to management of not only the ancient forests in the Pacific Northwest but all forests on taxpayers' (YOUR) land.

T. H. W.

* * *

ENVIRONMENT AND HEALTH

— 5 —

Twentieth-Century Living: Environmental Illness

Carolyn Gorman

> We do not have to quake helplessly in the face of cancer, "hoping" to escape its clutches. We do not have to sit by passively, watching our loved ones succumb to this disease. We do not have to spend our life savings, undergoing painful and devastating treatments that do little or no good. We are blessed now with the knowledge which enables us to make clear, life-giving choices. We need only to make them in time.
>
> John Robbins, *A Diet for a New America*

The twentieth century has been a century of phenomenal achievements for humankind. Advances in engineering, chemistry, and other sciences have enabled humankind to soar to outer space. Communications, once limited by wires, are now linked by satellites orbiting our shrinking Earth. Harnessing of electricity has progressed from kite string to atomic fission. Agriculture, once bound to house and plow and Earth, now encompasses sophisticated mechanized equipment, hybrids, grafts, chemicals, and irrigation. Medicine, once challenged by the bubonic plague and smallpox, now encompasses laser surgery, computerized body imaging, and transplanted organs.

The wonders of our victories are amazing, and the human race seems limited only by its imagination. However, the discoveries and the miracles of progress may be proceeding too rapidly. Rapid change has stressed the social, economic, and cultural fibers of society and the resources of the Earth. Overpopulation, irresponsible use of Earth's resources, and a total disregard for the delicate balance of the ecosystem have created problems that require the genius of humankind for solution.

For many, these advances make life in the twentieth century exciting, rewarding, bountiful, and fulfilling. For an increasing number of individuals, life on twentieth-century Earth is one of continual struggle to avoid illness. These people are victims of the twentieth century. Their struggle is with their environment; their condition is called environmental illness.

This new illness is a result of the body's reaction to inhalants (e.g., pollens, dust, mold), food, water, and chemicals. The symptoms of the illness are the result of the interplay of the body's reaction to the many physical and psychological stressors affecting it. The condition reflects the unique metabolic characteristics and nutritional status of the body, the biological individuality, genetic background, and the integrity of the immune and enzyme systems of the body.

Symptoms of environmental illness are as varied as the causes. Many people fail to perceive the cause and effect relationship between the substance and symptom. It has been estimated that as much as 60 percent of all illness may be linked or influenced by these environmental triggers.

Forty million Americans have pollen sensitivities, and an additional twenty million have food reactions of some kind. Many more may have either food or pollen sensitivities of which they are not aware. For example, if a person eats beef occasionally, he or she may notice a runny nose or coughing after ingestion of the beef. But if the food is eaten daily, symptoms may not be noticeable, illness may develop, and the person may be unaware of any systemic response to the offending food. Sneezing, runny nose, watery eyes, sinus pain and pressure, and asthma are common symptoms of the inhalant sensitive. Indigestion, joint pain, headaches, diarrhea, nausea, depression, and even asthma can be linked to food sensitivity.

These varied symptoms may occur as a vigorous response to naturally occurring substances encountered every day. The food we eat and the pollen, dust, and mold we breathe have existed for ages and are not products unique to the twentieth century. There is another aspect of environmental illness that enhances the body's response to food and air and water. This is the body's reaction to a myriad of chemicals that increasingly permeate our world. The presence of chemicals in air, food, water, and soil is an unnatural addition to the natural environment and is a major factor in the development of twentieth-century illness.

Chemical Sensitivity

Environmental illness is illness characterized by sensitivity to a variety of environmental substances. This sensitivity is heightened, and successful management of the symptom response becomes complicated and difficult, when the body also reacts to chemicals that may contaminate our food, water, and air. The chemicals in the air can complicate inhalant sensitivities because both can affect the same organ or area of the body. As an example, formaldehyde affects the eyes and respiration system, just as do pollen and mold. Chemicals in the form of dyes and preservatives can create symptoms irrespective of the existence of any sensitivity to the substances that contain them.

Chemicals not only complicate sensitivities, they can create reactions of their own. Individuals can exhibit sensitivities to cigarette smoke and perfume, car exhaust, and carbonless paper. Management of chemical sensitivities is difficult when avoidance is the treatment of choice.

The impact of chemicals on a life-style can be tremendous if, for example, one works in a smoke-filled office eight hours a day handling carbonless paper. The knowledge of the cause and effect of chemical exposure is frequently difficult to detect because of the continual contact with several chemicals. Even if one suspects a sensitivity problem or illness related to chemical exposure, acknowledgment tends to be slow as the individual strives to maintain job performance. This continuing contact may lower the body's level of tolerance, resulting in an increase in sensitivities and symptoms. Eventually, immune and detoxification systems can dysfunction, and environmental illness can become a reality.

Chemicals

Chemicals are an integral part of our world. They are part of the technological and industrial revolutions and, therefore, progress. However, we haven't always used them prudently with restraint and respect. Knowledge of their impact has not always been sufficient. We have enjoyed their benefits without due concern for the full effects of their use.

Chemicals have permeated almost every aspect of our ecosystem. They have become part of us. In one study of one hundred patients, levels of volatile organic chemicals such as benzene and ethylbenzene, known carcinogens, were found in every patient. Chlorinated pesticides such as DDT, dieldren, and chlordane were found in all but two of the subjects. According to the Environmental Protection Agency (EPA) studies, most Americans have over one hundred foreign chemicals in the fatty tissues. None of these chemicals should be in the blood, fat, or brain of anyone. These statistics are evidence of a major health threat that should be a concern to everyone.

How do chemicals enter our body? We absorb these substances through the food we eat, the water we drink and bathe in, and the air we breathe. Pesticides are one of the main contaminants of food. A pesticide is a highly toxic chemical used to kill insects, weeds, and pests on food crops. During the last three decades, pesticide usage has increased tenfold while the number of crop insects has doubled. The United States Department of Agriculture predicted that 439 billion pounds of pesticide would be used on ten major food crops in 1989. The use on corn alone would consume 226 million pounds of pesticide, soy beans 112 million pounds, and cotton 37 million pounds.

Many pesticides sold today have not been fully tested by the EPA, especially for their long-term health effects. Until 1970, pesticides did not have to pass stringent health or safety standards before being placed on the market. In 1972, Congress initiated more stringent health requirements for registering pesticides. These included tests to determine the long- and short-term effects on human health and environment. The EPA has faced a difficult task of reregistering and retesting over six hundred active ingredients in products registered before 1972. This review process is expensive and arduous, and the EPA estimates it will take another fifteen to twenty years to evaluate the pre-1972 pesticides. EPA considers only three hundred of the twelve hundred known inerts to be safe, while one hundred others are considered to be of toxicological concern.

The National Academy of Science reports that only about one-fifth of all pesticides sold in the United States have been adequately tested for cancer risk, only about one-half for their role in causing birth defects, and only about 10 percent for adverse effects on the nervous system. A group of seventy-five EPA experts ranked pesticide residues among the top three environmental cancer risks. Tested or not, health risk or not, these pesticides still remain on the market and pose serious risk to the young, the old, and people with health problems.

Food

Pesticides are extensively present in food. The EPA estimates that 100 percent of nonorganic grocery store food contains pesticides. These residues are known or suspected carcinogens and may affect central nervous system disorders. The Food and Drug Administration (FDA) and the California Department of Food and Agriculture

(CDFA) have detected pesticide residues in 63 percent of all strawberries, 55 percent of all peaches, and 53 percent of all celery.

The five most commonly detected pesticides in food are known or suspected carcinogens. Organochloride pesticides such as chlorophanothane, DDT, benzene hexachloride (BHC), and dieldren have been banned from usage in this country. However, because of their persistence in the soil, they are still part of the food chain. Captan, considered by the EPA to be a "probable human carcinogen," is still in legal use, and 33 percent of strawberries sampled by the FDA had Captan residues. Chlorothalonil, classified as another "probable human carcinogen" by the EPA, is still in use and was found on one-half of the celery sampled by the FDA in conjunction with the CFDA.

The organophosphates are another class of pesticides present in the food chain. These pesticides attack the central nervous system by inhibiting the enzyme, acetycholinesterase. This causes overstimulation of the central nervous system, thereby creating stomach upset and other nervous system symptoms. In one study, three or more organophosphates were found to be among the five most common pesticide residues on one-half of all foods sampled.

To this list of residues in food, add antioxidants, antimicrobials, steroids, hormones, dyes, and antibiotics. In February 1987, the Center for Disease Control stated that 60 percent of all cattle, 90 percent of all pigs and veal calves, and 100 percent of all poultry ate antibiotic-spiked feed. Antibiotics such as penicillin and tetracycline are used to control infection or disease in the host. Because of continued exposure, bacteria in the animal can become resistant to these antibiotics. If a person becomes ill after consuming a meat containing a resistant bacteria, treatment with these antibiotics may not destroy the bacteria. Treatment alternatives may be difficult, and illness may ensue. A National Academy of Science report of May 1987 concluded that many bacteria-laden chickens passed USDA inspection. Americans for Safe Food say at least one-half of all chickens contain salmonella. Visual inspection of birds will not detect the bacteria, and chemical tests that detect it are too slow to be used. These facts concerning antibiotics in food make it much less appetizing.

Hormones such as progesterone, estradiol, and testosterone, fed to animals to increase muscle and weight, may also increase cancer risk since certain hormones already present in the body are carcinogens. Therefore, the Federal Drug Administration (FDA) has advised that no one consume more than one percent of these hormones that are already present in the human body. Because a delicate hormonal balance exists in the human body, the addition of these residual hormones makes maintenance of a correct hormonal balance more difficult, thereby creating a serious health risk. Therefore, the USDA requires a fourteen-day waiting period between a hormone dose and slaughter in the hope that the hormone has been eliminated by the host. This is not always the case. In Puerto Rico, very young prepubescent children were experiencing changes attributed to puberty. Girls were developing breasts, and boys' voices were lowering. These occurrences were finally linked to hormones in chicken feed. The problem of hormone usage certainly should cause concern for individuals who eat meat, eggs, milk, and poultry.

Artificial food coloring, added to numerous gelatins, cereals, meats, pudding, and canned fruits and juices, is made from coal tar or petroleum. Dyes in our foods, while making them attractive, add undesirable chemicals that can create multiple sensitivity reactions. Food colorings have been linked to hyperactivity in children. Tartrazine, a yellow dye, has been known to cause reactions from hives to laryngeal edema. Red dye #3 has been named as a possible carcinogen. Therefore, the eye appeal that they give food may also cause a potential life-threatening sensitivity response to the colorings.

Sulfites added to salads, potato chips, soups, relishes, and wines may spark serious asthma attacks in steroid-dependent asthmatics. Butylated hydroxyanisole (BHA) and butylated hydrozytoluene (BHT) — common preservatives found in breakfast cereals, donuts, and potato chips — can cause eczema, hives, and asthma in sensitive individuals.

Because of the complexity of the problem, all people must exercise self-protection. The person who has elevated levels of pesticides in the blood and fat must strive to reduce additional exposure or face increased health risk. If regular grocery store food is used, careful selection must be exercised. Organ meats are to be avoided as they may contain concentrations of chemicals. Foods from foreign countries and the southern and eastern United States may contain more fungicides and pesticides than those from the western United States. Washing fruits and vegetables removes some pesticides, as does removing the outer leaves of lettuce. Peeled fruits usually contain fewer pesticides since the peeling removes some of the chemical.

In spite of every effort, some pesticides will remain in nonorganic, grocery-store food. Therefore, the safest alternative for all, and especially for those at-risk individuals, is organically-grown, less-chemically contaminated fruits, vegetables, and meats, purchased either from an organic producer or grown in your own garden. The choice becomes one of life or illness, maybe death for those with environmental illness.

Water

Another nutrient essential for our survival is water. Another source of chemical and pesticide contamination may be water. Water usage and consumption, one of life's necessities, for some may now be a life risk.

Water contamination is not new. The Delaware River was so polluted during World War II that President Roosevelt considered it a threat to the national security. He feared that gases from the water might cause corrosion at a nearby radar installation. Since World War II, water contamination has increased. This is due to population increase, and also parallels the chemical and technological revolutions.

Home and industrial waste disposal and chemical and petroleum production, usage, and storage may be major contributors to water contamination. The increased use of nitrate fertilizers and pesticides in agriculture may further add to the problem of water source contamination. The EPA estimates that 70 percent of the 1.2 billion pounds of pesticides used in the USA each year are used in agriculture. Pesticides, because of their persistence in the soil and their water solubility, have high potential for leaching into groundwater. Sandy soils and shallow water tables make groundwater contamination from nitrate fertilizers and pesticides a major concern.

Landfills and hazardous waste sites also have high potential for water contamination. In 1982, an EPA study revealed that of 929 hazardous waste sites, drinking water was contaminated at 128 sites and contamination suspected at 213 additional sites. This same study reported confirmed or suspected groundwater contamination at two-thirds of the hazardous waste sites.

Eight out of ten Americans live near these toxic waste sites according to the Council on Economic Priorities, and 49 percent of Americans drink groundwater. These toxic sites can and do contaminate groundwater. In 1984, the US EPA's National Water Quality Inventory reported forty-four hundred incidents of groundwater contamination in twenty-one states, which caused closure of private, public, or industrial wells and forced users to find alternative water sources.

Underground storage tanks of petroleum, gasoline, and chemicals can leak and lead to groundwater contamination. The Texas Water Commission estimates there are fifty thousand to one hundred thousand underground storage tanks in Texas. The EPA estimates there are three to five million nationwide.

Twenty-five percent of US households dispose of their residential wastewater through cesspools and septic systems. Individually of minimal significance, these disposal methods become important if drinking water wells and septic systems are located near each other. Contamination of the drinking water with bacteria, nitrates, and viruses can occur. Serious health problems may ensue.

Seven hundred organic, inorganic, biological, and radiological contaminants have been detected in US water supplies, yet by 1986 only twenty-three contaminants were being regulated by the EPA. Understanding of the health risks from long- and short-term chemical exposure and advances in analytical testing capabilities led to the realization that drinking water standards were grossly inadequate. Because of the EPA's slow regulatory pace, the US Congress, in 1986, passed amendments to the Safe Drinking Water Act. Fifty-three additional drinking water contaminants were required to meet contamination standards, and the EPA was also required to review and revise existing standards.

Added to the list of microbiological contaminants, such as guardia and viruses, and the organic chemicals, such as arsenic and lead, is an increasing list of organic and synthetic volatile chemicals. To meet the standards of the Act and its revisions, many cities may require new and better filtration equipment. This added financial burden may strain existing city budgets. While some larger metropolitan systems are equipped to meet the requirements of the Safe Drinking Water Act, 35 percent of community water systems have been cited for failure to meet the established standards for maximum contaminate levels. Another problem of smaller communities is that their systems are not equipped to even monitor for such a large number of volatile organic chemicals. This, plus the need for water treatment update, makes compliance difficult and health risk probable.

Even if compliance is met and the standards are achieved, the danger of exposure to carcinogens in drinking water still exists. Only six pesticides are regulated by the EPA, and regulation of pesticides in groundwater has been slow in evolving. This was due to the belief that pesticides would break down in the soil or be bound to it. Such is not the case. In 1985 EPA reported that seventeen unregulated pesticides had been found in the groundwater of twenty-three states. This measure of exposure of carcinogenic chemicals appears intolerable.

The EPA's standards for carcinogens allow high risk for cancer. The EPA standard for a substance is a cancer risk in the range of one to ten thousand to one in one million. A one in ten thousand risk would allow twenty-four thousand additional cancer cases in the entire population. These risk numbers apply to each contaminant separately. Thus, the risks are greater for each additional contaminant that is present in the water supply and in the body. Since we daily drink water containing many of these contaminants, these standards appear to fall far short of health assurance and protection.

Woburn, Massachusetts, is an example of drinking water contamination, industrial pollution, and the risk involved when volatile organics are present in drinking water. In Woburn, the incidence of childhood leukemia was more than twice as high as what could be expected. Within a half-mile radius it was 7.5 times higher than it should have been. The health hazard that existed was from high levels of the chemicals trichlorethylene, tetrachlorethylene, and chloroform that had contaminated the wells supplying water to the community. This case points out the risk of well-water consumption and the tremendous need to continually sample well water and small municipal water supplies.

Industrial and agricultural pollution occurring on land can contaminate groundwater and thus drinking water. But this pollution is creating major concern for our oceans, their inhabitants, and our food sources. From Portland to Morehead City, North Carolina, fishermen are hauling in lobsters and crabs with ulcerous lesions. Oysters in Chesapeake Bay are experiencing a fungal disease. According to a report in *Time* magazine (August, 1988), shellfish beds in Texas were closed eleven of the previous eighteen months due to pollution. In Louisiana, 35 percent of the state's oyster beds were closed because of sewer contamination. Pesticides and chemicals fill New York's marine waters.

It is now a health risk to eat some bluefish, flounder, and striped bass. This pollution of water, a lifeblood, is devastating and cumulative. Dangerous minerals, chemicals, and pesticides enter the water and are concentrated when we eat fish and shellfish. Laws and agencies exist to protect and prevent this. However, the contaminants are numerous and the pollution vast, and we are not yet concerned enough.

Because probable carcinogens are present in contaminated food and water, contact and exposure must be minimized. Filtered or bottled water and organically grown food are necessary alternatives. We may avoid or minimize our ingestion of chemicals, microbiological organisms, and undesirable minerals in food and water, but what a price the ecosystem must pay! Will the balance ever be restored?

Air

Pesticides and organic hydrocarbon chemicals are in food and water, but the threat to us doesn't end there. Residues of these chemicals are also present in the air we breathe. These chemicals exist in the air in our homes, our offices, and outside of them. The pollution of air takes on a new magnitude when we consider the fact that we may drink two liters of water a day but may breathe ten thousand to twenty thousand liters of air a day.

The air contains pesticides, volatile organics, monoxides, sulfates, and radioactive particles that rise from farms, factories, and automobiles and traverse the globe in a toxic wind. The magnitude of the problem was illustrated in the case of Lake Siskiwit, a small lake on an island in Lake Superior. Toxaphene, polychlorinated biphenyls, and DDT were found in the mud at the bottom of the lake, that itself is an isolated ecosystem with no sewage, farm runoff, or toxic dumps to contaminate it. The EPA concluded that these chemicals came from the atmosphere. They speculated that some had traveled from the southern cotton fields to be deposited into the lake's waters, others like DDT were from Central America, Asia, and Russia.

Pesticides can ride on dust or ride the wind in a gaseous state. Carcinogenic solvents can travel as vapor or be dissolved in moisture. Metals can even be vaporized from incinerators and ride the wind currents. The EPA has reported that possibly one thousand different chemicals enter the Texas air each year. These may react with each other to form ten thousand chemicals — unregulated, even unnamed.

There are an estimated 162.5 trillion grams of human-made organic chemicals spewed into the air each year across the United States. Each of these chemicals may pose a serious health threat, yet many interact to form complex new chemicals whose effect is unknown. For example, when benzo-a-pyrene, a coal tar product of woodburning stoves and furnaces, is combined on the skin of a mouse with a solvent, dodecane, its cancer-causing effects are increased a thousandfold.

Near industrial centers the problem is frequently intensified. Oil refineries and chemical plants along the Gulf Coast have been known to produce their own clouds and low-pressure weather systems that can help spread pollutants. The incidence of leukemia has been found to be higher in these areas. Near Midland, Michigan, where herbicides are produced, there are high rates of soft-tissue sarcomas.

Even the polar bears of the Canadian high arctic have the pesticide chlordane in their fatty tissue. The forests along the eastern seaboard are dying from acid rain. The Great Lakes are ecologically dying. The use or production of the forty-nine thousand chemical compounds is not a localized threat. Chemicals and their effect circle the globe, shrinking its size, making it a timeless village of toxins.

Workplace Air Pollution

Indoor air contamination has been a problem since Ben Franklin's day. He stated, "No common air from without is so unwholesome as the air within a closed room that has been breathed and not changed." Since we spend 80 percent of our time indoors, indoor air contamination is an important health issue. Indoor air is not an exact reflection of outdoor air. Indoor air can have much higher concentrations of chemicals than outdoor air, and there are some contaminants indoors that pose little or no problem outdoors. Indoor air does contain some of the pollutants found outdoors, but the indoor pollutants measured with the highest levels are those that arise from within buildings and their substructures.

One of the most common indoor air contaminants in home and office is cigarette smoke that can contain formaldehyde, cadmium, acrolein, benzopyrene, ammonia, and pesticides. In 1985, *Newsweek* reported that British researchers had discovered that 85 percent of tested nonsmokers were found to have measurable levels of tobacco substances in their urine, even though only one-half thought they had been exposed to cigarette smoke. Cigarette smoke is a definite health hazard to those who smoke and to those who don't but breathe it. It is especially troublesome to those with respiratory ailments and a sensitivity to it.

Heating systems that burn natural gas, kerosene, oil, and wood emit various quantities of respirable particles along with carbon, sulfur, and nitrogen oxides and trace organic chemicals. Other indoor air contaminants include volatile aromatic, aliphatic, and chlorinated hydrocarbons, asbestos, pesticides, and formaldehyde. Fungi, dust, bacteria, and other disease-causing organisms add to the indoor air contaminants that can make breathing hazardous to one's health.

American industry uses an estimated five hundred thousand chemicals to produce many of the benefits of twentieth-century living. Twenty million Americans work with one or more of these chemicals that can damage the nervous system. Workers exposed frequently to methyl n-butyl ketone, a solvent used as an ink thinner and machine cleaner, have suffered varying degrees of nerve damage to the lower limbs. Continued exposure to paint solvents can impair intellectual capacity and affect coordination. Toluene, a paint additive and solvent, and trichloroethylene, a degreaser and dry cleaning agent, not only can cause peripheral neuropathy but they also can be addictive. Methylene chloride, a solvent and spray can propellant, can produce hallucinations. It is also an active ingredient in paint strippers and pesticides and is the chemical blamed for the death of a pest-control worker who died while spraying pesticides in a poorly ventilated crawlspace. This is a chemical considered harmless outdoors. Acetone, a chemical used in cellulose production, can produce vertigo. Carbon disulfide, used in rubber vulcanization, can cause numbness and tingling in the lower limbs, psychosis, and memory loss. Frequent exposure to dibromochloropropane, a soil fumigant, can induce sterility. Methyl-bromide, a popular termiticide, likewise is a known neurotoxin. Anesthesiologists and dentists routinely inhale halothane, chloroform, cyclopropane, and nitrous oxide.

Workers and professionals can be exposed to these neurotoxins daily. The EPA and OSHA have a difficult job regulating the one-half million chemicals in use in industry today. What we don't know about them and their synergetic effect is greater than what we do know. Only a small percentage have been adequately tested because the regulating agencies are not given enough authority, money, and staff to perform the task. Another complicating factor is the fact that many chemical companies do their own product testing, and this can lead to fraudulent behavior. The consequences of these facts are indoor pollutants which can cause irreversible damage to the health of the unsuspecting worker.

Even if no spray or volatile organics are introduced into the indoor air, the structure itself can be a source of contaminates. Chemical companies manufacture nine billion pounds of formaldehyde each year, making it a common contaminant of indoor air. It is found in some glues, cleaners, carpets, fabrics, and wood products such as plywood, pressboard, and chipboard. Formaldehyde is a potent eye, upper respiratory, and skin irritant and is a probable carcinogen. Significant amounts of trapped formaldehyde are released from new products into indoor air. Then the hydrolytic decomposition of formaldehyde occurring over years maintains undesirable levels of it in the closed building. This continuing release of formaldehyde into the air can make it a major contributor to indoor air pollution and the "sick-building syndrome."

Unlike other contaminants that are found in water and outdoor air, there is no regulation that requires home or office buildings be monitored for indoor pollutants. Virtually all cases of unhealthy indoor air or "sick-building syndrome" have been discovered by the human body's adverse response to this pollution. For example, in many instances the building was new or had recently been remodeled. The occupants may have expressed a myriad of complaints. The air in the structure was then sampled, and sometimes one of the culprits found in the sample was a formaldehyde level above the standard .1 ppm. Removal of the formaldehyde-containing agents or increased ventilation have sometimes improved the air pollution problem. However, occasionally the structure contained excessive levels of numerous pollutants, and the symptoms of the occupants were severe. The decision was then made to declare the structure unfit for occupancy, and the building was closed.

Even the duct work of our homes and offices can be a source of indoor air contamination. Fungi, bacteria, and dust mites can invade the heating and cooling systems to create illness and sensitivity responses.

Home Air Pollution

Practically all of these chemicals that are part of an everyday work environment are also present in homes. Paints, cleaners, and glues also are used in the home. Add to the neurotoxic effect of these chemicals the effect of insecticides and termiticides, and the home can be anything but the safe haven it is considered to be. *U.S. News and World Report* in September 1986 quoted the EPA as stating that toxic chemicals in the home posed three times the cancer risk of airborne contaminants even in an area next to a chemical plant. Lance Wallace, an EPA scientist, reported chemicals ingested in the home make it more of a toxic waste dump than a nearby chemical plant.

Chlordane is a common subterranean termiticide. It remains in the soil for about twenty years after application. Studies on the health effects of chronic low-dose exposures to this chemical are almost non-existent. Its potency and capacity to cause illness was illustrated in the case of the Bergen family of Dallas, Texas. The Bergens moved into a new home that had been treated to prevent termite infestation. The Bergens experienced a multitude of health effects over a period of eighteen months before the home was suspected as the cause of the problem. Members of the family experienced nausea, headache, shortness of breath, phlebitis, and blood clotting. Although proof that the termiticide caused the illnesses suffered by members of the Bergen family was difficult and debatable, the toxicity of the chemical cannot be denied.

Americans do not want their investments destroyed by termites. They do not want roaches, ants, fleas, or spiders in their homes or offices. They do not want weeds or insects destroying their lawns. The answer to these insect problems has been spraying. These insecticides and herbicides can produce health effects from allergic responses to neurological problems to death. When chemicals are extensively used in the home, concentration of environmental toxins poses serious health considerations.

Other building and home contaminants can be natural gas or coal-fired furnaces, stoves, and appliances that can increase carbon, sulfur, and nitrogen oxides to levels the equal of outdoor freeway emissions. Studies have indicated increased incidence of respiratory diseases and lower pulmonary functions in people residing in homes with gas-burning appliances.

Radon gas, a carcinogenic radioactive gas product of uranium, permeates many American homes. At high levels, this product exposes us to as much radiation yearly as was experienced by those people living in the vicinity of the 1986 Chernobyl nuclear power plant disaster.

To minimize indoor air contamination we can increase our knowledge of chemicals. A wise alternative is to use products low in formaldehyde or volatile hydrocarbons. Pesticides from natural sources can replace organophosphates and organochlorides, and alternative energy sources can be used. Asbestos-containing products can be removed. Air-conditioning ducts can be periodically cleaned, and filtration media used. Changes such as these are not choices, they are necessities. Even with changes made to reduce indoor air contamination, the effects of numerous chemicals present in air, food, and water remain a serious health problem. Many are probable carcinogens, or they may affect the central nervous system, heart, brain, liver, kidney, and stomach.

The health effects of exposure to some chemicals can take years to develop. Others can produce immediate illness with symptoms persisting indefinitely. For some individuals, improved health returns after chemical exposure ceases. But even though exposure ceases, the chemical can remain. As stated earlier, EPA studies indicate most Americans have over one hundred foreign chemicals in their fatty tissues, an indication of perhaps unknown exposure occurring over a lifetime at home or at work.

For a chosen few, the chemical exposure so sensitizes the individual that exposure to other chemicals in food, air, and water causes many symptoms, some of which can be intolerable. Health is severely compromised, and the maintenance of a normal life-style becomes increasingly more difficult. The victim of a twentieth-century environment is created, and EI (Environmental Illness) is born.

To try to regain health and become symptom free, some individuals need to retreat to an environment in which chemical exposure is minimized. Housing becomes a major problem because of the chemicals present in many construction products. An inability to find an area completely free of air pollutants complicates the problem. The use of less toxic products in every aspect of life becomes a necessity. Natural fibers are needed to replace synthetics, and perfumes, hydrocarbons, pesticides, and aldehydes must be avoided.

This retreat does not always unable the EI to improve quickly.

Initially, it enables the individual to endure. For a period of months, the environmental illness victim may notice increasing sensitivities. As contaminant exposure is minimized, the victim becomes more aware and notices sensitivities to items once considered inoffensive. Environmental tolerance narrows, and more items and activities are removed from the life-style. Gradually, perhaps after years of a reduced body-stress load in this austere environment, the immune and enzyme systems improve, and sensitivities and symptoms lessen. The need for minimal chemical exposure still remains, but some semblance of a normal life-style is achieved.

The retreat may be an answer for some. It is not a solution to the contamination of air, water, and food. Control of these must not be left entirely to government agencies. Stewardship must be exercised by all to protect the world, the balance of the ecosystem, and its inhabitants. Product choices are required by each of us, and solutions must be found to reduce exposure to toxic chemicals. Our dependence on toxic chemicals and our insistence on their use must stop. Available alternatives must be used, and new ones must be found.

At a conference of virologists in May 1989, attendees expressed deep concerns about the convergence of factors that could set the stage for new epidemics. Two such conditions are the population growth resulting in millions of people now living in crowded squalor. Second, various environmental and ecological changes could influence the emergence of viruses — some which health officials may not effectively be able to control.

Choices made today will protect tomorrow. Wrong decisions made today will still affect our air, food, soil, and water for many tomorrows. If we do not develop a real sense of responsibility, and exercise it through thoughtful action, we will increasingly find ourselves victims of the twentieth century, and our fragile world, burdened by contamination, will shatter.

C. G.

* * *

TAKING ACTION

1. If at all possible, grow your own vegetables. If you don't have the space, buy as much as possible from your local produce suppliers. Learn what chemicals have been applied to produce by asking the growers in your area.

2. Avoid buying fruit and vegetables out of season. Very likely they are imports from Central and South America and contain considerable pesticide and preservative applications, some of which — e.g.,

DDT — have been banned in the US. The safest out-of-season food to buy is usually frozen.

3. It is advisable to know just what chemicals are in the meat you buy. If your grocer doesn't know and can't find out where the meat is from and what's in it, it's best to find a store that does. If you can't get information, at least avoid veal. Most of the veal offered in stores is the product of factory-farming processes that leave considerable chemicals in the tissue.

4. Likewise, check sources of fish, especially in the Great Lakes and coastal areas where hazardous waste and sewage have washed up on the beaches and where corporations have dumped industrial waste.

5. Buy wood that hasn't been chemically "treated." Much of the trendy wood — that which is supposed to last forty years — contains highly toxic chemical preservatives that inevitably seep into the ground. One of the most popular contains arsenic and should not, for example, be used to border a vegetable garden. These woods are also dangerous for pets and backyard birds and animals. Find out what preservative was used and the possible side effects before you invest in something which could be harmful.

6. Give up the suntan — it isn't healthy any longer because of the depletion of the ozone layer in certain areas. If you're going to be in the sun, avoid exposure from 10:00 AM to 2:00 PM, wear a hat and long-sleeved clothing, and use strong sunscreen.

7. Where does your water come from? Have you had it tested? What are you drinking? It would be a good idea to know your water source. And if it isn't adequate, there are now a number of water processors that will take chlorine and other harmful elements from your water.

8. Get political. Support enforcement of the Clean Air Act and the Clean Water Act. Keep in touch with your local and state representatives to see what they're doing about providing for enforcement in your area.

9. Plant trees that produce fruits and nuts. Not only do you have the advantage of trees that hold the soil in, offer shade, and contribute to cleaner air, you can have the advantage of fruits and nuts. Check with your local garden shop or one of the conservation organizations about toxic-free pesticides. (Soapy water — such as used dishwater — poured at the base of some fruit trees will keep away most "pests.")

— 6 —

Silent Spring or Sustainable Agriculture?

Terry Gips

There was once a town in the heart of America where all life seemed to live in harmony with its surroundings... Then a strange blight crept over the area and everything began to change.... Mysterious maladies swept the flocks of chickens; the cattle and sheep sickened and died.... There was a strange stillness.... The few birds seen anywhere were moribund; they trembled violently and could not fly. It was a spring without voices.

Rachel Carson, *Silent Spring*

More than a quarter century ago, Rachel Carson's words first alerted the world to the dangers of pesticides such as DDT and launched the modern environmental movement. Despite her warnings, pesticide applications in the US have doubled since 1964, reaching more than one billion pounds of active ingredients valued at $6.6 billion in 1985.[1] Worldwide, the $14 billion pesticide industry[2] produces five billion pounds of pesticides annually — approximately one pound for every person on Earth.[3]

The effects have become evident everywhere from the Bhopal tragedy in India and the poisoning of the Rhine River in Europe to the contamination of American supermarket foodstuffs with pesticides such as EDB and heptachlor. Other less publicized pesticide problems continue to mount:

86

- A 1983 United Nation's report estimated that there are approximately two million pesticide poisonings annually, nearly four per minute worldwide.[4]

- Between 1972 and 1982, pesticide poisonings among US farm laborers and field hands doubled, and as many as 313,000 farm workers suffered from pesticide-related illnesses each year.[5]

- Seventeen pesticides now contaminate drinking water in twenty-three states, forcing the closure of thousands of wells from California to New York.[6]

- Thirty-nine percent of the wells tested in Minnesota were found to be contaminated with one of more pesticides.[7]

- Forty-four percent of California's fresh produce has been found to be contaminated by residues of nineteen pesticides, including such carcinogens as DDT and dieldrin.[8]

- DDT is now present in virtually all living things around the world, contaminating mother's breast milk in Central America at levels forty-two times above the World Health Organization's safe standard.[9]

- The National Research Council estimates that pesticide residues in the US food supply could add as many as 1.4 million total cases of cancer.[10]

We seem to be fighting a losing battle. In the past thirty years, pesticide use in the United States has increased twelvefold while crop losses to pests have nearly doubled.[11] The National Academy of Sciences has found that pesticides have become increasingly ineffective as pests have become resistant. The number or resistant species of insects and mites has grown from seven to 447 in less than half a century.

Additional Problems with Present Agriculture

Every year, six million hectares of land is permanently degraded to desert-like conditions, with another twenty-one million hectares providing no economic return because of the spread of desertification due to farming and grazing practices.[12] Agriculture has been a major contributor to the destruction of 40 percent of the world's mature tropical forests.

It is estimated that the US has lost one-third of its topsoil from cropland in use today,[13] and that a third of US cropland is suffering soil losses "too great to be sustained without a gradual but ultimately disastrous decline in productivity."[14] For every bushel of grain harvested by American farmers, at least five bushels of topsoil are lost. In 1979, the US Department of Agriculture estimated that such erosion results in annual plant nutrient losses of $18 billion.[15]

Water erosion caused the loss of four billion tons of American soil in 1972, equivalent to a fully-loaded, 633,000-mile freight train that could reach to the moon and back or encircle the Earth twenty-four times.[16] In the continental US, three billion metric tons of this sediment ends up in waterways, causing an estimated $6.1 billion in damage.[17]

To help compensate for soil loss and boost yields, world fertilizer use has grown nearly tenfold since 1950, reaching 135 million tons in 1988[18] or 59 pounds for every person. In the US, 40 million tons of commercial fertilizers are applied to fields every year, with over a million metric tons of nitrogen contaminating surface and groundwater.[19] This results in decreased oxygen levels for fish, choking plant growth, destruction of soil microorganisms, nitrate contamination, and methemoglobinemia or "blue baby syndrome."

In addition, our short-sighted agriculture destroys fish and wildlife habitat, increases energy dependence, depletes groundwater aquifers, causes salinization and siltation, confines farm animals in inhumane conditions, spreads bacterial resistance to antibiotics, and contributes to global warming.

Has this destruction been worth the price? Has it succeeded in boosting production and reducing hunger? No! World hunger has actually increased 14 percent in the decade ending in 1980[20] and is continuing to worsen in the face of environmental destruction and the debt crisis. Approximately thirty-five thousand people die every day from hunger and related causes, the equivalent of 100 jumbo jets filled with children and their parents crashing.

A New Perspective Is Required

As hunger grows and the environment decays, it becomes clear that something is terribly wrong with our present approach to agriculture. In fact, the root of the problem goes far deeper and can be found in our relationship with nature. As ecologists Bill Devall and George Sessions have pointed out, "the dominant worldview of technocratic-industrial societies regards humans as isolated and fundamentally separate from the rest of Nature, as superior to, and in charge of, the rest of creation."[21]

This is in direct contrast to the holistic, interconnected view of existence shared by many traditional religions and belief systems. The Vedic culture of ancient India stressed the unity of humans and nature, as well as the imminence of one divine spirit in all life.[22] According to Islam's holy Koran, "There is not an animal on earth, nor a flying creature on two wings, but they are peoples like unto you."[23] In similar fashion a Hindu dictum states that "the Earth is our mother, and we are all her children."[24]

Unfortunately, the more mechanistic worldview of Francis Bacon, René Descartes, and Isaac Newton has dominated[25] with the attribution of its evolution ranging from a misreading of God's granting humans dominion over all living things[26] to the creation of patriarchal societies based on male-dominated hierarchies.[27] Regardless of the source, farmer/poet Wendell Berry has warned that such a worldview leads to alienation and wrong answers:

> Once we see our place, our part of the world, as surrounding us, we have already made a profound division between it and ourselves. We have given up the understanding . . . that we and our country create one another, depend on one another, are literally part of one another.[28]

The simplistic thinking of the reductionist approach to agriculture (separating various segments of the ecosystem rather than considering their interrelatedness) leads to the "magic bullet" solution of spraying pesticides to kill all "pests" (any insect or plant not desired by humans) because they seemingly interfere with a narrowly-defined goal of maximum yield. It assumes that if the pest can be eradicated, the problem will be solved. However, the pesticides may kill not only an essential food source for beneficial insects, but likely, the beneficials as well, thus leading to secondary pest outbreaks.

Also, while the pesticides certainly eliminate the symptoms, they may mask more serious, underlying problems with soil management and agro-ecosystem balance. For example, a lack of balanced soil nutrition contributes to unhealthy, weak plants to which insects are attracted. Ironically, it has been shown that some pesticides weaken plant immune systems and make them so attractive to pests that even more pesticides must be used.[29]

The dominant worldview not only separates nature from humans and contributes to an expensive and hazardous "pesticide treadmill" but also leads to an even more damaging result: nature is seen as a brutal force that must be fought, dominated, and exploited. Wendell Berry has addressed "the agricultural crisis as a crisis of culture," noting, "We are all to some extent the products of an exploitive society, and it would be foolish and self-defeating to pretend that we do not bear its stamp."[30] As Rachel Carson wrote in *Silent Spring:*

> The "control of nature" is a phrase conceived in arrogance, born of the Neanderthal age of biology and philosophy, when it was supposed that nature exists for the convenience of man. . . . It is our alarming misfortune that so primitive a science has armed itself with the most

modern and terrible weapons, and that in turning them against the insects it has also turned them against the earth.

It is clear that we must rethink not only our approach to pest control but to agriculture and life as we know it.

The Emergence of "Sustainability" and "Sustainable Agriculture"

It is a central component of traditional Iroquois thinking to base decisions on what their effects will be on the seventh generation to come.

Since the mid-1970s, the concept of sustainability has received increasing attention worldwide. The need for a sustainable agriculture has been underscored as environmental contamination has grown, health hazards have mounted, pest control practices have faltered, rural economies have deteriorated, and hunger has spread. Many states, such as California, Minnesota, Wisconsin, and Iowa have each created multi-million dollar sustainable agriculture programs.[31] With funding from the Agricultural Productivity Act, the federal government has now established a $4 million "low-input, sustainable agriculture" program.

Definitions of Sustainable Agriculture

According to *Webster's Dictionary*, sustain means "to keep in existence; keep up; maintain or prolong; to provide sustenance or nourishment for."[32] The International Alliance for Sustainable Agriculture and an increasing number of researchers, farmers, policy-makers, and organizations worldwide have developed a definition that unifies many diverse elements into a widely adopted and comprehensive working definition: A sustainable agriculture is ecologically sound, economically viable, socially just, and humane.[33] Such a system is productive in both the short and long terms while enhancing our environment and health.

This definition establishes four basic standards by which widely divergent agricultural practices and conditions can be evaluated and modified, if necessary, to create sustainable systems. The result is an agriculture designed to last and be passed on to future generations.

Principles of a Sustainable Agriculture

The four components of sustainable agriculture form a circle of life, functioning much like the spokes of a whole wheel, each essential to the system's integrity, strength, and balance.

1. ECOLOGICAL SOUNDNESS

The first criterion for sustainability is that the system be ecologically "sound," or "healthy...and in good condition."[34] This applies to the vitality of the entire agro-ecosystem from humans and plants to wildlife and soil organisms.

While the commandment in Genesis 1:28 providing humans with dominion over the fish, fowl, cattle, and all the Earth often has been misused as a pretext for exploitation, St. Francis of Assisi and most Christian scholars have generally interpreted "dominion" to mean an acceptance or responsibility and stewardship for God's Creation.

The concept of the "agro-ecosystem" is essential to an agriculture that is ecologically sound. There are two components necessary to achieve a whole, healthy agro-ecosystem, both of which are based on mimicking processes in nature: self-regulation and resource efficiency.[35] To achieve self-regulation and resultant stability, species diversity is essential.[36] Primary attention must be given to assuring the health of the soil, a precondition for healthy plants. Soil health is achieved by such practices as balanced crop rotations, cover crops, addition of biomass, proper tillage practices, and sound water management.

It is also important to maintain the health of the surrounding flora and fauna. Again, species diversity is critical as are proper habitats for the species.

An ecologically sound agriculture also must conserve precious resources, avoid system toxicity, and decrease costs. Central to such efficiency is the cycling of resources.

An ecologically sound system should be designed so that energy, nutrients, and other resources are recycled and not lost with an emphasis on renewable resources that allow greater self-reliance.

Trees can play an essential role in resource efficiency by meeting multiple purposes: providing building materials, cooking fuels, food and other products; protecting soil from wind and water erosion; assuring proper habitat; making deeply buried nutrients available; offering shade and beauty; and, perhaps most important, transforming carbon dioxide into oxygen to help overcome the greenhouse effect.

Not only will an ecologically sound agro-ecosystem be able to adapt, grow, and continue into perpetuity, but its health will provide the basis for the health of all its parts, including humans. The agro-ecosystem should produce thriving, nutritious plants that nourish humans in all respects: physically, mentally, and spiritually. Thus, such an agriculture is both sustainable and sustaining.

2. ECONOMIC VIABILITY

The second test of a sustainable agriculture is that it be economically "viable"; an economy must be able to maintain itself and grow over both the short and long term.

There are additional costs and subsidies, often hidden, that are not accounted for in the determination of economic viability. Loss of wildlife and health care costs from chemical exposure often are not considered in decision making because their determination is difficult.

In only a short time, conventional agriculture has used up nearly all of nature's historic "capital investment" through its depletion of millions of years of fossil energy, erosion of thousands of years' development of topsoil, and loss of invaluable, centuries-evolved germ plasma. Burning the candle at both ends, conventional agriculture has borrowed against the future by passing on tremendous public health and environmental costs in the form of various "toxic timebombs."

Also ignored in current accounting are numerous subsidies that make agriculture appear economically viable, such as taxpayer-subsidized research and extension efforts with agrichemicals and biotechnology; an indemnity program that paid beekeepers millions of dollar for their massive loss of bees from pesticide spraying; and US taxpayer-funded irrigation schemes that provide water to California farmers at extremely low prices.

Subsidies for pesticide production and sales in the third world are widespread, ranging from 15 to 90 percent of total retail cost. These subsidies cost third world governments hundreds of millions of dollars annually and "undermine efforts to promote the most cost-effective methods of integrated pest management."[37] And just as significant is a less direct pesticide subsidy provided by a stream of corporate profits gained from the export of banned, restricted, and unregistered pesticides to the third world.[38]

3. SOCIAL JUSTICE

The third requirement for a sustainable agriculture is that it be socially "just," or "equitable ... right or fair."[39] Quite simply, the system must assure that resources and power are distributed equitably so that the basic needs of all are met and their rights assured.

This standard is frequently overlooked, often because assessing power, privilege, and exploitation is an uncomfortable process that threatens the status quo. We must, however, confront the issue.

Social justice is explicitly part of Judeo-Christian teachings. God's commandment of a sabbath for the land every seventh year: "In the seventh year you shall let it lie fallow" (Exodus 23:10–11), requires the owner to let the land "provide food for the poor of your people." The prescription goes even further and calls for the remission or cancelation of all debts at the end of every seventh year (Deuteronomy 15:1–2). In other words, "It is a basic human right to have *regularly* a fresh chance to succeed, without being forever weighed down by the past."[40]

According to eminent Biblical scholars, the sabbatical and jubilee years together "represent a unique Israelite attempt to combat the social evils that had infected Israelite society and to return to the idyllic period of the desert union when social equality and fraternal concern had prevailed."[41] A similar balance of control can be found in Isaiah 5:8, which forbids the concentration of large blocks of land in a few hands.

There are two essential components of social justice: equitable control of resources and full participation. Regarding the first, access to land is necessary in order for a majority of the world's population to escape poverty and grow the food it requires. As important to success in this effort as equitable land tenure is the availability of adequate resources including capital, technical assistance, and market opportunities. At the same time, the rights of landless farm workers and the urban poor must be recognized. This requires fair wages, a safe work environment, proper living conditions, and the right to nutritious, healthy food.

Unfortunately, there is widespread injustice. Today, in a majority of third world countries, 80 percent of the land is controlled by only 3 percent of the population.[42] Although women provide 66 percent of the total working hours, they receive only 10 percent of the world's income and own only 1 percent of the world's property.[43] A 1988 study found that North American farm workers faced working conditions that were as hazardous as their third world counterparts, with 43 percent of those interviewed reporting they had been poisoned by pesticides and only half receiving medical help.[44]

The second essential component of social justice is the right to full participation. Whether in the field, market, or voting booth, all people must be able to participate in the vital decisions that determine their lives. This right is particularly important in the case of women, indigenous people, and others who historically have been discriminated against and kept out of the decision-making process.

In many countries, federal farm policy is designed to eliminate family farms while providing subsidies to large, corporate farms. Farmers have been unable to gain increases in minimum prices of many products. Farmers and consumers have little influence on commodity pricing policies or agribusiness boards.

4. HUMANENESS

The fourth and final requirement for sustainability is that it be "humane," or have "what are considered the best qualities of human-kind: kind, tender, merciful, sympathetic, etc."[45] Most often, the term is applied to our treatment of animals. While this is certainly an important component, a humane agriculture must embody our highest values in all aspects, from respect for life to the protection of diverse cultures.

The doctrine of "ahimsa," or noninjury to sentient beings, was originally specified in the Vedas, India's five-thousand-year-old year old Sanskrit scriptures. The Vedic literature of Hinduism, the oldest of all Asian religions, has very clear teachings regarding universal compassion. The Vedas say that if one cares for all living creatures, then one naturally cares for humanity as well. The Vedic viewpoint is that a person should see the same life force in all living entities and that those who cannot understand the principle of life in lesser beings may then eventually misunderstand what the life force is altogether and lose their sense of humanity.[46]

Humane treatment of animals is required by Jewish law. According to Jewish tradition, the prohibition against inhumane conduct towards animals is one of the seven commandments given to the sons of Noah, and therefore is binding to all humanity.[47] Although no work is permitted on the sabbath, exceptions are made if the purpose is to relieve the suffering of an animal. In fact, kindness to animals is one of the few virtues that the Jewish tradition specifically associates with the promise of heavenly reward.[48] In Ecclesiastes it is written:

> For that which befalleth the sons of men befalleth the beasts. Even one thing befalleth them: as the one dieth, so dieth the other; yea, they have all one breath, so that a man hath no pre-eminence above a beast.[49]

In fact, the Bible not only calls for respect of all living things, but requires humans to learn from all other life. God spoke to Job and commanded.

> But ask now the beasts, and they shall teach thee; and the fowls of the air, and they shall teach thee: Or speak to the earth, and it shall teach thee.[50]

Twentieth-century writer, theosophist, and Indian independence leader Annie Besant explained the humanitarian ideal:

> All the misery we inflict on sentient beings slackens our human evo-lution and makes the progress of humanity slower towards the ideal that it is seeking to realize ... you cannot isolate yourself while you are

trampling others down. Those that you trample on retard your own progress. The misery that you cause is as it were mire which clings round your feet when you would ascend; for we have to rise together or fall together.[51]

While humans clearly have an interdependent relationship with animals — from their physical labor and companionship to their invaluable recycling of organic matter and provision of foods — too often animals are seen only as objects to be exploited. Humane agriculture must be based on a fundamental respect for animals and a recognition of their rights.

In an extensive treatise, leading animal rights advocate Tom Regan has made a cogent argument that "animals have certain basic moral rights, including in particular the fundamental right to be treated with the respect that...they are due as a matter of strict justice...and their equal prima facie right not to be harmed."[52]

Ecologist Thomas Berry has called for a shift from a limited human or anthropocentric perspective to a bio-centric one: "The reduction of the earth to an object simply for human possession and use is unthinkable in most traditional cultures.... The earth belongs to itself and to all the component members of the community."[53]

Despite this thinking, animals are subjected to inhumane conditions on "factory farms" with laying hens jammed into tiny battery cages, veal calves kept in small, dark stalls and fed anemic diets, and hogs confined in unhealthy buildings and fed antibiotics to assure extra weight gain.[54] While countries such as Switzerland and Sweden have banned battery cages and legislated other reforms, inhumane practices still persist worldwide.

It is equally important that the highest values apply to human interactions as well. The fundamental dignity of all human beings must be recognized, and both relationships and institutions must incorporate such essential human values as trust, honesty, self-respect, cooperation, self-reliance, compassion, and love.[55] We must balance the society's predominant, aggressive patriarchal traditions with qualities such as nurture, sensitivity, and reverence, which are drawn from our female sides or what Native Americans term "the Great Earth Mother."

The increasing substitution of the term "agri*business*" for "agri*culture*" reflects a fundamental shift to an economy in which everything, including human beings, is assigned a certain value. These "inputs" are viewed as expendable and replaceable. The human is lost. Farmers become competing production units whose sole goal of efficiency is a system that rewards those who can manage to "get one up on another."

Rather than encouraging a sense of community, such a system leads to an increased competition, isolation, and alienation. As rural societies break down, their values, once the backbone of the larger society, are lost. Without such values, agriculture is neither humane nor sustainable.

Aldo Leopold cited the lack of any underlying ethic to the relationship of humans to the land and the animals and plants that grow upon it: "There is as yet no social stigma in the possession of a gullied farm, a wrecked forest, or a polluted stream, provided the dividends suffice to send the youngsters to college."[56] The need for such an ethic is essential to counter "economic self-interest" which "tends to ignore, and thus eventually eliminate, many elements in the land community that lack commercial value, but that are (as far as we know) essential to its healthy functioning."[57]

But to embody the highest human values requires even more. Wendell Berry has said: "An agriculture that is whole nourishes the whole person, body and soul. We do not live by bread alone."[58]

A New, Common Ground — Sustainable Agriculture

Sustainable agriculture represents a positive response to the limits and problems of both traditional and modern agriculture. It is neither a return to the past nor an idolatry of the present. Rather, it is a balance of old and new. It seeks to take advantage of best aspects of both traditional wisdom and the latest scientific advances. This results in integrated, nature-based agro-ecosystems designed to be self-reliant, resource-conserving, and productive in both the short and long terms.

The Many Faces of Sustainable Agriculture

Sustainable agriculture encompasses a surprising diversity of farming systems. These systems possess different names, and their practices vary greatly. This is a function of their unique histories, geographic locations, and cultural associations. Some of the most common names for such systems are: organic, biological, alternative, ecological, resource-efficient, low-input, natural bio-dynamic, regenerative, and permacultural.[59]

The first four place a primary emphasis on the ecological soundness of the system, although their proponents often incorporate the other principles of sustainable agriculture. Resource-efficient and low-input systems focus even more narrowly on the actual input use. Finally, the proponents of biodynamic, natural, regenerative, and permacultural approaches address many, if not all, of the sustainable agriculture principles in a holistic manner.

Sustainable agriculture also embodies components from many disciplines and concepts, including agro-ecology, farm-systems research, agro-forestry, and integrated pest management. These systems and approaches are briefly described in *Breaking the Pesticide Habit.*[60]

Many of the traditional methods of farming are unsustainable for various reasons from population pressure and lack of productivity to government policies. As the decline of great Mayan and Mesopotamian civilizations has shown, traditional agriculture is not inherently sustainable and can lead to ecological ruin.[61]

Sustainable Agriculture Grows with Public Concern

As many as one hundred thousand of America's 2.1 million farmers are practicing sustainable agriculture and their numbers are growing rapidly as farmers struggle to cut costs and reduce soil erosion, health risks, and environmental contamination.[62]

The movement has received a major boost from mounting public concern about pesticide residues in food, as reflected in a Harris Poll conducted in November, 1988, that found 84.2 percent of Americans saying they would buy organic food, if available, and 49 percent would pay more for it.[63] This concern sharply escalated following a CBS-TV's "60–Minute Special" on February 26, 1989, in which actress Meryl Streep released a Natural Resource Defense Council study presenting the health risks to children from twenty-three pesticide residues in produce, including alar in apples.[64]

As a result, some twenty big US supermarket chains have started stocking organic produce. While organic produce still accounts for less than one percent of the nation's sales, some distributors have more than doubled their sales in the past year and some are having difficulty obtaining an adequate supply.[65] Estimates on the size of the national organic industry vary from $1 billion annually to as high as $10 billion.[66]

In response to consumer demand, farmers have begun a wholesale shift toward organic farming, which encourages proper soil health and forbids the use of all synthetic pesticides and fertilizers. Nationwide, such big suppliers as Sunkist Growers, Inc,. and Castle and Cooke's Dole Foods subsidiary are starting to grow organic produce.[67]

Generally, organic farming systems make up less than one percent of the farm operations in most industrialized nations. A 1980 US Department of Agriculture report found that the nonchemical control methods used by these farmers were "reasonably effective" and that the farms obtained yields at net income comparable to chemical-intensive farms.[68]

An Example of Sustainable Agriculture in Iowa

On a typical, all-American farm in the heart of Iowa's cornbelt, Dick and Sharon Thompson successfully grow 300 acres of corn, soybeans, oats, and hay, while also managing a 90-row-farrow-to-finish hog operation and a 90-head cow-calf herd. While their yields are the same as their neighbors — 120 to 145 bushels per acre of corn and 40 to 45 bushels per acre of soybeans — their costs are $90 lower with less than half the soil erosion.

What's their secret? Regenerative agriculture. In 1968, the Thompsons changed from their practice for fifteen years of farming with heavy fertilizer and pesticides applications that had led to levelling yields, mounting agrochemical bills, worsening weed problems, and growing animal illnesses. Their shift from continuous corn production to a rotation of corn-soybeans-corn-oats-hay, along with the adoption of ridge tillage and other sophisticated planting practices, works to control weeds and insects while maintaining yields.[69,70]

Dick Thompson actually feels weeds can be used as an asset: "Not only will they help hold soil, water, and plant nutrients, but we're learning that their roots (particularly foxtail) may chemically inhibit the germination of broadleaf weedseeds in the lower soil profile."[71] He then uses his Buffalo-Till planter to remove the top two inches of soil from the ridge in order to both form the seedbed and push the foxtail between the rows where it can be controlled later by a cultivator. He plants high densities of fast-growing soybean varieties in order to create a dense canopy for shading out weeds.

The Thompsons also changed their animal-rearing practices from total confinement in which, as Dick said, animals "sleep on slatted, concrete floors over fuming manure pits in buildings with no sunlight and stale, moist air" and "are fed a steady diet of corn and soybeans mixed with a variety of drugs, antibiotics and synthetic vitamins and minerals."[72]

Instead, they build open-air finishing units (with straw bedding instead of concrete) at a 75 percent savings compared to the cost of a conventional, $80,000 confinement facility. By using lime in the ground, corncob bedding material, and a diversified feeding ration containing grasses, legumes, and beneficial lactobacillus bacteria, the Thompsons have eliminated the need for iron shots, antibiotics, and disinfectants. A single dust bag — filled only once a year — is hung in the gateway for beef cows and calves to control bace flies and grubs.[73]

An Impossible Dream?

President John F. Kennedy once dared to share a seemingly impossible dream: to land a human being on the moon. Many laughed at the impracticality, but Kennedy was able to inspire people to join together to make the dream become a reality.

Now it is time for us to return home and accomplish another dream: the creation of a sustainable future for the Earth. This dream can and must be achieved if humans are to continue living on spaceship Earth. As Adlai Stevenson said:

> We travel together, passengers on a little space ship, dependent on its vulnerable reserves of air and soil; all committed for our safety to its security and peace; preserved from annihilation only by the care, the work, and, I will say, the love we give our fragile craft.

T. G.

* * *

TAKING ACTION

1. Consider how production of food affects the environment. Think about rain forest beef, the shrimp fishing that kills thousands of turtles, the tuna fishing that kills thousands of dolphins, and the veal for which calves are treated inhumanely in many instances, subject to significant doses of medication in order to be kept alive.

2. Know what you're buying — read the labels. If you don't know what an ingredient is, find out. You may be getting more chemicals in the food than you realize.

3. Do not buy fruit and vegetables out of season. More than likely, the out-of-season produce contains a considerable number of chemicals because they may have been grown in Central or South America, areas that allow DDT and other toxins banned in the United States. In addition, the further food travels the more preservatives are required to keep it fresh-looking.

4. Give up "designer" food. The prettier an item looks, the more likely it is to contain chemicals in order to keep the bugs and insects away. Organically grown food is far more likely to have blemishes, but it is free of chemical toxins. Think more deeply about "the perfect apple."

5. Eat more vegetables, fruits, and grains; decrease your consumption of meat and animal products. If Americans reduced meat eating

10 percent, the 12 million tons of grain saved annually could feed all people on Earth who starve to death. Animal agriculture is responsible for: 85 percent of topsoil loss; 260 million acres of forest destruction; over half our water consumption; and 215 times the fossil fuel needed to produce the same amount of protein in grain. (Source: *Utne Reader*).

6. Grow a garden of your own and use either no chemicals, or, if you must, organic chemicals. At least two companies are making organic chemicals available: Safers and Natural Guard. Ask your local nursery or flower and garden shop for information. Also organic gardening books are available.

7. Plant fruit and nut trees. Not only do trees help in environmental efforts to provide clean air and counteract the greenhouse effect, the fruits and nuts produced are great treats.

8. Support grocery stores and food markets that offer organically grown food and be sure that the food is certified organic.

9. Learn who, in your area, is practicing sustainable agriculture and support them by buying their products.

10. If you can't find a sustainable farm, it is still better to shop locally. Ask the farmers what chemicals were used on the produce they are offering.

— 7 —

Air Pollution:
Can Our Planet Survive?

Lewis G. Regenstein

Major changes in the chemistry of the earth's atmosphere are taking place, with potentially calamitous effects for all mankind....

If after all, what you're doing is stopping the systems which support life and enable life to continue on this planet, it's much more important than just stopping smoking. It means that life may not be able to continue in its present form unless you do it.... Life won't go on existing as we know it unless we tackle the very nature, the very atmosphere that sustains life on this earth.
British Prime Minister Margaret Thatcher,
Interview on "Nightline," March 7, 1989

The pollution of our air and atmosphere is a problem of almost unimaginable dimensions that may ultimately affect our future on this planet.

In recent years, a variety of government studies and expert scientists have demonstrated beyond question that the current situation presents a serious danger not only to the lives and health of many millions of Americans but to the very survival of our civilization.

Harmful chemicals regularly discharged into the air may be killing hundreds of thousands of Americans each year; threatening the lives of some thirty-five million Americans; warming the Earth to temperatures humans may not be able to endure; causing acid rain that is killing off lakes, forests, and food crops; and destroying the globe's protective ozone layer that makes life on Earth possible.

101

One graphic example often cited of the damaging effects of air pollution is that of Cleopatra's Needle, the striking granite obelisk that was placed in New York's Central Park in 1883, after some thirty-five hundred years in the Egyptian desert. During less than a century in the park, it has lost several inches of granite and undergone greater depletion than in the thirty-five centuries it spent being pounded and ground by the sand and wind, and baked by the hot Egyptian sun.[1] This same air — which has eaten away part of this solid granite object — is breathed in and out of the lungs of each of New York's seven million residents at the average rate of sixteen thousand quarts a day per person. It is thus hardly surprising that three decades ago, the American Public Health Association estimated that some ten to twenty people a day were dying from air pollution in New York City. We now know that, nationwide, the figure may be in the hundreds of thousands.[2]

Caution: Don't Breathe the Air

Air pollution is hardly a new phenomenon; some cities, such as London, have experienced it for centuries. Indeed, in 1952, an atmospheric inversion there claimed some four thousand lives. Ten years later in London, seven hundred people died during another period of heavy air pollution. Other lethal air pollution episodes occurred in New York City in 1953, where two hundred people were killed; the Meuse Valley, Belgium, where sixty-three died in 1930; and Donora, Pennsylvania, where twenty were killed in 1948.[3]

Breathing polluted air can bring on chronic, irreversible, and often fatal lung damage in even the healthiest individuals, causing such obviously-induced diseases as "black lung" from coal dust in coal miners and "brown lung" from cotton dust in textile workers. At lower levels of pollution, the effects are less apparent and not as well understood, but nevertheless result in more subtle effects such as shortened life spans, disability, cancer, increased asthma attacks, and generally poor health. The May 1980 report to the President by the inter-agency Toxic Substances Strategy Committee states:

> Of all urban dwellers, one in five — more than 35 million people — are at special risk from such illnesses as emphysema and bronchitis as a result of exposure to air pollution because of age or health. In general, industrialized, densely populated metropolitan areas have higher cancer mortality rates than rural areas, especially for lung cancer....In Great Britain, lung cancer rates declined first in areas where the clean air laws were applied.[4]

Dr. Marc Lavietes, a professor specializing in pulmonary medicine at the New Jersey College of Medicine and Dentistry, has had extensive first-hand experience treating patients with lung disease. He has observed, "The most common diseases I treat are, to a major degree, caused by environmental pollution — asthma, bronchitis, and lung cancer. . . . Research in the laboratory proves *beyond any doubt* that air pollutants can cause these diseases."[5]

Recent research indicates that people with cancer who live in cities with polluted air face a greater risk of their cancers spreading. (Over half of all Americans, some 60 percent, live in cities where the air violates federal clean air standards, and thus are at higher risk for lung damage, cancer, and other diseases.) A study released in March, 1990 suggests that air pollution, especially nitrogen dioxide from car emissions and cooking gas, harms the body's immune system and its ability to fight cancer.[6]

Air pollutants also produce lesions in the lungs that promote tumor growth and the spread of cancer to the lungs. This research provides further evidence that such pollutants as ozone and nitrogen dioxide, as well as cigarette smoke, are factors in the approximately 150,000 cases of lung cancer that occur each year, resulting in over 140,000 deaths.

According to the American Academy of Pediatrics, smog levels in most American cities can permanently scar the lungs of children. And experts from the Harvard School of Public Health report that air pollution is a contributing factor in one out of every twenty premature deaths in this country.[7]

Over 22 Billion Pounds a Year

On April 12, 1989, the US Environmental Protection Agency (EPA) reported that American industry was emitting a "startling and unacceptably high" volume of deadly chemicals into the air, land, and water.

This first national inventory of toxic releases into the environment found that US manufacturing facilities of major size released or dumped at least 22.4 billion pounds of toxic substances in 1987 — roughly one hundred pounds for every man, woman, and child in the country.

Approximately 2.7 billion pounds of these chemicals were released into the nation's air; the rest was disposed of in streams and other waters (9.7 billion pounds); underground wells (3.2 billion pounds); landfills (2.7 billion pounds), and waste treatment and other disposal facilities (2.6 billion pounds).

Since the report covered only 329 chemicals, and did not include all of the large manufacturers, or any of the smaller ones such as dry cleaning establishments, the actual volume of toxic emissions is substantially higher than indicated in the study.[8]

Some of these chemicals being routinely emitted into the air are incredibly toxic. In Kansas, releases included almost 70,000 pounds of the deadly nerve gas phosgene, which was used to kill thousands of soldiers during the chemical warfare attacks of World War I. Indiana's air was polluted with 143,097 pounds of methyl isocyanate, the gas that killed some three thousand people in Bhopal, India, in 1984.[9]

With the volume of deadly substances being released into the air each year amounting to some ten pounds for each American, it has been suggested that the air we breathe should carry a health warning from the Surgeon General.

As Congressman Henry Waxman (D-California) observed after releasing the report, "High levels of toxic releases are sure to be accompanied by high levels of human suffering — yet EPA is doing nothing to regulate them."[10]

Indeed, the impact of this pollution on the public's health is bound to be enormous if not yet quantifiable. A 1986 EPA study found that just twenty air pollutants could be causing two thousand cases of cancer every year. EPA has also concluded that living near chemical plants significantly increased one's risk of contracting cancer.[11]

But with tens of millions of pounds of poisons being released into our air every day, no American is safe from breathing these toxins, no matter where he or she lives.

Another Bhopal: Could It Happen Here?

On the night of December 2–3, 1984, a chemical accident at the Union Carbide pesticide plant in Bhopal, India, caused the release of methyl isocyanate fumes, resulting in the worse chemical disaster the world has even seen. At least 2,000 to 3,000 people were killed by the fumes, with an estimated 30,000 experiencing crippling injuries, including blindness and severe breathing difficulties. Over 550,000 people filed damage claims for injuries received during the accident.[12]

Many people fear that a similar accident could happen in the United States. Indeed, smaller-scale Bhopals occur with regularity in America, killing and injuring hundreds of people every year. An EPA study released in December 1985 documented an astonishing 6,928 major accidental chemical releases into the air between 1980 and 1985 in the United States. These accidents resulted in 138 deaths,

4,717 injuries, and over 200,000 people being forced to evacuate their homes.[13]

Another EPA report released in April 1989 found 11,048 toxic chemical accidents from 1982 to 1988, which resulted in 11,341 injuries and 309 deaths in the United States. In the last twenty-five years, according to the study, there were seventeen potentially catastrophic industrial accidents that released deadly chemicals at greater volumes and toxicity than occurred at Bhopal.[14]

Moreover, the health of many millions of Americans is endangered by the regular, routine release into the air of literally *billions* of pounds of toxic chemicals annually from factories, industrial facilities, and cars, trucks, and buses.

Sulfates: 187,000 Deaths a Year

Sulfates are among the most damaging air pollutants, and a 1978 study found that up to 212,000 adult Americans may be killed each year just by the presence of sulfates in the air. The study by Professors Robert Mendelsohn of the University of Washington in Seattle and Guy Orcutt of Yale University estimates that the annual number of adult white deaths from exposure to airborne sulfates is between 163,587 and 211,781 with the expected level put at 187,686. Sulfur dioxide causes between 7,730 and 39,782 deaths each year with the probable level put at 23,756. Equally lethal is carbon monoxide, killing between 7,416 and 35,389 white males, or probably 21,403. The authors conclude that "there appears to be a definite association between pollution and deaths from heart and circulatory failure."

Their research also found that the most polluted air was found in the northeastern and north central areas of the country, and that residents of those areas have about *twice* as great a chance of dying from air pollution as people in the rest of the country. The worst single area identified was in eastern Ohio, which had the greatest concentration of sulfates, probably from the presence of many major power plants. The cleanest air was found in states west of the Great Plains.[15]

Numerous other studies also demonstrate that sulfates cause breathing difficulty and various adverse health effects. A number of research papers published by EPA on this subject document an association between sulfate levels in the air and such effects as increases in mortality, heart and lung disease symptoms, chronic bronchitis, asthma attacks, lung disability, and susceptibility to viral disease of the respiratory tract.[16]

Rains of Death

Sulfates are also a major factor in the phenomenon called "acid rain," acidic precipitation in the form of rain, snow, hail, dew, and frost that is occurring throughout large areas of the United States, Canada, Europe, and Japan. In the northeastern United States, during the past twenty-five years, the acidity of rainfall has increased some fiftyfold! It is now one hundred times more acid than normal rainfall, and typical summer rains have the acidity of lemon juice, according to an EPA study released in mid-1980. As a result, tens of thousands of lakes in the United States and Canada have become damaged or "dead" — devoid of fish and plant life;[17] and trees and forests, especially at high altitudes, have been killed or damaged.

Acid rain takes place when smoke emissions from a variety of sources (e.g., tall stacks at power plants, smelters, car exhausts) containing oxides of sulfur and nitrogen are transformed in the atmosphere into sulfuric and nitric acids. Because of high smokestacks, these pollutants are often transported hundreds or thousands of miles before falling to Earth as acid rain.[18]

Thus, pollution from the huge concentration of coal-fired power plants and industries in the Ohio River Valley — which are responsible for one-fifth of all sulfur dioxide emissions across the United States[19] — ends up killing fish and forests in New York State.[20]

Acid rain is a worldwide problem. Winds from Great Britain kill salmon and other fish in Scandinavia. In Greece, Rome, and elsewhere in Europe, priceless and historic buildings, statues, and monuments, built centuries ago, are disintegrating because of acid rain and other air pollution. In one well-known incident in 1974, a storm in Scotland produced rain that was the acidic equivalent of vinegar.[21]

The economic impact of acid rain is incalculable but will certainly affect every American in the form of increased inflation, higher taxes, health and insurance costs, food and lumber prices, damage to private property (such as automobile paint corrosion), and loss of tourism to affected areas.[22]

And if acid rain is not bad enough, scientists have recently discovered the frightening phenomenon of "dioxin rain" in several areas of the United States.

Dioxin (tetrachlorodioxin, or TCDD) is the most deadly human-made compound known, and EPA considers it the most powerful carcinogen it has ever tested. In October 1984 a study by Indiana University researchers was released, showing that dioxins were found throughout the atmosphere and were being spread and distributed by winds and rain. High levels of dioxin were found in dust, apparently from incinerators used to burn trash, which produce dioxins when plastics are subjected to high temperatures or burned. As more and more municipalities and states turn to incineration to dispose of their solid waste, the spread of "dioxin rain" can be expected to continue.[23]

Catastrophic Climate Change

The burning of fossil fuels, such as coal, gas, and oil, and the discharge of certain industrial chemicals into the atmosphere, are changing the world's climate in a way that could threaten human civilization, and endanger the Earth's ability to support higher life forms.

With the accelerating depletion of the Earth's protective layer of ozone, and the warming of the atmosphere due to increased levels of carbon dioxide (the so-called greenhouse effect), were are facing a serious climatic crisis, the ultimate effects of which are unforeseeable but potentially catastrophic.

The heat and drought of recent summers may grow even more intense as such conditions become a permanent feature of our summer season. As the polar icecaps melt and sea levels rise over the coming decades, coastal cities and settlements could be flooded and might have to be abandoned.

Such scenarios sound alarmist and unreal, but when the scientific projections are put in layperson's terms, this is what the experts fear may be coming.

While increasingly more carbon dioxide (CO_2) is being produced by the burning of fossil fuels and forests, the accelerating destruction of forests worldwide means there are less trees to absorb the increased CO_2 levels in the atmosphere.

Because atmospheric carbon dioxide allows sunlight to pass through to the Earth but absorbs and traps some of the heat given off by the globe, it tends to raise the temperature of the planet, much as a greenhouse operates.

The early potential effects of the greenhousing of our atmosphere are projected to include rising sea levels and the disappearance of Bangladesh and other low-lying areas; the inundation of coastal regions, including New York City, much of the East Coast, and all of Holland; and the desertification of the American midwest and Central Europe.[24]

These relatively short-term effects are projected to occur in the next few decades. Over the long term, the next century or two, the rise in the Earth's temperature will simply "burn up" agricultural areas and make it impossible for most life forms, including humans, to survive.

One of the government's leading experts on climate and atmosphere testified before Congress that the nation's 1988 drought and heat wave — then the most severe in recorded history — was the beginning of the greenhouse effect. As Dr. James E. Hansen, of the National Aeronautics and Space Administration, told a congressional committee on June 23, 1988, "It is time to stop waffling so much and say that the evidence is pretty strong that the greenhouse effect is here.... It is already happening now."[25] Indeed, the five warmest years of the past century occurred in the 1980s with 1988 being the hottest of all. The first half of 1990 continued to set records for high temperatures throughout the world. Scientists fear that future drought could be "catastrophic" for the world's food supply, resulting in a depletion of dwindling grain supplies and widespread starvation.[26]

Depletion of the ozone layer will have equally dire results. In recent years, it has become all too apparent that the planet's protective layer of ozone gas, which makes life on Earth possible by shielding us from the sun's ultraviolet radiation, is being depleted at an alarming rate. A hole the size of the United States, containing only half the normal amount of ozone, now appears regularly over Antarctica. Overall, about three percent of the world's ozone layer is thought to have disappeared in the last decade; the damage already done, and still being done, may be permanent and irreversible.[27]

EPA has projected that if current trends continue, the increase in ultraviolet radiation hitting the Earth could cause Americans to suffer forty million cases of skin cancer and eight hundred thousand deaths in the following eighty-eight years, plus twelve million eye cataracts, in addition to the far greater numbers of such ailments that would occur worldwide.[28]

The ozone layer is vanishing largely because of an increase in production and use of gases known as chlorofluorocarbons (CFCs), which are used in refrigerators, air-conditioning systems, foam insulation, food packaging (such as styrofoam containers), and in aerosols outside of the United States (where such use in now largely banned).

Senator George Mitchell (D-Maine), after co-chairing congressional hearings on the subject, said that "CFCs threaten the very ability of the planet earth to support life as we know it."[29] Such warnings may be overly pessimistic, but can we risk gambling our future when the stakes are so high? As a Canadian government official working on the issue put it, "We can't afford to be wrong on this one. There's no recovery, no turning back."[30]

In September 1987 several dozen nations met and reached an

agreement to freeze, and later reduce by up to 50 percent over the next twelve years, consumption of CFCs. However, developing countries can continue to increase their use of CFCs by 10 percent a year for ten years; and the Soviet Union can complete its CFC plants already under construction. Conservationists had hoped for a phaseout of 95 percent of CFC production, a position the Reagan administration originally supported but abandoned under pressure from industry.[31]

It is projected that the plan agreed to will prevent an estimated 130 million excess skin cancer cases over the next century that would have occurred at the current rate of increase. But even these reduced levels of CFCs will allow an additional two percent loss of the ozone layer in the next seventy years, causing some seven million excess cancers. It is estimated that each one percent decline in high altitude ozone could cause twenty thousand additional cases of skin cancer in the US.[32]

On March 2, 1989, the twelve nations on the European Community agreed to eliminate their production and use of CFCs by the end of the century. But a few days later, on March 7, an international conference in London on protecting the ozone layer, attended by 123 countries, ended without agreeing on a timetable for a worldwide ban on CFCs. Scientists at the conference had warned that even if all ozone-destroying chemicals were banned immediately, the ozone layer would continue to deteriorate until the end of the century, and that it might take centuries for the layer to restore itself.[33]

Fortunately, there are numerous steps that could be taken to address the problem. The global tax on CFCs would discourage their use and encourage the search for alternatives. And such simple steps as redesigning automobile air-conditioner seals and valves to reduce leaks and using CFCs with shorter atmospheric life spans could effectively reduce CFC levels. We might even be able to live without plastic foam containers for our fast food, if it meant saving the planet.[34]

The Threat from Raising Livestock

Many people are surprised to learn that America could prevent vast amounts of energy use and the resulting pollution and warming of the atmosphere by simply cutting back on the raising of livestock and the consumption of meat.

As the Humane Society of the United States (HSUS), of Washington, DC, documents in its "Close-Up Report" on factory farming of livestock, raising animals for food uses huge amounts of energy to keep the animals warm in winter, and cool in summer, to transport feed to them, to haul away wastes, etc. The amount of fossil fuels needed to raise one pound of feedlot beef would produce forty pounds of soybeans.[35] According to HSUS, "Supplying the world population with a typical US diet (assuming petroleum as the sole energy source) would deplete world oil reserves in 12 years." But if all humans had a vegetarian diet, the reserves would last for 260 years.

The burning of fossil fuels is the largest single cause of global warming, which is being brought about mainly by concentrations in the atmosphere of carbon dioxide (CO_2), methane, and nitrous oxide. Large amounts of all three of these gases are produced by raising beef.

The clearing and burning of forests, much of which is being done to supply pastureland for cattle, produces carbon dioxide, while eliminating trees that suck up carbon dioxide and produce oxygen. Nitrous oxide comes from chemical fertilizers used to grow grain, 90 percent of which is fed to livestock. And methane is expelled by farm animals in tremendous quantities through their excrement, contributing to the destruction of the ozone layer.[36]

Since much of the clearing of tropical rain forests in Central America is being undertaken to raise beef for fast-food outlets in the United States, it is estimated that each four-ounce hamburger represents about fifty-five square feet of rain forest destruction.[37]

In his book, *Diet for a New America,* author John Robbins estimates that some 260 million acres of forest have been cleared in the United States to create cropland to produce a meat-centered diet. He projects that every time someone gives up eating meat and becomes a vegetarian, an acre of trees is spared.[38]

Saving Money by Cleaning the Air

Although opponents of strict environmental regulations often cite the expense involved in tightening standards, cleaning up and preventing pollution saves much more money than it costs. Numerous studies have documented the substantial savings that can be attained through enforcing EPS regulations and controlling certain pollutants.

It is estimated that air pollution is annually causing some $60 to $100 billion in damages to the environment. The American Lung Association projects that illness and death caused by dirty air costs Americans up to $40 billion a year in health care and related expenditures.[39]

In April 1980, the President's Council on Environmental Quality

(CEQ) issued a report estimating that fourteen thousand lives and billions of dollars were saved in the United States in 1978 alone as a result of improvements in air quality since 1970, the year the Clean Air Act was passed.

The report, prepared for CEQ by economics professor A. Myrick Freeman III, concludes that "national benefits which have been realized from reductions in air pollution since 1970 lie in the range from roughly $5 billion to $51 billion per year," with the best estimate of air quality improvement benefits attained in 1978 being $21.4 billion. Such savings include reduced damage to human health, crops, forests, vegetation, buildings, and other property.

If the "best estimate" for 1978 benefits is used — $21.4 billion — this represents almost $5 billion more than the costs of complying with the Clean Air Act, and more than $2 billion greater than *all* spending on air pollution control for that year.

These figures are considered to be quite conservative since they do not include actual benefits from preventing further degradation of air quality or benefits accruing to Canada and Mexico. In addition, Freeman estimates that "between 2,780 and 27,800 lives are saved per year as a result of air pollution control. The most likely number is 13,900."[40]

An earlier study by Lester Lave and Eugene Seskin, *Air Pollution and Human Health,* calculated the cost benefits of regulating air pollution, and came up with similar figures. They conclude that controls on stationary pollution sources (such as power plants) yield over $16 billion in savings on health costs (not including property damage) at a cost of only $9.5 billion, producing a net benefit in dollars of $6.5 billion, to say nothing of the savings in terms of deaths and illness prevented. They estimate that if all health benefits from improved air quality (such as increased earnings) are included, the combined savings to society amount to "some $23 billion a year (or) considerably higher," in addition to an increase in life expectancy of almost one year for the average person.[41]

In 1990, the American Lung Association, one of the most effective groups leading the fight against air pollution, published an important report entitled, "The Health Costs of Air Pollution," which summarized widely-varying studies discussed below demonstrating the enormous savings that can be achieved by cleaning up our air.

A 1984 EPA study found that health cost benefits of implementing new federal standards for fine particulates (in 1988 dollars) were between $5.3 and $9.6 billion with total benefits varying from $533 million to $222 billion.[42]

A 1985 EPA report determined that limiting lead concentrations in gasoline would provide annual health benefits (in 1988 dollars) of over \$6 billion by preventing high blood pressure in middle-aged males and cognitive development problems in children. The study found that the health benefits of the lead reduction program (\$34 billion) would exceed its costs (\$3.1 billion) by a factor of more than ten to one.[43]

A 1987 study examining the health effects on the US population from exposure to automobile and truck exhaust emissions found the estimated health costs in 1985 to be between \$4 and \$85 billion.[44]

A 1988 EPA study on air quality standards for sulfur dioxide found that exposure to sulfates may be the largest cause of adverse health effects. It estimated (in 1988 dollars) mortality benefits as high as \$432 billion from sulfate reductions required by the current federal sulfur dioxide standard (assuming "worst case" correlations between sulfate pollution and premature deaths).[45]

The savings that can be achieved by controlling pollution are summed up in a 1987 EPA report, "EPA's Use of Benefit-Cost Analysis: 1981–86," which concluded that proposed new EPA regulations would provide over \$10 billion in net economic benefits, mostly by reducing health costs from pollution.[46]

Wasting Half Our Energy

By practicing energy conservation, Americans can save money, reduce pollution, enhance our national security, and strengthen our economy, while maintaining our present standard of living, and even reducing taxes and inflation.

America wastes about half of the energy it uses. This means that realistic energy conservation measures could effectively double our energy supply. Such a course of action could be undertaken without Americans changing their basic life-styles. In fact, other countries with comparable standards of living use and waste far less energy. America, with some 5 percent of the world's population, accounts for over 30 percent of the world's energy consumption.[47]

As an environmental task force put it in *The Unfinished Agenda* (1977), each baby born in America is equal to several dozen born in underdeveloped nations in terms of energy used and pollution generated:

> each new American consumes... 60 times as much energy as the average South Asian. Thus, the 1.3 million Americans added each year through natural increase (not counting immigration) constitute at least as much of a burden on the global resource base as the annual increase of 12 million in India.[48]

Put another way, the average American used 57 times as much commercial energy in 1974 as the average citizen of India and 122 times more than the average Nigerian, according to the United Nations *Statistical Yearbook* for 1975.

In 1979, the Harvard Business School issued a report, *Energy Future,* concluding that over the long run, the United States can use up to 40 percent less energy with "virtually no penalty for the way Americans live":

> If the United States were to make a serious commitment to conservation, it might well consume 30 to 40 percent less energy than it now does, and still enjoy the same or an even higher standard of living. That savings would not hinge on a major technological breakthrough, and it would only require modest adjustments in the way people live.[49]

And according to the tenth annual report of the President's Council on Environmental Quality:

> technology is now available to increase US energy productivity in an economical manner. More efficient buildings can save the home owner several dollars for every dollar judiciously invested in energy-conserving features. By selecting vehicles with more efficient designs, automobile users can economically reduce fuel costs by 50 percent or more. A wide variety of conservation technologies available to industry today can often provide a 30 to 50 percent per year return on investment.[50]

National legislation requiring a deposit on soft-drink bottles in order to encourage their recycling would save an estimated one hundred thousand barrels of oil a day, in addition to reducing litter. And 165 million barrels of oil a year could be saved if American homeowners simply installed and used windowshades, according to a 1980 study by North Carolina State University. The study found that shades could save the average home $168 a year in fuel and utility costs, and $314 a year in areas with extreme temperatures. In the summer, it was estimated, lowering the shades before sunlight pours in could reduce summer utility bills by $100.[51]

Another way of saving enormous amounts of energy is through effective appliance efficiency standards, which were largely eliminated by the Reagan administration. As Public Citizen pointed out in its 1984 report, "a Safe Energy Platform":

> Residential appliances consume one-third of all domestic electricity, as well as oil and gas equal to 50 percent of US oil imports on a heat-content basis. Effective appliance efficiency standards for furnaces, boilers, central and room air conditioners, water heaters, refrigerators, freezers, cooking ranges, clothes dryers, and lighting

equipment...could displace 100 large coal or nuclear power plants over the next two decades....

The savings to US consumers over the next two decades would be in excess of $100 billion, cutting the average home electricity bill of $1,500 in half.

Foregoing these coal and nuclear plants will also prevent land degradation, air pollution, and increases of toxic sludge dumps and radioactive waste sites. Acid rain emissions would be reduced by two million tons per year.[52]

Perhaps the most successful single conservation measure of all has been the fuel efficiency standards legislated in 1975, requiring cars to achieve an average of 27.5 miles per gallon (mpg) by 1985.

In 1981, the National Highway Traffic Safety Administration (NHTSA) reported that these fuel standards have saved the average buyer of a 1980 car $1,700 in gasoline costs, with the purchaser of a 1985 model saving an additional $1,600.

NHTSA has estimated that such improvements will save the United States about a trillion dollars in imported oil over a twenty-year period. And by producing vehicles that can attain 60 mpg, the US would save five million barrels of oil per day.

Unfortunately, the Reagan administration repeatedly granted the automobile industry exemptions from these requirements, allowing a 26 mpg standard from 1986 through 1988, and a 26.5 mpg rate for 1989. These are tremendous improvements over the 14 mpg the average car was getting at the time of the 1973 Arab oil embargo. But stricter standards along the lines of 50 or 60 mpg, which NHTSA has said are technologically and economically feasible, would save huge amounts of energy.

Indeed, just increasing the fuel standards from 26 to 27.5 mpg would save FOUR TIMES MORE OIL than could be expected to be produced from Alaska's Arctic National Wildlife Refuge, a pristine sanctuary that the oil industry is attempting to open up to oil exploitation.[53]

As the Natural Resources Defense Council points out, a real commitment to energy conservation could prevent environmental disasters like the *Exxon Valdez* oil spill in Alaska's Prince William Sound and eliminate the need to drill for oil in ecologically sensitive areas:

Merely improving the efficiency of existing oil and gas and water heaters to the fullest cost-efficient extent would save the equivalent of 4.5 billion barrels of oil. This is roughly the same amount of oil that is believed to underlie the most sensitive areas (Alaska's Arctic National Refuge and Bristol Bay fishery; the Florida Keys; New England's George's Bank Fishery; and portions of the Pacific and Mid-Atlantic

Coasts)....Moreover, aggressive weatherization programs for America's 53 million oil- and gas-heated homes would save twice the oil believed to be in these areas.

Finally, an increase in fuel efficiency of cars to 40 mpg and of trucks to 30 mpg by the year 2008 would save more than three times the amount of oil in these areas.[54]

Solar Energy: Clean, Cheap, and Renewable

Solar energy provides an environmentally benign way of meeting America's and the world's energy needs. In its 1978 report, "Solar Energy: Progress and Promise," CEQ concluded that "the nation could meet as much as one-quarter of its energy demands from solar sources by the end of the century and perhaps as much as one-half by the year 2020.... For the period 2020 and beyond, it is possible to speak of the United States' becoming a solar society — one in which solar is not a supplementary source but rather a primary source of energy."[55]

Unlike the United States, many other countries already make extensive use of solar energy. According to Denis Hayes, former head of the federal Solar Energy Research Institute:

> About one-fifth of all energy used around the world now comes from solar resources: wind power, water power, biomass, and direct sunlight. By the year 2000, such renewable energy sources could provide 40 percent of the global energy budget; by 2025, humanity could obtain 70 percent of its energy from solar sources.[56]

The Clean Air Act and Its Nonenforcement

The main reason that our nation's air remains so dangerously polluted is that the EPA has never adequately enforced the laws regulating air pollution, especially the Clean Air Act.

Attempts by environmentalists to strengthen the law's provisions and enforcement, particularly on acid rain, have repeatedly been stymied by Congress and the executive branch. The eight years of the Reagan administration were characterized by strong hostility to increased protection for the environment and public health. A stronger Clean Air Act was most effectively opposed by the Reagan administration; by the automobile, steel, oil, gas, and chemical industries; some of these industry's unions; and by Congressman John Dingell (D-Michigan), chairman of the House Energy and Commerce Committee and an ardent supporter of the automobile industry. Legislation to strengthen the act has been introduced in Congress almost every year for the past ten years preceding 1989, and each time these efforts have been defeated.

In the twenty years since the Clean Air Act was passed in 1970, EPA has stubbornly resisted enforcing the law. It has set emission standards — and weak ones at that — for just seven cancer causing air pollutants! The only major fuel additive it has even partially regulated is lead, which is still allowed in gasoline and remains in the air and a danger to the health of many Americans. Lead is especially dangerous to children, causing brain damage and a variety of behavioral, mental, and learning disorders, such as decreased IQ, hyperactivity, and inability to concentrate or pay attention in school.

With the election in 1988 of George Bush, who promised to be "the environmental President," prospects brightened that a new and stronger Clean Air Act could be enacted. And as of late spring 1990, a significantly strengthened law was working its way through Congress.

But amid charges of "closed-door, back-room deals," the Bush administration and the Senate leadership in April, 1990, agreed on compromise legislation that many environmentalists, citizens groups, and congressional leaders attacked as far too weak to address adequately the problems.

Senate Majority Leader George J. Mitchell (D-Maine), a leading supporter of environmental protection and of strengthening the act, explained that he was forced to conduct "back room negotiations" with Bush administration officials who opposed a tougher law because he did not have the votes to block or end a threatened White House-supported filibuster to kill the legislation, or to override a veto by President Bush.[57]

Attempts to amend and toughen key portions of the bill were voted down, resulting in a significant weakening of provisions in the original Senate bill to control automobile emissions (a primary cause of urban smog and the greenhouse effect), acid rain, and the release of toxic, cancer-causing chemicals. In May 1990, the House of Representatives passed a similar compromise bill. Nevertheless, the legislation represented a real improvement over the current law, albeit one far too weak to effectively protect the environment and the public's health.*

---

*On November 15, 1990, a compromise bill was signed into law, putting *some* significant controls on *some* types of pollution, but falling short of what was needed to adequately address the problem.

The Future of Our Nation — and Our Planet

As a result of the government's inaction over recent decades, urban smog has greatly worsened and reached record levels in 1988, the worst year ever recorded. Some 150 million Americans — three out of five of us — now live in areas where EPA considers the air quality to be unsafe.[58]

A report released by the World Resources Institute in September 1988 showed that air pollution was doing some $5 billion a year worth of damage to crops such as soybeans, peanuts, kidney beans, cotton, and winter wheat, in addition to immense damage to trees and forests.[59] But the greatest cost of air pollution is in terms of human health.

On February 28, 1989, several medical authorities and federal environmental officials appeared before congressman Henry Waxman's House subcommittee, holding hearings on strengthening the Clean Air Act, to give alarming testimony on how air pollution was threatening the public's health, especially children. This is particularly true of ozone pollution, formed when hydrocarbons from automobile exhausts and factory emissions react with sunlight to form urban smog, which reaches a peak on hot, sunny days.

Dr. Philip Landrigan, representing the American Academy of Pediatrics and the American Public Health Association, testified that exposure to ozone at certain commonly-found levels could affect the lung functions of children. He stated that if children's outdoor play was not limited in such situations, they could suffer pain, shortness of breath, and other respiratory problems.[60]

Dr. Thomas Godar, President of the American Lung Association, told the subcommittee that "ozone can cause immediate short term changes in lung function" and other respiratory problems "in healthy adults and children who exercise moderately or heavily during periods of elevated ozone concentrations." Exposure for as little as one hour can cause pain, coughing, shortness of breath, and other problems, he testified, adding that there was growing medical evidence that repeated exposure could cause permanent lung damage.[61] And a study released in May 1990 revealed that autopsies of one hundred Los Angeles area youths aged fourteen to twenty-five showed twenty-seven had suffered severe lung damage, and so had serious tissue abnormalities. If they had lived, most of the youths would have developed lung disease in less than twenty years, according to Dr. Russell P. Sherman, Professor of Pathology at the University of Southern California.

It is thus clear that the price we will pay for our failure to control air pollution will be a costly one, both in terms of dollars and cents, and the lives and health of millions of Americans. It is impossible to put a price tag on the loss of children's health, or their freedom to play outside. But as *Atlanta Journal-Constitution* columnist Jim Fain puts it, "Any tolerance for those who sanction polluters vanishes with the dry rasp of a child's struggle for breath in the night."[62]

Yet these costs, heavy as they are, pale in comparison to the horrors that lie ahead if we allow the greenhouse effect and the destruction of the world's protective ozone layer to proceed. Indeed, what is at stake in the fight against air pollution is the very survival of our planet, and ourselves.

But unless our senators and congressional representatives, and the administration of President George Bush can be persuaded to take the necessary action to protect us from poisons in the air, there will be a dim future, if there is one at all, for coming generations of Americans.

L. G. R.

* * *

TAKING ACTION

1. In March 1989, EPA made public a report stating that manufacturing facilities collectively emitted 2.4 billion pounds of toxic air pollutants in 1987 — equivalent to ten pounds of toxic material per American. The estimate is conservative since only nineteen thousand of the thirty thousand industrial facilities met the requirement and supplied EPA with their toxin inventories. (The list on the following page shows state ranking in total toxic air emissions). Learn what industries around you are doing with their toxic waste. If they don't have a convincing disposal program, notify the EPA, Greenpeace, Earth First!, National Wildlife Federation Natural Resources Defense Council, and other organizations. (Addresses in the Appendix.)

2. If every American family planted one tree, over a billion pounds of "greenhouse gases" would be removed from the atmosphere every year. (*50 Simple Things You Can Do to Save the Earth*, The Earthworks Press)

3. Chlorofluorocarbons are emitted in the manufacturing of styrofoam products such as cups, plates, and fast-food sandwich containers. Encourage your office and social organizations to eliminate the use of these products.

Total Toxic Air Emissions
(measured in millions of pounds)

1. Texas	239.0	26. Iowa	39.2
2. Ohio	172.7	27. Oklahoma	36.4
3. Louisiana	138.3	28. West Virginia	35.6
4. Tennessee	135.0	29. Alaska	31.7
5. Virginia	132.4	30. Massachusetts	30.1
6. Michigan	116.4	31. Connecticut	26.1
7. Indiana	112.9	32. Kansas	24.7
8. Illinois	99.2	33. Oregon	20.9
9. Alabama	98.3	34. Maryland	20.2
10. North Carolina	94.6	35. Arizona	16.6
11. Georgia	93.6	36. Maine	14.6
12. New York	89.4	37. Nebraska	14.4
13. Pennsylvania	87.5	38. New Hampshire	13.0
14. California	82.7	39. Colorado	11.0
15. Utah	77.3	40. Delaware	8.0
16. South Carolina	64.2	41. Rhode Island	5.9
17. Mississippi	57.3	42. Montana	5.3
18. Arkansas	54.6	43. Idaho	4.2
19. Kentucky	52.7	44. New Mexico	3.6
20. Missouri	50.6	45. Wyoming	3.2
21. Florida	50.2	46. South Dakota	2.4
22. Wisconsin	48.7	47. Vermont	1.4
23. Minnesota	42.1	48. Hawaii	1.1
24. New Jersey	42.0	49. North Dakota	0.9
25. Washington	40.6	50. Nevada	0.7

(Source: *Garbage,* September–October 1989)

---

4. A number of cities are now requiring residents to limit the use of fireplaces due to pollution from the burning of wood, especially during atmospheric inversions. Cooperate, and if your area doesn't have such a program, ask the local health officials about initiating such a program, which would apply during certain weather conditions.

5. Some of the most common pollution comes from the burning of fossil fuels. Limit the use of cars, and cut down on energy used in your employment and home.

6. Plant trees. Trees are a great source of clean air in addition to being storehouses of carbon.

— 8 —

How We Use and Abuse Water

Robert W. Adler, Natural Resources Defense Council

> We can help clean up our water. It's as simple as realizing that what we sweep into a gutter may end up in the water on a beach, that the fertilizer and pesticides we put on our lawn can run off into a river.
>
> Shouldn't we demand that companies be shut down, not just fined, for dumping toxins into our water? That developers be stopped cold from building over wetlands? That there be no more extensions granted to cities that violate clean water laws?
>
> There's not much time left for tolerance.
>
> Hugh Downs, ABC News, September 8, 1988

> If there is magic on this planet, it is contained in water.
> Loren Eiseley, *The Immense Journey*

Most Americans take water for granted. We take water for granted because it is so common. Just turn on the tap.

Increasingly, however, the average American is becoming aware that clean, ample water supplies are in serious trouble. Sometimes we are reminded by natural phenomena, such as the nearly nationwide drought of 1988. Sometimes we are reminded by our own folly, as in the Ashland oil spill that polluted drinking water for hundreds of miles down the Ohio River, or the catastrophic *Exxon Valdez* oil spill that slaughtered birds and marine mammals in its path.

But these incidents are episodic. Only when we recognize daily threats to our water will we begin to treat water with proper respect.

America's water is in trouble. Aquifers that supply the world's breadbasket are running perilously low. Drinking water is contami-

120

nated with chemicals that cause cancer and birth defects. We are told that even fish from our protected natural areas, such as the Everglades National Park, are not safe to eat. Shellfish beds are closed all along the Atlantic and Gulf coasts. Medical wastes and plain garbage wash up on our beaches.

These problems will require strong medicine to correct. But these steps will not be accepted unless we understand why they are needed. We all need to understand better how we use water, and how we abuse it.

How We Use (and Overuse) Water

Americans use more water per person than people in virtually any other country:

Country	Water Used Per Person Each Year (in gallons)
United States	571,000
Canada	396,500
Soviet Union	351,000
Australia	345,000
Japan	244,000
Mexico	238,000
West Germany	177,500
France	160,000
United Kingdom	134,000
Sweden	126,500
China	122,000
Israel	118,000[1]

In the home alone, we each use an average of between 140 and 168 gallons of water a day (estimates vary); the average household uses over 100,000 gallons of water a year. This water is split about equally between indoor and outdoor use.

How do we use so much water? Water use for common household tasks (using standard fixtures) may seem surprising:

Task	Water Use (gallons)
Flush toilet	5–7
Shower	25–50
Brush teeth	2
Shave	10–15
Wash dishes (hand)	20 (with water running)
Dishwater	2[2]

But even considering these figures, only about one out of ten gallons of water used in the United States is in the home. The rest goes to uses such as agriculture and industry.[3]

By far the largest use of water in the United States is irrigated agriculture. In seventeen arid states west of the Mississippi, irrigation accounts for more than nine out of every ten gallons of water used. Irrigated agriculture is extremely important to our economy. While only one out of seven cultivated acres is irrigated (a total of forty-five million acres — about the size of North Dakota), this acreage produces about a quarter of total US crop value. The amount of irrigated acreage has tripled since World War II and is still increasing.

Industry takes over thirteen trillion gallons of water out of rivers and out of the ground each year — enough in a decade to fill Lake Erie. This accounts for nearly half of the country's water withdrawals. But very little of this water is actually consumed; most is released — generally with a mixture of pollutants — back to the environment. Nevertheless, industry accounts for roughly 10 percent of US water consumption, about the same amount as municipal water use.

The average citizen might say: "So what?" To many, there appears to be no shortage of cheap, clean water. It is true that in total amount, the United States is water-rich. While we use more water per person than almost any other country in the world, we also possess more renewable fresh water than almost any other country in the world except Canada, Brazil, China, Indonesia, and the Soviet Union.

But much of this water is concentrated in certain regions. Other areas, most notably dry agricultural regions that rely on heavy amounts of irrigation water, are rapidly running dry. Yet these dry areas continue to "mine" water at an alarming rate, causing perilous drops in groundwater tables.

A prime example is the Ogallala aquifer,[4] which supplies irrigation water in eight states (Texas, Oklahoma, Kansas, Nebraska, South Dakota, Wyoming, Colorado, and New Mexico) and supports a $30 billion a year agricultural economy. The aquifer itself is about the size of California and contains about as much water as Lake Huron, the second largest of the Great Lakes.

By all accounts, the Ogallala is in trouble. The first irrigation wells were sunk into the Ogallala about ninety years ago, and intensive irrigated agriculture began just after World War II. But in just this short period, the level of the aquifer has dropped dramatically. Because we pump far more water from the aquifer than is replenished by rainfall and other sources, we are depleting the aquifer at the rate of about a trillion gallons a year. Already millions of acres of land have been taken out of irrigation because of this decline, and by the year 2020, an area the size of New Jersey will have to be taken out of irrigation.

The Ogallala aquifer is not alone. Water tables are falling beneath one out of four acres of our irrigated cropland. Between 1978 and 1982 alone, net irrigated area in the United States dropped by over 1.6 million acres, an area bigger than Delaware.

In terms of declining groundwater levels, the worst problems are in relatively dry states with heavy agricultural irrigation. But the great drought of 1988 shook virtually the whole country, bringing surface waters to their lowest levels in decades. Water levels plunged in the nation's three largest rivers — the St. Lawrence in the Northeast; the Mississippi in the Midwest; and the Columbia in the Northwest.

While the 1988 drought was extreme, droughts are becoming far more frequent. In 1989, New York City announced its third drought emergency of the decade and banned all lawn watering, car washing, and filling of private swimming pools. Businesses were asked to reduce water use by 20 percent.[5]

What can be done to reverse this trend? Most often, the government deals with water shortages by increasing supply,[6] often without regard to economic or environmental costs. As a result, we build tremendous irrigation projects that do not pay for themselves. Already farmers in the West who use federal water projects pay only *one fifth* the true cost of that water.[7] The rest comes from our taxes. The Congressional Budget Office estimates that 170 major water systems in the country will need more supply by the year 2000 at a cost of \$2.5–\$3.1 billion per year. Even greater sums are needed to fix aging urban water systems, especially in the urban Northeast.

Major water projects can also hurt the environment. In one dramatic example, thousands of fish and water fowl were killed by toxic irrigation drainage water in California's Kesterson National Wildlife Refuge. These harmful effects are beginning to be recognized. EPA recently vetoed a major water project designed to supply water to Denver, Colorado-based on environmental concerns, including the loss of important wetlands along the South Platte River.

Fortunately, there is often a far better solution to the water supply crisis: a gallon saved is a gallon earned. We can save by using water more *efficiently*, that is, by growing or producing the same amount, or by doing the same job, with less water. Not only are water efficiency alternatives available and affordable; in many cases they can actually *save* money, energy, and other resources important to our national economy.

Efficient Agriculture[8]

Irrigated agriculture can be extremely inefficient. Worldwide, only thirty-seven out of every hundred gallons of irrigation water, on average is actually used by the plants. The rest is lost to the air, to groundwater, or to surface water. Fortunately, much progress has been made to improve irrigation efficiency. The following methods improve the percentage of irrigation that actually is used by plants:

Water recycling — recovery and reuse drainage water can pay for itself in reduced (pumping) costs.

Precise levelling of fields can substantially reduce water runoff. Some farms actually use lasers to level their fields, reducing water use by 10–40 percent.

Sprinklers generally are more efficient than ditch irrigation. Special "drop tube" sprinklers and other advanced techniques can improve efficiency to the point where nine out of every ten gallons of irrigation water is actually used by the plants.

Special planting methods such as reducing the amount of tillage, or "furrow diking" (placing mounds at intervals within each furrow) can improve water use even where more traditional irrigation techniques are used.

Selecting drought resistant crops can reduce the need for irrigation water. For example, alfalfa requires about nine times as much water per season as lettuce.

We know how to use less water without sacrificing our agricultural production. It is simply a question of getting more farmers to save water by using these techniques.

Efficient Industry

Industrial water use can also be reduced substantially *without* compromising production. The key to industrial water conservation is recycling water within the factory. It is simply a question of getting American industry to use these methods.

Currently, the average gallon of water in US factories is used between three and four times before it is discharged back into the environment. This reflects a substantial improvement over the past three decades, but water efficiency potential in US factories has barely been tapped. The following examples from other countries demonstrate this point:

- Due to extreme water shortages, Israel more than doubled its amount of industrial production per gallon of water used between 1962 and 1975.

- Sweden, where paper mills account for 80 percent of total water use, cut its paper mill water use in half while doubling its paper production between the early 1960s and the late 1970s.

- Six oil refineries in arid areas of the Soviet Union do not discharge *any* of their water.

Efficient Communities

Like industries and agriculture, the American communities throw away huge amounts of water that could be put to good use.

Most of this water is in the form of sewage treatment plant discharges. These discharges are rich in nitrogen, phosphorus, and other nutrients needed to grow various crops. Replacing these nutrients, in turn, uses scarce oil reserves that we convert into chemical fertilizers.[9] So by dumping sewage effluent into our rivers, lakes, and coastal waters, we throw away valuable water and valuable fertilizer nutrients while polluting further our water. Similarly, trillions of gallons of runoff water pollutes our surface waters each year.

Again, there is a far more logical solution. Adequately treated sewage water and storm water can be reused as irrigation water for crops, forests, parks, and other areas. In fact, sewage water reuse can improve agriculture because nutrients are released slowly and continuously, rather than in a single large dose, as is the case with chemical fertilizers.[10]

There are over one thousand wastewater reuse projects in the United States in which water is reused for irrigation, industrial cooling and processing, and groundwater. For example, Los Angeles and Orange Counties, California, reuse about two-and-a-half million gallons of water a day for irrigation, cooling water, and groundwater recharge. But despite this effort, only about a fifth of one percent of water use in the United States is met by reclaimed water. By comparison, reclaimed water met 4 percent of Israel's water needs in 1980 and is expected to reach 16 percent by the year 2000.

Communities can also decrease their overall water use by finding leaks in water supply systems. Many US cities are losing a quarter or even a half of their total supply just through leaks in the pipes! New York City, for example, loses about 150 million gallons of water a day to leaks, enough to serve a city of a million people!

Efficient Individuals

Individual water users can also can save money while helping to protect water supplies. Efficient plumbing fixtures are now available that can help the average homeowner save about four out of every ten gallons of water used in the home. This saves money not only on monthly water bills but, in the case of water-saving shower heads, on energy bills as well.

Water Savings by Using Efficient Plumbing Fixtures[11]

Device	Water Use	Percent water saved
Toilets	1.6 gallons	50–75
Showerheads	2 gallons/minute	30–50
Faucets	0.5–2.0 gallons/minute	50–80

Many of these devices are used in other industrialized countries. This may explain why water use per person in many European cities is less than half of the US average.

Another explanation may be the cost of water. Despite the fact that we use so much more water than do European countries with similar standards of living, we pay about half as much for the privilege. Water is still so cheap to the average homeowner that there is little incentive to save.

More important, the cost of saving water may be far lower than the cost of providing more water. Tucson, Arizona, a city with severe water problems, promoted water conservation with price increases and price structures that encourage water use at times when the total water demand is low. Peak pumping rates declined by more than a quarter in less than a decade, allowing the city to save $45 million in new water system costs.

If we want to squander our public water supplies, at least we should be required to pay the real cost of that water. More likely, we will begin to think twice before turning on the tap.

How We Abuse Water

HOW WE POLLUTE OUR RIVERS, LAKES AND OCEANS

For centuries we have used our rivers, lakes, and oceans as dumping grounds for society's wastes. Just how much pollution is dumped into our waters? And where does it come from?

The typical picture of water pollution is a large factory spewing noxious chemicals into pristine waters. To some extent, this is still true. Despite considerable progress in pollution control over the past two decades, factories continue to release large amounts of dangerous pollutants into surface waters.

But individuals are also responsible for water pollution. Each time we flush the toilet we send from two to ten gallons of our own pollution to public sewage treatment plants, which generally release their wastes into public waters, or into our private septic tanks, which release wastes into groundwater.

We also cause pollution simply by where and how we live. At least half of all water pollution comes from sources other than factories and sewage plants such as runoff from farms, city streets, construction sites, and other areas. We add to this pollution when we build our homes close to coastlines or rivers. We pollute water when we thoughtlessly dump used oil or paint thinner into our local storm drains, or when we use too much fertilizer or chemical pesticides on our lawns.

These three major sources of water pollution — factories, sewage, and poison runoff — are taking a drastic toll on our public waters. Nationwide, at least a quarter of our rivers, lakes, and coastal waters are not safe for fishing or swimming.[12]

POLLUTION FROM FACTORIES

How much factory waste reaches our waters? About seventy-five thousand factories nationwide dump their wastes directly into rivers, lakes, and coastal waters. The thirteen hundred factories that discharge wastes to coastal waters alone dump a total of about five trillion gallons a year. More important, how clean is this water when it is returned to the nation's waters? Factory water can be badly polluted. It is often mixed with thousands of different chemicals, producing a "toxic soup" by the time it reaches the end of a factory.

The 1972 Clean Water Act established the basic principle that no one has a "right" to use our waters as dumping grounds. Various tools were required to clean up polluted factory water before it is dumped back into the environment. Eventually, Congress directed that the release of polluted factory water was to be ended altogether.

EPA was slow to act. But a 1976 NRDC (Natural Resources Defense Council) lawsuit forced EPA to regulate over 125 toxic pollutants discharged by the nation's largest industries. All told, these controls require industry to reduce their discharges of toxic pollutants into coastal and other waters by over one thousand *tons* a day.[13]

Despite this progress, we still have a long way to go and we are nowhere near the elusive goal of ending factory pollution altogether.

Hundreds of millions of pounds of uncontrolled toxic pollutants are released into US waters each year, and NRDC recently filed another major lawsuit to end this pollution.

SEWAGE POLLUTION

What happens when we flush the toilet? In some cases our sewage is treated by septic systems below our front lawns. Such systems can create environmental problems of their own, generally by polluting groundwater.

Often our toilets are connected to a public sewer system, especially if we live in cities or areas where soils are too rocky or too sandy to allow septic systems. This sewage is sent to a public treatment plant, where solids are removed, biological wastes are broken down, and bacteria are killed by disinfection.

But the sewage treatment process if far from perfect. The end-product of the sewage treatment process includes wastewater, which is generally discharged back to coastal and other waters, and sewage sludge, which consists of most of the solid material. While federal law encourages communities to reuse wastewater for irrigation and similar uses, most areas have elected the easy path of using our public waters as dumping grounds.

The liquid waste generated by sewage plants is released in large amounts into rivers, lakes, and coastal waters. These discharges amount to over thirty-six billion gallons of sewage waste a day, adding up to about thirteen trillion gallons a year.

Even properly treated sewage still contains considerable amounts of pollution, including biological wastes and nutrients such as nitrogen and phosphorus. But many public sewage plants also accept wastes from factories, which include the same type of toxic soup as is present in other factory wastes. Most of these toxics are not removed during the sewage treatment process, which is designed primarily to treat household sewage — not toxics.

Worse, some sewage dumped into coastal waters does not even receive full treatment! Some of our sewage discharged to coastal waters receives only the initial stage of treatment, removing only the grossest contaminants. And large amounts of sewage are actually dumped into rivers and oceans without any treatment at all. This latter problem is caused when sewers designed to carry household and other sewage are combined with storm sewers. When it rains, these combined sewers overflow, carrying large amounts of raw sewage (and other wastes) directly into waters used for fishing and swimming. EPA estimates that twenty-five million Americans are served by sewer systems that overflow.[14]

Sewage plants are the biggest cause of water pollution from biological wastes and nitrogen. These pollutants reduce oxygen levels in coastal waters, literally choking the life out of many productive waters. And sewage wastes are also major sources of other pollutants such as bacteria, oil, phosphorus, and toxics.

A lot of progress has been made over the past twenty years in reducing pollution from sewage treatment plants. The federal government alone has spent over $40 billion on new or improved sewage treatment plants.

But we have a long way to go. According to EPA's most recent survey of sewage treatment plant needs, another $70 billion will be needed to meet the sewage needs of our current population alone.[15] Accounting for expected population growth over the next twenty years, this price tag rises to over $80 billion. And as the population grows, even more pollution from domestic sewage may be released into our public waters.

POISON RUNOFF

While we all know about water pollution from factories and sewage treatment plants, our surface waters are also polluted by a more pervasive type of pollution — poison runoff from city streets, farms, building sites, and other common uses of land.[16]

In fact, poison runoff causes *at least half* of the nation's water pollution and is the leading source of some contaminants. And as with sewage, we all contribute to this problem.

The major culprit is simply growth and development. More and more people live near our rivers, lakes, and coastlines, causing more and more poison runoff. While the amount of growth has much to do with the amount of poison runoff, the way in which we use the land also contributes to poison runoff. For example:

- We use more fertilizer and dangerous pesticides than needed to grow food and other crops. These chemicals run off farms and pollute our waters.

- Our homes, shopping centers, and other buildings are surrounded by acres of pavement. And America depends on its massive road system. Rainwater that runs off these surfaces collects oil, chemicals, and toxic metals from cars and other sources, and dumps these pollutants into our waters.

- Timber companies cut trees to make wood, paper, and other products that we use at work and at home. But cutting trees and building logging roads too close to the water causes erosion that pollutes our water.

- We don't control erosion of sediment and other pollutants from farms, mines, and other activities.

Large amounts of sediment in the water smother fish gills, which prevents fish from breathing properly. It also covers the important bottom habitat in which fish lay their eggs. High levels of nutrients (nitrogen and phosphorus) in polluted runoff causes excess growth of tiny water plants — a process known as eutrophication. These blooms lower oxygen levels and literally choke the life out of large water bodies, such as lakes and estuaries. Large fish kills often result.

Poison runoff also contains toxic pollutants that are dangerous in even small amounts. EPA found at least sixty-seven toxic pollutants in polluted runoff from city streets and other areas.[17] Other toxic pollutants are bound to sediment that runs off mining sites. These pollutants contaminate fish and shellfish, and can be toxic to birds and other fish and wildlife.

Far less progress has been made in cleaning up poison runoff than pollution from factories and sewage plants. Unfortunately, stopping poison runoff will be even harder because it is caused by a much larger number of sources. Each source alone contributes only a small amount of pollution. But taken together, our rivers, lakes, and coastal water are slowly but surely being suffocated by poison runoff.

How We Contaminate Our Groundwater[18]

Pollution also affects groundwater, underground supplies of water held in porous rocks, and other formations that can be "mined," by pumping, for human use. While groundwater pollution has been of concern for years, it took public health scares such as the Love Canal for most Americans to wake up to the threat of groundwater pollution.

Warning signs of surface water pollution can be obvious, such as fish kills, odors, and discoloration or cloudy water. Pollution of groundwater can be equally dangerous to human health, but much harder to detect. In fact, except for obvious problems with taste or odor, the only way to detect serious groundwater contamination is through expensive chemical testing.

One out of every two Americans obtains drinking water from the ground. Not surprisingly, groundwater use is concentrated west of the Mississippi and in rural areas, and some states rely almost entirely on groundwater for public water supplies.

How much of our groundwater is polluted? Even more than for surface water, the answer is a resounding, "We don't know." Some groundwater contamination has been reported in all states, and at least twenty states report that groundwater pollution is a major concern. But the exact extent of this pollution is not known.

Because of the high cost and complexity of groundwater testing, only a tiny fraction of our groundwater supplies have been tested for the full range of possible contaminants. And due to this uncertainty, government agencies such as EPA and others can only "estimate" how much of our water is polluted.

According to these very rough estimates, only 1 to 2 percent of our groundwater is currently contaminated by major sources of pollution such as hazardous waste sites and landfills. While this may sound small, it means that millions of Americans regularly drink water that may cause cancer, birth defects, and other health problems. Plus, this EPA "estimate" does not include more widespread but dispersed sources of groundwater pollution, such as agricultural pesticides and fertilizers.

More important, our existing monitoring information may only be catching the tip of the iceberg. As with surface water pollution, virtually everything we do on land can pollute groundwater. The following is a partial list and description of the activities that can pollute our groundwater supplies:

Septic tanks — sewage from a third of the American public is treated by twenty-two million septic tanks. Each tank releases between fifty thousand and seventy-five thousand gallons per year of sewage, for a national total of more than a trillion gallons a year. This wastewater penetrates and can contaminate groundwater with nitrates, bacteria, and chemicals that we dump down our toilets and drains. Septic tank contamination is most prevalent in densely populated areas where too many tanks discharge to a small area. A particularly disturbing problem caused by septic tanks is nitrate contamination, which has been linked to infant crib death syndrome.

Underground storage tanks — Many states cite leaking underground tanks as the leading cause of groundwater pollution. There are literally millions of these tanks buried around the country, holding billions of gallons of chemicals, some of which are hazardous. Many tanks are old, and many were built with materials that do not resist corrosion. Thousands of these tanks have leaked, polluting soil and groundwater.

Accidental spills — Thousands of accidents occur each year in which dangerous chemicals are spilled. Especially when local fire departments or others respond to the spill by flushing it away, these chemicals can pollute groundwater (or surface water).

Agricultural chemicals — Millions of tons of pesticides, fertilizers, and other agricultural chemicals are used each year on American farms. A recent, preliminary EPA survey found seventy-four pesticides in the groundwater of thirty-four states, and EPA expects to find even more contamination when this survey is expanded. Overuse of chemical fertilizers causes excess nitrogen, phosphorous, and other chemicals to penetrate into groundwater. Ironically, farmers could save money by changing many of these practices — by using integrated pest management techniques that reduce the need for expensive pesticides; and by using organic fertilizers that release nutrients more slowly than chemical fertilizers, increasing crop yields; and by nutrient management plans that calculate how much fertilizer is actually needed and when and how it can most effectively be applied.

Waste disposal sites — Most of society's garbage is dumped in or on the ground. And "garbage" includes everything from your household wastes to hazardous wastes produced by industrial processes. The array of landfills, impoundments, lagoons, and other sites used to store or dispose of waste is staggering. There are almost one hundred thousand active landfills in the United States, including over seventy-five thousand industry sites and almost twenty thousand municipal dumps. Added to this are about two hundred active and an astounding twenty thousand abandoned hazardous waste sites. Why so many sites? We generate over 150 million tons of garbage a year nationwide! And while we often fear the pollution that can be caused by hazardous wastes from factories, even normal household garbage includes large amounts of toxic chemicals from everyday household products. If not properly handled, pollutants from society's garbage end up in our groundwater and sometimes right back in our drinking water.

Well injection — One frequent "solution" to the nation's waste disposal problem is to dispose of chemical and other liquid wastes by injecting them into wells that go below the earth's surface. There are more than two hundred thousand of these injection wells around the country, including almost three hundred used to get rid of hazardous wastes. Unfortunately, much of this injection is simply "out of sight, out of mind." Many states have reported groundwater pollution in aquifers near well injection sites, most frequently in connection with the disposal of oil and gas wastes.

There are many other sources of groundwater contamination, caused by activities we see every day or by producing products we use every day. Chemicals spilled at construction sites; wastes produced at oil, gas, and mining sites; salts and other chemicals used to de-ice roads; pollutants in sewage sludge used to condition soil — all can find their way into groundwater supplies. In short, wherever we live and work, we threaten our groundwater. Clearly, we need to do a far better job of protecting this resource.

R. W. A.

* * *

TAKING ACTION

1. Use less water. Take showers of less than five minutes instead of a bath. Don't let the water continue to run as you wash your hair, shave, brush your teeth, or rinse dishes. (Source: *Utne Reader,* November–December 1989)

2. Wash your car on the grass. The lawns will make use of the water and the soap will eliminate unwanted "pests" the natural way.

3. Consider the use of toilet dams, a single rubber device which installs in seconds and saves up to four gallons of water every time you flush. Annually, that's thirteen thousand gallons of water a year for the average household. (Available from Seventh Generation, 800-456-1177.)

4. Available also from Seventh Generation is the Low Flow Showerhead, which uses 70 percent less water and saves an estimated $100 a year on your hot water bill.

5. Be sure to check your water supply for pollution. Private and public laboratories are available for this service. If your water contains elements that are harmful, look into the many companies that produce water filter systems which eliminate contaminants.

6. Repair all leaks and drips as soon as they occur. Letting them go can waste considerable water.

7. Landscape with vegetation that requires little or no irrigation.

8. Buy phosphate-free, biodegradable soaps and detergents. If your grocery stores do not carry them, ask that they do. These products also are available from Seventh Generation.

9. Keep paint residues, used oil, and other household chemicals out of storm drains, sinks, and toilets; instead, save these chemicals for the hazardous waste facility in your area. Better yet, switch to nontoxic household products that are increasingly becoming available to consumers.

10. If you farm, use a nutrient management plan to save money on fertilizer and to increase yields, and use integrated pest management to save money on expensive pesticides.

11. If you farm, explore how you can increase profits by using state-of-the-art irrigation devices and by planting crops that require less irrigation.

12. Use lawn fertilizers sparingly and only when needed.

13. Demand laws that require those who use the most water, or who use water inefficiently, to pay their fair share of the bill.

14. Insist on stronger laws and regulations to stop the continuing pollution of our rivers, lakes, and coastal waters.

15. Demand tougher action to prevent the contamination of our groundwater supplies by toxic chemicals.

GARBAGE: ON LAND, IN WATER

— 9 —

Where Are We Going to Put All this Garbage?

George Baggett

> For too long, waste "management" in America has been a matter of picking up trash and burying it in the ground...maybe after burning part of it first. As we keep pouring in more trash than the system can handle, the "waste stream" is simply overrunning its banks.
>
> Environmental Defense Fund, 1988

If you are not aware that there is a solid waste crisis, it might be best that you skip this chapter and return to it when you are asking yourself, "Where are we going to put all this garbage?" Surely you have heard about the trash problem. Perhaps you saw stories about the Islip garbage barge touring the world, looking for a place to dump. We each generate three to five pounds of garbage a day. We see it along our highways, and the garbage truck comes once or maybe twice a week, and hauls "IT" away. Where is "Away"? Is it a small town in New Jersey or just anywhere out of sight and out of mind?

We create millions of tons of garbage. We put it in landfills that leak, we dump it at sea, we burn it, and these methods are not solving the problem. These methods are creating a major liability for future generations. The solid-waste crisis has had its hand held high, begging for a solution, and we must find that solution before the toxic ramifications of our actions consume us.

The first rule a mathematician learns when trying to solve a problem is that it is necessary to define the problem correctly. If the problem is defined incorrectly, you will always get the wrong answer. This is exactly what has happened to the problem of solid waste. We have defined solid waste as one material, one garbage mess. City planners have done feasibility studies based on so many tons per day of garbage. New York is a 28,000 tons-per-day market target of garbage. Just figure: 28,000 tons per day x $150 per ton = $4,200,000 per day x 365 days per year = $1,533,000,000 per year. Trash is big business.

The fact is that garbage is not one thing in black bags or roll-off containers. Trash is made up of inorganic materials, metals, plastics, yard waste, food waste, rubber, wood, newspaper, mixed paper, glass, and God only knows what else. By mingling these materials together, we are following a recipe that will lead to toxic brew. This is why landfills do not work, and why incinerators are not the answer to the problem. These measures fail to define the problem correctly.

Another rule in mathematics is that when you are trying to solve a complex problem, it may be necessary to solve the problem in phases. The answer to part of the problem in an early phase will provide a number to be plugged into an equation down the line. If you try to solve the latter equation by guessing, you are only giving it your best guess. The more complex the problem, the less desirable it is to make a guess. Proper solid waste management is a complex problem. We have tried guessing already.

The solid waste crisis is acute in the East. Land is at more of a premium near Eastern cities, and high-population-density cities like Newark, New York, and Philadelphia are experiencing landfill shortages. These shortages are coupled with excessive disposal charges. The garbage crisis has forced Eastern communities to make hasty decisions, and incinerator vendors were more than ready to meet the market demand. This has resulted in numerous "waste-to-energy" garbage incinerators both under construction and in operation today.

The term "waste-to-energy" became the sales-pitch bullet, as they say in the advertising industry. A bullet is a catchy phrase that has an element of truth in it, but that is primarily meant to sway the minds of people who are not intimately involved and do not know, or do not want to know, the details. In this case, people and local politicians were sold the idea that they could turn garbage into electricity. It sounded too good to be true, and it is. People were led to believe that the community could build a new power plant to make electricity that would be fired by trash. But believe me, there is no free lunch in solid waste.

As it turns out, garbage is one of the worst possible fuels. Combustion of garbage releases toxic gases, transforms heavy metals in their most biologically available (oxide) form, makes a toxic ash, and is the most expensive method of handling solid waste.

The recent history of the trash-incinerator industry is one of environmental and economic disaster. Heavy metals like mercury and hexavalent chromium, as well as toxins like dioxins and phosgene (nerve) gas, are just a few of the toxic substances released into the air as a result of burning garbage, and current emission standards are not adequate to protect the air we breathe. Incinerator ash also fails the EPA test for hazardous substances, and is hazardous waste.

Since incinerators are the most expensive option for waste reduction, many cities have incurred tremendous debt in making hasty decisions to build these facilities. Having done so these cities have hindered recycling for a period of ten to twenty years since they are committed to burning their trash, and must pay for the incinerator. The sales pitch fails to mention that incinerators do not remove the need for a landfill, and schemes like using ash for road-bed materials are environmentally irresponsible.

As mentioned before, most people remember the nightly news reports about the Islip garbage barge, but there were two other barges afloat that did not make the nightly news. These barges were filled with incinerator ash from the Philadelphia trash incinerator. The first barge was dumped in Nigeria, but when the second went into Nigeria to be dumped, the ship was met by the Nigerian military. The ship towing the barge was under a Norwegian flag, so the Nigerians arrested the Norwegian ambassador; he was released only after the ash was removed. The barges were ultimately dumped at sea, and Philadelphia is still trying to figure out what to do with their ash. The problem of what to do with the ash is remarkably similar to the nuclear-waste problem.

Citizen action groups are now beginning to form as a result of the trash mess. It is my personal belief that such citizen action groups are the beginning of a major grass roots movement similar to the civil-rights movement or the movement against the Vietnam war. Let me suggest that if we act, black and white together, hand-in-hand, we shall have a clean environment some day.

Citizens must take the bull by the horns on the issue of solid-waste management. It may be a generalization, but, in most cases, politicians should not be determining the outcome of the solid-waste issue. A core group of a few citizens can organize groups comprised of a variety of people with only one thing in mind: a clean environment to leave our children.

One lesson some environmentalists and most industrialists have learned is that if you educate your local politicians to group concerns, the more likely these politicians will conform to the needs of the people. Tell them what you want! In most cases, it helps to do some — if not all — of their homework for them.

With this in mind, it is necessary to outline a strategy for dealing with solid waste, develop flow charts, and discuss a plan for action. Consultants and community planners need arrows, charts, direction, and a gentle nudge. Local grass-roots groups can gain the upper hand by providing guidance.

We begin by defining the problem. Surely, we know that recycling technology is a major part of any plan to manage waste, but what and where do we recycle? A market for a material does not appear because that material can be separated from our waste. We need to develop a market. Then what? What do we need to do next and where do we go from here?

We need to break down the tasks and actions into parts and find solutions for each part. Then we must organize these issues, prioritize them, and then put them together. Community-based waste management is when a community approaches this problem in phases and separates tasks into manageable units.

The first priority of a recycling plan is to develop markets for recyclable materials. State, local, and federal agencies as well as private industry should buy recycled paper products. We then need to encourage traditional economic-development organizations like the Chamber of Commerce to promote product manufacturing that utilizes recycled materials. We need to locate and list regional facilities that handle and process waste materials that otherwise would only contribute to what we call a "waste stream."

Along these lines, we can promote and develop buy-back centers. These centers will pay citizens for aluminum cans, glass, and paper.

We need to establish a program for waste reduction to eliminate unnecessary packaging, particularly plastics and foam containers. Further, we need to encourage backyard composting of yard wastes. (Facilities for composting materials that cannot be composted in the backyard will be discussed under the section "Composting.") Another part of waste minimization is the development of deposit programs and ordinances governing disposal of batteries and problem containers such as solvent cans. Cities should also be encouraged to participate in rapidly-growing federal and state consumer-education programs to minimize waste.

Development of neighborhood curbside recycling programs is a must. Some cities ask citizens to separate waste into three, and sometimes as many as five, different containers. However, many cities are finding that they achieve greater participation rates by using a two-container system. One container is used for collection of recyclables, and the other receives waste that cannot be recycled. The recyclables are first taken to a centrally-located separation facility. The materials are separated and characterized both at the source and then more extensively at a centrally-located materials processing facility.

There are various means of handling household hazardous waste. One way is to have a special drop-off center; another is to collect these materials in the recyclable container. Regardless of methods, it is very important to remove for special handling potentially hazardous materials from the waste. These items include immediately hazardous products like paints, solvents, wood preservatives, waste oil, pesticides, and household cleaners.

Items that are hazardous when burned could be separated in this system. This would include such things as household batteries, electronic components, advertising inserts, magazines, PVC, and vinyl plastics.

The commercial and industrial sector has seen the profit in recycling. In fact, much of what is being recycled at the present time are materials from industry. They know a good deal when they see one. Industries are also mandated by law to reduce waste and develop waste minimization programs. What is needed now is another attempt at an industrial-waste exchange, like those tried in the early 1970s, where industries were brought together to find uses for each other's by-products. In the industrial sector, communities may need to develop a special waste-disposal facility for sludges generated by pretreatment waste waters discharged to city sewers.

After recycling, composting, and waste minimization programs are in place, then, and only then, can we determine optimum disposal methods for remaining waste. As I see it, we will have four choices. We can use incineration for the remaining materials that are safe to burn, landfill these materials, develop advanced recycling techniques, or a combination of all three options.

Extending the mathematical analogy each of these parts of the problem requires work and a solution. In this case, discussion among groups is necessary to determine how each part fits into your community's equation. How will waste minimization fit? Will people participate in recycling voluntarily or will participation need to be mandatory? As you can see, people need to talk these issues out, and this is a task in which churches can and should play a major role.

Public participation. The public should be involved in every step of development and implementation of an integrated waste management plan. Communities should develop a recycling commission made up of neighborhood leaders chosen by their respective boards. This commission should also include city-council and county-appointed representatives. This commission could assist employees of public-works departments and other agencies in the implementation of an integrated waste management system to include recycling and composting programs and the development of a materials processing facility. Recycling programs should involve charitable organizations, which can be an integral part of such a commission.

Markets. This is the most exciting part of an integrated solid-waste management program because opportunities are created for small businesses to expand and new businesses to develop. Since the processes involved are relatively low-tech, facilities can be up and running in a surprisingly short amount of time. In the past year, industries that recycle tires, plastics, and mixed paper have grown dramatically; in recent months, the number of mills using scrap steel has burgeoned.

To give you an idea of the volume of resources available, the Environmental Defense Fund has recently published a pamphlet on recycling. EDF notes that this issue is one of the eight most important current issues. The EDF information states that every Sunday, more than five hundred thousand trees are used to produce the 88 percent of Sunday newspapers that are *not* recycled. They also note that the amount of aluminum Americans do *not* recycle is enough to rebuild our commercial airline fleet every three months. Further, the EDF informs us that we throw away enough glass bottles and jars to fill the 1,350 foot twin towers of New York's World Trade Center every two weeks — and we go through 2.5 million plastic bottles every *hour,* only a small percentage of which are being recycled.

It should not be assumed that materials should be recycled if and only if there is an existing local market, defined as someone willing to pay. Communities will have to consider *"avoided cost,"* or savings, when a salvager takes away material for nothing or for a charge, less than the cost of its separation and landfilling. However, the community will have to be watchful in order to prevent illegal dumping.

High priority should be given to recycling activities that result in the most resource-recovery savings. An example of this is seen in paper recycling. The amount of energy required to make a ton of paper from virgin materials is sixty thousand kilowatt hours. While the amount of energy required to make a ton of paper from recycled paper is only sixteen thousand kilowatt hours, the process of recycling conserves forty-four thousand kilowatt hours of energy per ton of paper. However, the amount of energy that could be recovered by burning a ton of paper is only six hundred kilowatt hours.

One method of recycling plastic is a process whereby mixed plastics are ground into fluff, heated, and formed into usable products like fence posts, building materials, and industrial flooring. This is an excellent recycling process.

The same can be said of rubber from tires. We can make this rubber into products that conserve a nonrenewable resource or it can be used to make rubberized asphalt. In this process, the rubber from tires is ground off discarded tires and sent to an asphalt plant, where it is added to asphalt for road paving. In a world in which oil resources are dwindling, conservation of nonrenewable resources may play an important role in recycling and waste management. In other words, we need to treat our waste as a resource. Some call it urban ore.

Many American cities and states have taken a much expanded view of recycling. A number have adopted goals of at least 50 percent reduction through integrated waste management. Results of recycling efforts in the city of Buffalo, New York, indicate that over 80 percent reduction is feasible, which is greater than the 70 percent reduction capability claimed by proponents of mass-burn incinerators. Recent studies have found that incinerators can divert only 51 percent of the waste from a landfill.

Waste minimization. Reducing the amount of waste generated is a key element in a community-based solid waste strategy. The EPA has proposed eliminating costly, useless, and polluting excess packaging as well as wasteful commercial and industrial practices. Integrated with maximum composting and recycling, waste reduction can extend the life of existing landfills and result in the lowest overall system cost. The community-based solid waste disposal plan outlined herein will not only solve the problem, but it will afford the best possible protection of our environment.

Recycling has demonstrated the feasibility of recycling as an alternative to incineration. The result of this integrated program, including composting, has demonstrated that over 80 percent of the waste stream is recyclable. Advanced recycling techniques are in the works that will improve the efficiency of recycling. Public participation levels have reached as high as 80 percent even in voluntary programs and 98 percent in mandatory programs.

Composting is another key element in a community-based waste management plan. Biodegradables are taken to a facility where they are ground into a mulch, mixed with hybrid bacteria, and placed into piles to let bugs do their work. Air is pumped through the mass to assist the decomposition process, and heat is produced as the matter is transformed. There are various schemes for accelerating the composting process, and it has been demonstrated that composting can reduce volume eight to one. Even if the resulting soil is used for landfill cover rather than sold, this process is one of the most efficient forms of waste reduction. Since composting requires very little capital investment and utilizes equipment that most communities have on hand, this element of a plan can be set in operation without delay. Cities should involve their parks department in the composting phase of the plan. Most parks departments have use for compost.

Materials processing facility. The materials processing facility should include recycling facilities, a separation plant, a flea market, a buy-back center, and a transfer station. The transfer station would transfer nonrecyclables to a landfill or other ultimate disposal such as an incinerator. The buy-back center would pay individuals for bringing recyclables to the facility. The separation plant could separate various waste items, and its operation would be enhanced by the sorting and grouping of specific items, i.e., paper from glass from aluminum, etc.

The facility would also have a flea market. The flea market would sell materials that have value without being processed. (Retail sales from the flea market at the Berkeley, California, recycling center have been on the average $47,000 per month.)

The separation facility is second only to the composting facility in importance. Large urban communities with thousands of tons of trash per day to separate will need to install systems that are quite elaborate. Rural communities have options ranging from transfer stations to detailed separation plants, which would concentrate on separating the minute waste particles. This action would reduce the need for disposal, which would reduce the cost to the community.

Public involvement and education is so important that it cannot be stressed enough. The public should be invited to be involved in all activities at the materials processing facility. Displays, models, and examples can demonstrate home-composting methods, waste minimization, consumer education, and challenges in waste handling and recycling. The education center could be a part of the flea market or the separation facility. Emphasizing this facet of the project can add an educational dimension and vastly increase public interest and participation.

Recyclable materials processing for transfer off-site. It is likely that portions of the waste stream will require transfer to regional recycling plants. Examples of these facilities would be the de-tinning operations, de-inking plants, tire recycling, and plastics reprocessing. To increase the likelihood that maximum materials are recycled, communities may, in some cases, subsidize the transfer of certain wastes to regional facilities. Necessary revenue could be generated from the more profitable recycled materials so as to avoid use of landfill disposal or incineration.

Landfill. As part of this plan, the only new landfill that could be recommended is one that would receive only waste called postprocessed residuals. This category of waste includes items that management from the materials processing facility deems nonrecyclable. Regardless of the waste management options taken by communities, a landfill will always be required. Many communities have experience with landfills, and most of these landfills are a major liability because the result of mixing various items of the waste stream is almost always toxic soup. Removing the biological activity before burial makes landfills safer in the future.

Household hazardous waste. Many programs to handle household hazardous waste have met with success. Household hazardous waste includes old solvent cans, pesticides, paint cans, old spray cans, mercury batteries, cadmium batteries, and other materials that are sources of toxins when landfilled or burned. Special pick-up days, monitored drop-off centers, and public education can keep these materials out of processing facilities, landfills, and incinerators. Mercury batteries can be collected at watch repair and service centers or sold to mercury recyclers. Paint can be made available to schools and theatrical groups. All nonrecyclable household hazardous waste should be handled in accordance with EPA guidelines — and these guidelines would be available at the education center.

Reducing waste and recycling are environmental activities in which each and every one of us can be involved. If you have not yet been involved in environmental programs, this is a good place to start. And we might remember that the less waste we create, the less we're going to have to deal with.

G. B.

Trash
by Volume

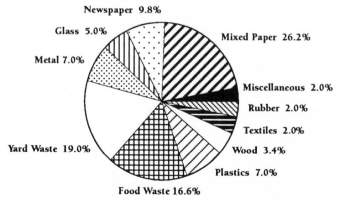

Newspaper 9.8%

Glass 5.0%

Metal 7.0%

Mixed Paper 26.2%

Miscellaneous 2.0%

Rubber 2.0%

Textiles 2.0%

Yard Waste 19.0%

Wood 3.4%

Plastics 7.0%

Food Waste 16.6%

FLOW OF MATERIALS TO RECYCLE TO
THE MAXIMUM EXTENT POSSIBLE

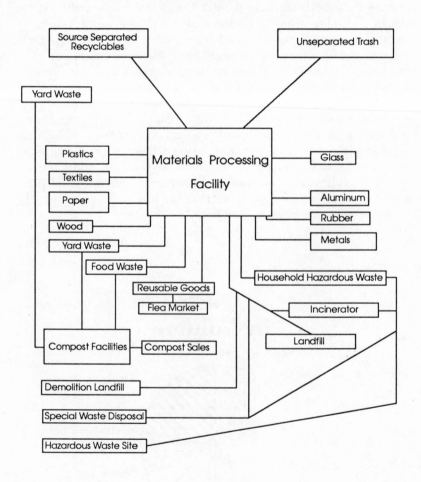

TAKING ACTION

1. Purchase bulk produce. The packaging around produce is unnecessary and is usually composed of a styrofoam plastic. Besides the destructiveness of styrofoam and wastefulness of the packaging, you don't get to select the produce. Look, first, for markets for organically grown produce, and if you can't find one in your area, select produce from bulk bins.

2. Plastic and paper diapers. These create an enormous load on the waste stream and can be a health hazard. They do not decompose, carry germs, and are made from nonrenewable resources. Use cloth diapers or a diaper service. If you must use throw-away diapers, purchase nonpolluting, biodegradable diapers from Seventh Generation. You may contact them at 126 Intervale Road, Burlington, VT 05401 or by calling (800) 456-1177.

3. Drinking containers. If you purchase coffee and soft drinks away on a regular basis, it is better to make a one-time purchase of either a hot or cold beverage container at a convenience outlet and take it back for refills. By carrying a permanent container, you will avoid using and disposing of numerous styrofoam cups and other throw-away containers — and adding to the landfill problems.

4. Back to cloth. Paper napkins and tissues require a tremendous amount of trees for manufacture and then eventually become a significant part of the waste stream, as they're not recyclable. Make or buy cloth napkins and handkerchiefs. Launder them along with your regular wash.

5. Informal dining. Save aluminum pie tins and other unbreakable wares for casual occasions rather than using styrofoam plates and cups, which are not biodegradable and add to the landfill problem. Using paper plates and cups also results in the cutting of too many trees.

6. For general cleaning. Again, avoid buying paper towels. Use old clothes as rags and keep them handy. They will pick up spills just as well as the paper towels and will not add to deforestation and the landfill overflow.

7. Shopping bags. The ideal shopping bag is reusable, such as those used for years by Europeans. They are available from Seventh Generation. Next best, take paper bags back to the store rather than using new bags each time you buy groceries. If you don't have a bag and are given the choice of plastic or paper, take paper.

8. Retail-store packaging. Refuse to take your purchases in sacks or bags. Carry your items out with the receipt or take your own sacks. Remove excess packaging materials and leave them at the store.

9. Avoid plastic or laminate furniture. Plastic doesn't decompose. Purchase wooden — homemade or second-hand — furniture and replace fabric when it is worn. Some older furniture has very good quality framing and is more substantial than some furniture manufactured in recent years. Plastics and laminates do not decompose and the articles will eventually end up in a landfill.

10. At home and at the office — use mugs rather than paper and particularly styrofoam cups. If your place of work is still going through dozens of styrofoam cups a day, encourage use of ceramic cups. Churches and social organizations should be especially interested in contributing to the demise of styrofoam since it is not only a landfill problem but also a major contributor to ozone depletion.

11. At the office, make double-sided copies. Considerable paper is wasted by making one-sided copies.

12. Buy beverages in returnable containers. A few smart legislatures have placed a monetary value on returnable single glass bottles.

13. Pressure fast-food chains. Ask that your purchases be wrapped in paper, not styrofoam containers. If they aren't willing to meet your request, there is nearly always another fast-food restaurant in the vicinity. Try them. Hardee's is particularly obliging.

14. Recycle! Recycle! Recycle!

— 10 —

Plastics in the Ocean:
More than a Litter Problem*

Kathryn J. O'Hara, Center for Marine Conservation

> The very survival of the human species depends upon the maintenance of an ocean clean and alive, spreading all around the world. The ocean is our planet's life-belt.
>
> Jacques-Yves Cousteau

The widespread presence of plastics in the oceans is a global problem that will require international cooperation to solve. But the roots of the problem stem from individual human carelessness in disposing of materials that are a part of our everyday lives. No one can point a finger at a particular country, region, industry, or group as the major contributor to the problem. The responsibility is shared by us all.

What Happens to Plastic Goods
When Their Useful Life Is Over?

It is common practice for crews on oceangoing vessels to throw their wastes overboard. Litter disposed of on land that is washed into marine areas via rivers and sewer systems contributes still more. Trash blown from landfills, tossed by careless beachgoers, or lost from other sources also adds to the problem. Most synthetic debris can create aesthetic or environmental problems, but the qualities

*Adapted from Kathryn J. O'Hara, *Marine Wildlife Entanglement in North America and Plastic in the Ocean: More than a Little Problem,* published by the Center for Marine Conservation, 1988.

that have made plastics so successful make plastic debris a particular threat to the ocean.

Plastic is lightweight, buoyant, and tends to float, causing a multitude of problems in the ocean. At least fifty species of seabirds are known to ingest small pieces of floating plastic, mistaking it for food such as plankton or fish eggs. Sea turtles ingest floating plastic bags and wrap, which can resemble prey such as jellyfish in color, shape, size, and motion. Ingested plastic may lodge in an animal's stomach or intestines, blocking the digestive tract. If large quantities of plastics are ingested, an animal may eventually die of malnutrition, caused by false feelings of satiation; they may simply stop eating.

Lost or discarded fishing nets and other plastic items suspended in the water column are known to entangle countless numbers of marine species. Entanglement refers to the interaction of a marine animal with debris that encircles its neck, flipper, tail, or other body parts. Entanglement may occur when an animal comes into either accidental or intentional contact with an item. Some entanglements have been attributed to the animal's inability to see plastic debris, especially fishing gear that is designed to be nearly transparent in water. In other cases, encounters with debris may be more deliberate. Young seal pups in particular are attracted to floating debris because of their curious and playful nature. Unfortunately, such curiosity may lead to entanglement.

Plastic is strong, and once a marine animal becomes trapped in a plastic strapping band, net, or other plastic item there is very little the animal can do to break free. Sea turtles entangled in a fishing line have managed to swim with this burden, only to become snagged on a rock, coral, or some other bottom structure. The line's strength prevents them from breaking free, and they eventually drown. Seabirds and waterfowl such as ducks and geese that become caught in fishing line have managed to fly, only to strangle after becoming snagged on a tree limb or power line.

This persistent nature of plastics is the greatest threat to the marine environment — plastic debris can continue to entangle and kill marine species for years after it is lost or discarded.

Types of Debris

Nets that are either accidentally or deliberately discarded at sea are killing marine wildlife, wasting fishery resources, and endangering human safety. An estimated thirty thousand northern fur seals die each year due to entanglement, primarily in net fragments. Lost nets that "ghost fish" continue to catch finfish and shellfish that are never retrieved by fishermen. One derelict gill net found off Alaska measured over nine miles in length. Entangled in the webbing were hundreds of valuable salmon and 350 dead seabirds. Nets and rope also can disable vessels after becoming wrapped around propellers. Several near-fatal accidents of scuba divers entangled in lost nets have been reported.

Fishing line is also a problem. For sea turtles and birds, discarded monofilament fishing line is lethal. One turtle found in New York had actually ingested 590 feet of heavy-duty fishing line. An ornithologist in North Carolina found the body of a laughing gull entangled in fishing line. He began to retrieve the remainder of the line to remove it from the beach. Twenty-five yards later he found five more birds entangled. Ospreys, gulls, and other birds even collect pieces of line as nesting material, creating death traps for their young. Fishing line also endangers boaters, who waste time and money on damage caused by line wrapped around propellers.

Cargo associated waste. Plastic is being used more and more in cargo transportation. Plastic strapping has replaced rope, and is rapidly replacing steel, because it is lightweight, does not rust, and is about half as expensive as steel.

Discarded plastic strapping becomes a problem when it is cast into the water, particularly when it is removed from a package without being cut, thus forming a ring that can entangle wildlife. Seals are the major victims. A synthetic "collar" of plastic strapping can cause lacerations prone to infection and, as the seal grows, the band will become more constricting, eventually causing strangulation.

Plastic pellets. Plastic pellets, the raw form of plastic, are transported in bulk to manufacturing sites and are made into consumer goods.

Plastic pellets have been found in concentrations of up to thirty-five hundred per square kilometer on the surface of the Atlantic Ocean, and up to thirty-four thousand per square kilometer in the Pacific — comparable to about fifty pellets on an area the size of a football field. But although pellets are not as abundant as other debris in the ocean, they composed about 70 percent of the plastic eaten by Alaskan seabirds examined in one study. Researchers speculate that the seabirds selectively choose plastic pellets over other debris because, to seabirds, these plastics may resemble planktonic organisms, fish eggs, or even the eyes of fish and squid. Nearly all the plastics ingested by seabirds float at the surface where these natural prey are found. Many plastic pellets are similar in size and shape to small crabs and other prey. Even researchers in laboratories have mistaken resin pellets for fish eggs.

Sewage and domestic plastics. Several items enter the marine environment through sewage and wastewater treatment plants, including plastic tampon applicators, condoms, thin pieces of plastic sheeting from sanitary napkins, and disposable diapers. (This is in addition to the widely-publicized incidents of used and AIDS-infected hypodermic needles washing up on East Coast beaches.) During a beach cleanup in New Jersey, for example, volunteers collected 650 plastic tampon applicators on a small section of coastline.

Domestic plastics include bags, bottles, lids, and a multitude of other consumer items. During a 150-mile survey of North Carolina beaches, more than eight thousand plastic bags were found in one day. Bags and sheeting are ingested by marine wildlife, who mistake these items for food. One turtle was found with fifteen plastic bags in its stomach; a whale was found with fifty. Plastic six-pack rings used to bind beverage cans are a threat to all kinds of marine animals. Researchers have found fish, birds, and even a California sea lion entangled in plastic six-pack rings. Along three hundred miles of Texas coastline more than 15,600 six-pack rings were found in one day.

Where Does It All Come From?

OCEAN SOURCES

More than a decade ago, the National Academy of Sciences estimated that ocean sources dumped fourteen billion pounds of garbage into the sea every year — more than 1.5 million pounds per hour. This figure includes all solid cargo and crew waste material (paper, glass, metal, rubber, and plastics) that were assumed to be disposed of by the world's commercial fishing and merchant shipping fleets, passenger cruise liners, military vessels, oil drilling rigs and platforms, and recreational boaters.

According to the Academy not only is the majority of ocean litter primarily concentrated in the Northern Hemisphere but the United States could be the source of approximately one-third of all the trash in the world's oceans. Hence, a reduction in the amount of litter generated by the United States would contribute significantly to a worldwide reduction.

LAND-BASED SOURCES

Untold quantities of plastic enter the ocean via rivers, drainage systems, estuaries, and other avenues. Sewage and wastewater treatment and disposal systems also dump plastic wastes into the oceans. In some areas sewer systems discharge plastic tampon applicators, diapers, and other items directly into marine areas. Sewage sludge also is a source of plastics. This is especially true in the coastal waters off New York and New Jersey, where during sewage treatment approximately

5 percent of the plastics escape screening and are dumped along with treated sewage sludge. In the late 1970s an estimated one thousand plastic tampon applicators were dumped with sewage sludge in the New York Bight every day. Present amounts are considerably higher.

People who visit the beach for recreation also contribute to the problem, leaving behind items that either remain as coastal debris or are easily transported offshore, adding to the litter in the sea. In Los Angeles County, California, beachgoers leave behind approximately seventy-five tons of trash each week.

Researchers have noted that beaches cleaned on a regular basis are often more popular than those that are not, even though they may be highly polluted areas. Others have noted that once an area appears visibly polluted by debris, people are more likely to leave their own trash behind.

Ultimately, the solutions to the problems of plastic debris depend on continued cooperation among industry, policymakers, and the general public. At no time in history has attention to the marine debris problem been greater. We must use this momentum to confront these problem areas and eliminate their contributions to the marine debris problem.

We all have the potential to do something to reduce the problems caused by plastics in the ocean. By reading this guide and becoming aware of the problem, you have already taken the first step. Now, become part of the solution![1]

K. J. O.

* * *

TAKING ACTION

The problems caused by marine debris stem from a broad range of sources both on land and at sea. But since each of us uses plastics in one form or another, each of us also has the opportunity every day to become part of the solution to the problems.

1. Properly dispose of plastic wastes. At home be sure not to dispose of plastics in sewer systems (plastic tampon applicators, for example). At the beach, be sure that plastic wastes are disposed of in trash facilities. Remember to break or cut the loops of plastic six-pack holders before disposing of them to ensure that if the ring escapes into the water, it will not entangle animals. This advice is recommended for anyone disposing of the plastic six-pack holders. Land animals have had hazardous experiences with the holders as well.

And look for degradable holders when making your purchases. As of 1989, eighteen states require that all six-pack holders be degradable and Anheuser-Busch has volunteered to change all its holders.

2. On a boat, be sure to stow your plastic trash and old fishing gear for proper disposal on land. If you are the captain, make it ship policy. In addition, consider using reusable items such as washable dinnerware to minimize the amount of plastic waste you generate. When you come to a port or marina, dispose of it properly.

Notify the Coast Guard if you see other boat crews dumping trash overboard. Be sure to get the vessel's name, number, location, and type of trash. Violators can be fined up to $50,000 and citizens can receive up to half of the imposed fines as rewards. State and local officials should also be informed of inadequate waste facilities in marine areas.

3. Investigate the problem in your area. What types of marine debris do you notice most frequently? The types of debris can often point to its sources. Are fishing gear, strapping bands, or plastic sewage-associated wastes prevalent in your area? Are there fishing fleets, marinas, or industries in your area that could be sources of this debris? If plastic litter indicates that land-based sources (e.g., plastics industries, sewage systems, and landfills) are contributing to the problem, inquire if any procedures to prevent plastic escapement are carried out by local industries, treatment plants, or landfills.

4. Inform others of the problem. Talk with children in your area about the problems caused by the improper disposal of plastic wastes. Encourage local schools to include the topic in their curricula. Zoos, parks, libraries, research centers, and other areas of high community visibility should have information available to the public. If they don't, tell them about the problem and encourage them to write to the Center for Marine Conservation, which can provide educational materials such as slide shows, brochures, photographs, and other information.

5. Publicize the problems caused by plastics in a local newspaper or community newsletter. If you are aware of projects underway in your community, publicize them well.

6. Become part of a larger group. Look for other individuals or organizations in your community that have an interest in this problem and may already be working toward and implementing solutions. For example, the National Marine Fisheries Service and the US Fish and Wildlife Service have granted permits to a number of individuals and

organizations that respond to marine mammal and sea turtle strandings. In fact, in every coastal state there is at least one group that responds to marine mammal, sea turtle, and, in some cases, seabird strandings, including those animals that have become entangled in debris. To assist their efforts you could make sure that their phone number is posted in marine areas. In many cases, they are in need of volunteers to respond to strandings. Even if you find an animal that has died, report it to your stranding network. Any and all information is important. Many state organizations sponsor activities to increase public awareness about the marine environment and debris during coast weeks, held every year in early fall.

7. Volunteer. Your state department of environmental conservation, natural resources, or fish and game may have other programs that use volunteers or publicize the importance of being a careful user of the environment. Contact them and find out how you can help. For example, does your area have annual sport fishing tournaments? Why not contact the organizers and volunteer to promote a "Stow It, Don't Throw It" theme at the tournament? You can offer to distribute information about the plastic debris problem at the tournament and ask fishermen to store plastic trash on board their boats for proper disposal on land.

LIVING WITH ALL CREATURES

— 11 —

Plight of the Ocean Animals

André Carothers and Andrew Davis, Greenpeace *magazine*

> The clubbing of baby seals, the running to death of mustangs with airplanes, the shooting of Alaskan and polar bears and mountain sheep with rifles fitted with telescopic sights, the poisoning of prairie dogs and of their enemy (but our friend) the coyote, the horrible whale slaughter....
>
> If one tries to define the psychological devices whereby some individuals can permit themselves to enjoy these hideous acts, it soon becomes clear that there is a complete *discontinuity* in their minds between pain as *they* know it and feel it, and pain as it is experienced by others, including animals.
>
> Dr. Karl Menninger, *Whatever Became of Sin?*

In May of 1988, the common, or harbor, seals in the North Sea began to die. Pregnant mothers spontaneously aborted their pups, and adult seals floated listlessly in the water, their lungs and vital organs failing. From the shores of Anholt, a tiny island off the coast of Denmark, the disease traveled through the far-flung seal colonies to those of neighboring islands and then to the mainland. By midsummer, seal bodies were scattered along hundreds of miles of North Sea coastline. In September, the disease was discovered among both common and grey seals on the Atlantic coast of Ireland.

Some people call it the black death of the sea. Of an original population of some eighteen thousand common seals, probably twelve thousand are gone. It is the largest die-off of seals anywhere in recorded history.

By the end of August, the killer had been found. The common seal is succumbing to a virus, probably canine distemper virus. But the virus did not, indeed could not, work alone. The accomplice, in this case, is toxic pollution. The North and Baltic seas are enclosed by some of the oldest and most heavily industrialized nations in the world. Today, the North Sea acts as a sink for some fifteen billion gallons of waste water discharged into the ocean or its tributaries each year, as well as uncountable quantities of runoff from cities and agricultural land. Swimming in this chemical-laden ocean, it is thought, damages the animals' immune systems; diseases that the seals would normally recover from thus become fatal. "A principal cause of their deaths is industrial pollution," says Professor Bernd Heydemann, the environment minister of a West German coastal state where a thousand dead seals have been found. "The immune system of the seals has been injured in a very serious way."

Although the seal die-off suddenly put the plight of the North Sea on the world stage, many of those who have observed the degradation of the ecosystem over the last three decades saw it coming. For them, the plague is not an isolated disaster; it is the latest in a series of crises that indicate something is drastically wrong with the ecosystem. "All signs point to a breakdown in the ecological balance in Danish waters," said Jens Kampmann, head of Denmark's environmental ministry.

The pollution problems that the region faces are compounded by geology. Shallow and partially enclosed, the North Sea holds relatively little water and renews itself just twice in a decade.

The Baltic, which flushes itself out only once every twenty to thirty years, resembles more a brackish lake than a sea. As a result, environmental insults, such as overfishing and pollution, have an enormous impact and are not easily reversed.

In the early 1960s, the North Sea earned the dubious distinction of being the first international body of water discovered to be contaminated with polychlorinated biphenyls (PCBs). The common seals of the Wadden Sea, off the coast of West Germany and the Netherlands, are among the most PCB-contaminated marine mammals in the world. Suspicions that PCBs can cause reproductive failures are borne out by the history of this population; from about three thousand three decades ago, the number of seals living off the Dutch coast has declined to about five hundred. As the seals that once inhabited the Rhine delta and southwest coast of the Netherlands have long since disappeared, it is entirely likely that once the plague has run its course, common seals will be eliminated from the Wadden Sea region.

But more than seals have been affected. A decade ago, the mussel beds off the coast of Sweden succumbed to mysterious poisonous algae, devastating the local shellfish industry. A year later, the coastal population of edgers mysteriously crashed. Several scientists attribute this seabird's plight, shared by the puffins on Britain's northeastern coast, to overfishing. The birds simply starved to death because their main source of food had been taken.

In May of 1988, a strangling bloom of algae spilled out from the coast of Sweden and Norway, causing massive fish kills and forcing fish-farming companies to haul their pens into the relatively safe waters of the fjords. Algal blooms are caused by an oversupply of phosphorous and nitrogen pouring into the sea from agricultural fields and the atmosphere.

As the algae grow, they deprive other sea life of oxygen. The process continues after the algae die, as decaying organic material consumes all the oxygen near the ocean floor, creating marine "dead zones." According to some researchers, as much as 30 percent of the brackish Baltic Sea is permanently deprived of oxygen.

The volume of pollutants these seas are forced to absorb is staggering. Into the North Sea's southern reaches empty the rivers that flow through central Europe's heartland — the Elbe, Rhine, Weser, Ems, and Scheldt. The Rhine, Elbe, and Weser carry more than 450,000 tons of phosphates and nitrates into the sea. The concentrations of these nutrient, which contribute to the lethal algal blooms, have increased fourfold over the last twenty to thirty years adding five to ten times the nutrients that derive from natural sources. Coupled with the industrial inputs of the Ems and Scheldt, these rivers annually channel some 50 tons of cadmium, 20 tons of mercury, 12 tons of copper, 10 tons of lead, 7,000 tons of zinc, 300 tons of arsenic and 20 million metric tons of sewage and other human detritus into the sea.

The list continues: the Thames River, whose estuary fans out from Britain's east coast, carries into the North Sea some 150 pounds of the pesticide Lindane and 225 pounds of DDT. Britain is the only North Sea nation to dump partially treated sewage sludge; roughly five million tons a year are poured into the ocean a mere eight kilometers from the coast.

Along the coast of Norway and Sweden, mines and old mining dumps, smelters, and refineries contribute a host of heavy metals to the water, while logging and paper mills are the largest source of persistent organochlorines, dioxins, and solvents. Atmospheric inputs, the clouds of heavy metals, sulfates and nitrates from cars, power plants, and other sources — add as much as 50 percent of the heavy metal burden absorbed by the sea, as well as tons of sulfur and nitrogen, the precursors of acid rain.

From the North Sea oil fields pour thousands of gallons of spilled oil and toxic drilling muds, roughly half a million tons since the industry started up in the late sixties, according to one estimate. In 1987 alone, the oil industry poured some thirty thousand tons of drilling muds into the North Sea.

At the second international conference on the North Sea, held in November and December of 1987, most of the North Sea states agreed to cut industrial emissions to the rivers of Europe by half. But East Germany and Czechoslovakia, two of the region's worst polluters, did not attend.

So far, most of the North Sea states are calling for action, but deeds too often fail to follow words. Many scientists are quick to point out that sufficient information existed in the 1960s to warrant vigorous action against the release of PCBs in the oceans, yet none was taken.

Environmentalists are demanding positive steps. A coalition of West German groups is filing a lawsuit on behalf of the seals against the government in hopes of setting a significant legal precedent.

Meanwhile, the situation remains critical. Today, according to some accounts, 80 percent of the female grey seals in the Baltic are known to be sterile. Roughly three-quarters of all Baltic seals examined show pathological changes in some internal organs and skin; some researchers suspect they will be extinct by the year 2000. Unfortunately, this experience is being repeated around the world. The plague parallels the infamous dolphin die-off along the United States' Atlantic coast. Since June 1987, as many as four of every ten dolphins that inhabit this region may have died. And concern is growing among scientists that the virus will hit the shores of North America very soon.[1]

* * *

To live we must daily break the body and shed the blood of Creation. When we do this lovingly, knowingly, skillfully, reverently, it is a sacrament. When we do it greedily, clumsily, ignorantly, destructively, it is a desecration.[2]

At the far end of the beach, a low white stucco building stands out, oddly square and sterile against the handful of brick and wood one-story dwellings that line the road and extend up the hill. On the other side of the building, Mexican laborers load dripping bags of meat, stacking them in rows in the back of a truck. Soon the truck labors up the hill, blood streaming from its open bed onto the dusty road.

This is the sea turtle slaughterhouse at Escobilla, north of Puerto Angel on the Pacific coast of Mexico. Here, for a few dollars a day, laborers cut apart thousands of endangered sea turtles each year. A fraction of the animal is kept for sale — the skin around the neck, sometimes the flippers or parts of the shell — the rest is piled in putrid heaps or allowed to drain into the dank, maggot-infested bay. In this way, perhaps one-and-a-half million Olive ridley sea turtles have died since 1966.

Sea turtles have existed on the Earth for 100 million years, outlasting dinosaurs and a couple of ice ages. Of the eight species in existence, three are rapidly disappearing — the Kemp's ridley, Hawksbill, and Atlantic Green. The other five are endangered. For the most part, they range over all the world's tropical oceans — at least they did, until human predation brought them to the edge of extinction.

In the fifteenth century, Christopher Columbus wrote of vast numbers of turtles congregating on the shores of the Cayman Islands, near Cuba — so many that he dubbed the islands "Las Tortugas." Several hundred years ago, sea turtles were an abundant, thriving part of the ecosystem, providing sustenance for indigenous coastal peoples around the world.

Then human exploitation began in earnest. Turtle eggs became an important source of protein for sixteenth- and seventeenth-century travellers; sea turtles, which stayed alive for weeks, were hoisted aboard ships to provide fresh meat during long voyages. Green turtle soup became popular in the courts of Europe.

In the twentieth century, international trade in sea turtle products has become a major concern. In commercial terms, there is more profit in a sea-turtle carcass than almost any other animal on Earth; a night of poaching can earn $200–$300, a year's income for some people.

The shell of the Hawksbill is the source of what is known as tortoiseshell — the polished, mottled sea-turtle carapace that is made into eyeglass frames, jewelry, and carved curios. Indonesia, Vietnam, Cuba, and Panama (through which much of the illegal Caribbean trade is "laundered") are major exporters of tortoiseshell. The vast majority of the raw shell is bought by Japan, where a single pair of tortoiseshell eyeglass frames can cost up to $1,000.

Calipee, the cartilaginous material found beneath the belly plate of Green turtles, boils down into a liquid that is the base for Green turtle soup. Sea-turtle leather is made into wallets and shoes in Italy, South and Central America, and Japan. Sea-turtle meat and soup are still imported to some countries in western Europe. Sea-turtle oil is used for skin lotions and cosmetics; the shells are often ground up for cattle feed. Stuffed juvenile turtles are sold in the Caribbean as curios.

Burgeoning native communities are looking to the dwindling sea-turtle population as a source of protein. Sea-turtle eggs are considered aphrodisiac, and command high prices in many regions; it is not uncommon to find a jar of turtle eggs on the bar in cantinas in parts of Central and South America.

In 1972, the Convention on International Trade of Endangered Species (CITES) came into force. Designed to protect wildlife from overexploitation, the agreement has been signed by ninety-two nations. Along with such species as the great whales, tigers, leopards, and giant pandas, sea turtles are on Appendix 1 of CITES, which means all trade is prohibited. But importing and exporting nations can take reservations to CITES rulings (Japan, for example, has objected to limits on tortoiseshell imports and is thus not legally bound by them). And several key nations such as Mexico have not signed the convention.

Thus, despite the international prohibitions, no animal listed under Appendix 1 of CITES is traded more often and in such huge volume than the sea turtle. The nation that trades most heavily in sea turtle products, both legally and illegally, is Japan.

The nesting habits of the turtles make them easy targets for poachers. The Kemp's and Olive ridleys practice the same patterns of nesting, a biological strategy known as predator satiation. The volume of the resource, in this case the turtle eggs, is so high that predators are overwhelmed and a critical number of hatchlings always survive. This strategy does not, unfortunately, foil the uniquely thorough predators known as humans.

The other sea turtle species are solitary nesters, arriving individually to lay their eggs before slipping back into the ocean. But all sea turtles share a unique talent — the ability to navigate so accurately that they return year after year to the same beach, often within sight of their nesting place of previous seasons.

Nesting for female sea turtles is a difficult, often life-threatening process. After pulling herself onto shore, she will pause, perhaps to smell the beach and water to verify the accuracy of her navigational abilities. If anything is amiss — a noise, the wrong smell, or a sign of predators — she will turn and slip back into the surf. Typically she wanders a bit until her instincts tell her the place is right. Only then does she begin to dig slowly and laboriously a deep hole in the sand in which to lay her eggs.

The life of a sea turtle hatchling is often short and brutal — if it manages to hatch at all. If it is not inundated by salt water and spoiled, the nest is likely to be dug up by wild dogs, raccoons, or other predators. The hatchlings emerge to a host of hungry animals including seabirds, foxes, and crabs; once in the water, they are prey to a wide variety of marine life.

Hatchlings focus on the reflective gleam off the night ocean to orient themselves after emerging from the nest, but on many beaches artificial light streams from nearby roads and buildings. Thousands of hatchlings die each year, crossing busy roads or from dehydration as they scramble instinctively in the wrong direction.

The toll exacted by disturbed turtle nests is aggravated by another hazard — shrimp nets. Towed by shrimp trawlers, these sock-shaped nets capture and drown sea turtles throughout the Gulf of Mexico. It is estimated that twelve thousand sea turtles die in the nets each year, including many gravely endangered Kemp's ridleys.

Fortunately, the National Marine Fisheries Service (NMFS) recently implemented regulations that require shrimpers to attach turtle excluder devices (TEDs) to their nets. Unfortunately, opposition from shrimp fishermen over the use of the nets continues to rage, and all the while the turtles continue to die.[3]

Today, Rancho Nuevo, a stretch of remote beach a few hours south of the Texas border and a major nesting area for the turtles, is patrolled by Mexican soldiers with M-16 rifles. A small settlement houses students and researchers who count and tag the Kemp's as they come ashore and move their eggs to the fenced-off areas of the beach. Scientists transport some eggs to Texas's Padre Island National Seashore in an attempt to start a new colony of Kemp's ridleys. In places such as Tortugero, a beach on the Caribbean coast of Costa Rica, and Les Hattes, on the Caribbean coast of French Guinea, environmentalists have made concerted efforts to save these endangered species.

A handful of projects such as these constitute the entirety of the human effort to save the sea turtle from extinction.

In just the last forty years, hunting, egg-collecting, and incidental capture by shrimp trawlers has driven the Kemp's ridleys to the edge of extinction. In 1986, barely two hundred females came to Rancho Nuevo to nest. At numbers as low as these, something called the allee effect comes into play. According to this ecological principle, the species cannot survive if the number of sexually mature adults falls below a certain number. Some biologists suspect that this may be the fate of Kemp's ridley, in which case the Mexican soldiers are more an honor guard than bodyguard, simply ensuring that this species' dignity is preserved through its last few years on Earth.

Of the eight species of sea turtle, the plight of Kemp's is the most dire. But extinction for the others, if present trends continue, is not far away. What is striking is how recently humans discovered sea turtles, in any sense other than commercial. We knew nothing about the remarkable animal, beyond its potential for exploitation, until twenty or thirty years ago. And a complete understanding of these creatures is still decades away.

As with all extinctions caused by human beings, the sea turtle tragedy brings us face-to-face with the vital question of humanity's place in nature. Our destruction of the Earth's plants and animals is progressing now at the rate of some 17,500 species per year. Such loss of species diversity will result in what renowned biologist Paul Ehrlich calls "a nuclear winter sort of denouement for civilization within the next hundred years."

We have driven yet another creature to the edge of extinction to satisfy the marketplace. The slaughter of sea turtles in particular strikes a chord, partly because — at the risk of being overtly anthropomorphic — the creature is so generous of itself. It is a slow and spectacularly fertile animal — fully capable, in a world of balanced predator-prey relationships, of providing sustenance for other creatures and easily maintaining itself. In short, a welcome addition to the ecosystem.

But in the world that includes humans — that animal which can and will rampantly consume resources for food, ornamentation, and profit — the sea turtle is the first to suffer. The sea turtle — so slow and docile, so governed by ancient instincts that it gives itself over to its exploiters — seems aloof from the danger it faces. It will go quietly, if we let it.[4]

* * *

Man, mankind, humanity, whoever and whatever you are, take note! Your ignorance can no longer be accepted in defense. You will forever live with what you do from now on.[5]

For a moment, only a pod of leaping dolphins creases the rippled stillness of the ocean. A score of the sociable mammals are swimming and diving together in a random migration that has endured for millennia.

Then, the chatter of a helicopter breaks the quiet, joined by the high-pitched whine of racing speedboats. Overtaking the dolphins, the boats pull in front and begin herding the now-terrified pod into a circle. Just behind, a two-hundred-foot fishing boat, the bizarre fleet's mother ship, turns to one side and begins laying a mile-long curtain of nylon net around the cauldron of churning water.

But it is not the dolphins that the fishermen are after. For underneath, in a hundred-yard column of crowded ocean, is a school of the dolphin's perennial ocean-going companions — yellowfin tuna. The reason behind their uncanny affinity is not understood by science, but for the fishermen who ply this region, called the Eastern Tropical Pacific, no explanation is needed. The dolphin serves as an expendable lure, nothing more.

It is a role with an awful price. Although wet-suited rescuers try to help them over the edge of the tightening net, many dolphins are left behind. As the net is cinched tight, flukes, flippers, and beaks become entangled, and the dolphins, gasping for air, slowly drown. Any of the mammals left alive when the net is winched aboard are crushed by the cascading tons of tuna on the ship's deck. In this way, over the last thirty years, more than six million dolphins have died.

What has proven so deadly to the porpoises and dolphins, and profitable for the fishermen, it the purse seine. First developed in the late fifties, this fishing technique helped boost tuna catches in this region from 115,000 tons in 1961 to an estimated 217,411 tons in 1985, according to the Inter-American Tropical Tuna Commission.

The number of dead dolphins, however, rose even more dramatically. In 1959, 71,000 northern offshore spotted dolphins, the fishing fleets' favorite target, were killed. A mere six years later, that number shot up to a staggering 365,000. By 1965, more than a thousand dolphins a day on average were dying in the nets of about one hundred fishing boats.

It was this senseless slaughter that helped create one of the most progressive, far-reaching pieces of environmental legislation ever drafted, the Marine Mammal Protection Act (MMPA) of 1972. Immediately upon passage, the MMPA made it illegal to "harass, hunt, capture, or kill" any marine mammal. It also placed jurisdiction over marine mammals in federal rather than state hands and banned the importation of marine mammals and marine mammal products such as seal-fur coats, scrimshaw, and spermaceti-based cosmetics.

Thanks to the MMPA, whales, walruses, polar bears, sea lions, sea otters, and dolphins finally were awarded long overdue protection. Some species demonstrated remarkable resilience: the harbor seal population of the Pacific Northwest appears to be increasing at an encouraging 7 percent per year and California sea lions at 5 percent.

But other species, for a variety of reasons, have not done so well. For almost as soon as the ink dried, the act became riddled with exceptions, loopholes, amendments, and exemptions. No mandate so sweeping as the MMPA's — which proposes in its preamble to protect all marine mammals "from the adverse effects of man's actions" — can hope to evade the pressures of business interests, particularly the international fishing industry.

Despite, or perhaps because of its ambitious intent, the MMPA has proven all too malleable. Its aims have been thwarted by legal challenges, special-interest lobbying, and the neglect of a recent administration that did little to hide its disdain for environmental concerns.

Although the MMPA states that dolphin mortality should be "reduced to insignificant levels approaching zero," the US tuna fleet is still sanctioned to slaughter 20,500 dolphins each year. For five years after passage of the MMPA, little progress was made and dolphins continued to die. In 1977, the National Marine Fisheries Service (NMFS), the government agency charged with enforcing the MMPA, was forced under the pressure of a lawsuit and public opinion to impose quotas and regulations.

Over the next four years, NMFS slowly clamped down on the number of dolphins allowed to die until it stopped, in 1981, at 20,500. In 1984, this quota was extended indefinitely and is still in effect.

The observer program, universally recognized as the best way to determine the rate of incidental kills, has been gutted by the fishing industry. The American Tuna Association claims to welcome government observers but, in 1981, it sued the US Department of Commerce and torpedoed plans to monitor the fleet.

Today, environmentalists fear that dolphins will never enjoy the protection envisioned by the creators of the MMPA. As the fleets of other nations grow in size and range, the impact of US legislation declines. To compound the problem, US ships are "reflagging" — registering their boats in other nations, such as Mexico and Panama, to avoid complying with the MMPA. This expanded "international" tuna fleet, largely out of reach of US legislation, is thought to be killing more than eighty thousand dolphins a year.

In 1985, the Marine Mammal Commission (MMC), a government agency that serves as the government's adviser on preservation of marine mammals, wrote to NMFS recommending measures to "identify and mitigate the cause of the continuing decline of the Pribilof Islands fur seal population."

These seals, once hunted to the brink of extinction for their pelts and other body parts, were governed by an international treaty rather than by the MMPA until 1984 when the treaty expired. Despite the new protection, the population continued to decline at an alarming 6 to 8 percent a year, falling from two million in the late 1950s to about eight hundred thousand today.

The National Marine Fisheries Service didn't respond until February 1986, and then only after the Marine Mammal Commission sent a second letter calling for the NMFS to address the problem. The MMC called the NMFS reply "not fully responsive" and concluded that "the National Marine Fisheries Service had not been doing everything necessary to determine and mitigate the cause of the continuing fur seal population decline."

Stories like these are fodder for charges often levelled at the NMFS — that an agency whose founding mandate is to protect the fisheries, and, by extension, the fishing industry, is not the ideal candidate to be simultaneously defending the rights of marine mammals.

Fisheries' mismanagement, declining stocks, and increased competition from foreign fleets have hurt the US fishing industry. Marine mammals have thus become a scapegoat for a problem that has many causes, the least of which is the appetites of a few seals and sea lions.

California sea lions, once hunted to near extinction, are now recolonizing former migration areas in the Pacific Northwest, largely thanks to the MMPA. Their old haunts, however, have since been altered by dams, development, and pollution, and the once flourishing fish populations have dwindled.

At the behest of fishing interests, NMFS biologists have mounted a program to scare away the sea lions with underwater explosives and loud noises, including tapes of heavy metal rock-and-roll and the collected speeches of Moammar Kadafy. This onslaught, not surprisingly, has significantly reduced the sea lions' share of the steelhead run.

But is has also proved expensive. During the last reauthorization of the MMPA (1988), government specialists recommended another approach — amending the MMPA to allow state and federal agents to kill animals that they decide are a "nuisance" to fishermen or fish stocks. The Pacific Marine Fisheries Commission (PMFC) issued a report recommending that state and federal agents be given carte blanche to kill "nuisance" animals.

The majestic black and white orcas are also targets for angry fishermen. Alaska's growing blackcod industry uses the "longline" technique — setting out a series of 750-foot lines trailing thousands of fishing hooks. Apparently attracted by the sound of the ships' hauling gear, the orcas are adept at removing the cod from the line.

Some fishermen, frustrated with the limited success of deterrents such as seal bombs and other acoustical devices, have resorted to guns and high-powered explosives. Under the MMPA, the long-liners held a permit to "take" up to one hundred small cetaceans (dolphins and whales) each year. NMFS later modified the permit to prohibit the use of plastic explosives and direct fire, but due to NMFS's limited resources, the rules are virtually unenforceable. In 1985, according to NMFS, eight orcas of the Prince William Sound pod sustained bullet wounds, and three of the pod's members subsequently disappeared.

A situation all too similar to the purse-seine catastrophe exists in the Pacific waters around the United States. The nets are unfurled at night from the stern of the boats. Stretching from ten to thirty miles, they hang as deep as twenty-five feet in the water, a nylon curtain that snares anything in its path. At dawn, the winches are started and the nets are hauled in. Along with the intended catch — generally salmon or squid, sometimes marlin and other bullfish — nontargeted species are also decked and then quickly tossed overboard. In this way, seabirds, sharks, whales, seals, Dall's porpoises, and other marine mammals die by the thousands.

The killer is the northern Pacific drift-net fleet. The Japanese, Korean, and Taiwanese salmon and squid drift-net fleets, comprising at least seventeen hundred boats, trail at least twenty thousand miles of net each night, with devastating effects. Some researchers estimate that as many as eight hundred thousand sea birds and tens of thousands of marine mammals are caught and drowned each year as a result of the drift-net fleets.

Not only do thousands of animals die in the course of routine fishing operations, but miles of discarded nets, called ghost nets, continue to kill fish and marine mammals for years until finally they sink to the bottom under the weight of the corpses.

Foreign fishing fleets must apply for permits if they are likely to kill marine mammals in US waters. Until 1987, the Japanese salmon fishermen routinely had been granted permits to take fur seals and as many as 5,500 Dall's porpoises each year. Due to the danger facing the Pribilof Island fur seals and the North Pacific's Dall's porpoises, the US Department of Commerce was forced to take action. The number of deaths allowed by Japan's Dall's porpoise permit has since been reduced, and the Pribilof Island's fur seals were removed from the permit completely. After Greenpeace filed a lawsuit, a judge voided Japan's permit and Japan's drift-net fleet has been temporarily banned from US waters.[6]

Greenpeace played a major role in the reauthorization of the Marine Mammal Protection Act in 1988. Greenpeace and a coalition of twenty-six environmental and conservation groups made significant progress to increase protection for seals, whales, dolphins, and other marine mammals. On April 13, 1990, the three largest sellers of canned tuna in the United States announced that they "would stop buying tuna that is caught in nets that also trap and kill dolphins." The three largest sellers of tuna are H. J. Heinz Co., which markets Star Kist; Van Camp Seafood Co., which markets Chicken of the Sea; and Bumble Bee Seafoods, Inc., marketer of Bumble Bee.[7] According to a direct mail letter from Greenpeace in June of 1990, however, the issue is far from over because "as much as 30% of the U.S. market remains outside the control of Star Kist and others."[8]

Greenpeace warned us. In August of 1987, the organization sent an appeal for help to its membership on the subject of offshore drilling. In part, the letter stated:

The Reagan Administration has plans to lease *hundreds of millions of acres* of America's offshore waters to oil companies.

The proposed sales involve enormous stretches of coastal waters ... off Florida's Gulf Coast and the Florida Keys, New England's Georges Bank, almost the entire coast of California, and the rich, teeming waters off southwest Alaska. So determined is the Administration to complete these sales while Reagan is President that Secretary of Interior Donald Hodel just dramatically lowered the minimum price companies must bid on oil-lease sites to only *$25 per acre.*

But by far the most insane of all the administration's plans is opening Alaska's Bristol Bay, in southwest Alaska just north of the Aleutian Peninsula, to offshore oil drilling. Bristol Bay is one of the world's richest remaining marine and coastal environments. Each year, six endangered great whale species — including the entire known population of gray whales — feed in the Bristol Bay Area. Bristol Bay also provides habitat for millions of birds and waterfowl, including black brant and emperor geese, as well as hundreds of thousands of marine mammals — Northern fur seals, walruses, sea lions, and ice seals. And it's one of the most productive salmon fishing grounds in the world — some years, more than a third of the world's salmon harvest takes place in Bristol Bay.

We have worked so hard to save the whales, the seals, the dolphins, and their habitats. We can't just sit back and let reckless oil-lease sales wipe out what we have worked years to accomplish.[9]

It was about Prince William Sound rather than Bristol Bay that the headlines on March 24, 1989, read:

"Under Oil's Powerful Spell, Alaska Was Off Guard"

"Spill Shows Dangers May Outweigh Benefits in Pursuit of Last Reserves"

"Oil Spill Account of Radar Altered"

"Exxon Concedes It Can't Contain Spill"

"Spill Could Pose a Threat for Years"

The eleven-million-gallon spill from the tanker *Exxon Valdez* was only one of many recent spills.[10] On December 22, 1988, a sea-going tug gashed a hole in the side of a barge, spilling 230,000 gallons of oil into Gray's Harbor on the coast of Washington State. Heavy seas and strong winds smeared the oil across three hundred miles of coastline, including the scenic parts of the Olympic National Park and the Pacific Rim National Park in Canada.

One month later, on January 28, 1989, the captain of the Argentine supply ship *Bahía Paraíso* ignored warnings and charted a course that ran his ship into rocks off Antarctica's Palmer peninsula.

The ship broke apart, spilling some 250,000 gallons of oil near thriving penguin, seal, and seabird colonies, and a US scientific research facility.

The EPA estimates there are some ten thousand oil spills a year in the United States alone, an annual gusher that costs some $175 million a year to clean up. And even this deluge is exceeded by the quantity of oil annually poured into coastal waters from what are known as "routine" releases — the bilge and oil-tanker cleaning, and the drilling-rig discharges that attend day-to-day oil development and transport.

An EPA report disclosed in March 1989 details a host of environmental problems at the oil complex on Alaska's North Slope, including overflowing waste disposal pits, toxic chemical spills, stacks of leaking drums, and a series of blatant violations of EPA regulations. In 1987, the US Fish and Wildlife Service reported that "fish and wildlife habitat losses from construction and operation of the pipeline system and the Prudhoe Bay oil fields were greatly underestimated in the environmental impact statement."

This litany of unexamined costs leaves out, of course, the environmental effects of the subsequent use of the fossil fuels, extracted with such dire effect. Nor does it touch on the economic convolutions required to make the keep-on-drilling philosophy appear reasonable. But, for the record, according to University of California energy expert Arthur Rosenfeld, the United States loses more energy each year through poorly-engineered windows than is provided by all the oil flowing through the Alaska pipeline. From this perspective, leaving it in the ground is far cheaper and less destructive than pumping it, burning it, and spilling it across oceans from Cape Horn to the Bering Sea.[11]

A. C.

A. D.

* * *

TAKING ACTION

1. Do not buy products that are the result of species slaughter and endangerment. This includes tortoiseshell, shrimp, tuna, and any product such as ivory of an endangered species.

2. Do not purchase any animal or animal product unless you know where it came from. Countless thousands of tropical birds die in

shipment as part of the illegal trade bound for individuals who deem it fashionable to own a rare species.

3. Gather information on toxic dumping into rivers, estuaries, and other sources of water which eventually enters oceans. Find out what industries are dumping poisons into our waters and alert local, state, and federal governments as well as Greenpeace and other organizations.

4. Because approximately 70 percent of the US population lives within fifty miles of one coastline or another, considerable pressure is being put on sea life because of the diminishing quality of our oceans. Keep track of what is happening through local environmental organizations and be a part of solving the problems.

5. Be energy efficient. Insulate your home, car pool, use less energy! Give up dependency on oil and, in the meantime, vigorously oppose drilling off the shores of the United States and in such pristine areas as Alaska and Antarctica.

6. Keep informed. Join Greenpeace, the Cousteau Society, Audubon Center for Marine Conservation, and other organizations working to preserve the integrity of oceans and coastal waters. Give them your money and your time. In return, they will give you information on what is happening, the chance to do more, and the knowledge that you have made a difference.

— 12 —

Extinction: Raiders of the Last Ark

Mike LaRue

> To meet the demand for 825 tons of ivory per year a minimum of 70,000 elephants have to die.... And that is only the elephants with tusks; thousands of calves also die because of the loss of their mothers, bringing the estimated total up to at least 80,000 elephants each year. The African elephant population is estimated at 800,000; at the current kill, the elephants have only ten years left.
>
> Cynthia Moss, "Elephant Memories"

> There is nothing man is doing on this planet that cannot be corrected by time, save this one thing: the extinction of a single species is the one permanent change man is capable of making in the Cosmos."
>
> Roger Caras, *Last Chance on Earth: A Requiem for Wildlife*

Extinction means the end. In a biological sense, extinction marks the end of a form of life. It is difficult for us to imagine gorillas becoming extinct, or tigers or elephants. Yet each year many species of plants and animals become extinct. In fact, as many as seventeen thousand species of plants and animals are being killed off each year. If the rate of extinction continues as it has recently, a million species might die out on this Earth in the next thirty years. So far gorillas, tigers, and elephants have been spared, but their numbers fall closer to extinction each day. Today most of the species that are becoming extinct live in the tropical areas of the Earth where destruction of the tropical forests is so great it is difficult to comprehend. The tropical forests could disappear in fifty to seventy-five years if the current destruction continues. Many of the species being killed by our abuse or neglect are not as glamorous as gorillas or tigers, but are such things as insects, spiders, and plants that have never even been described. They are no less important than gorillas, just less able to attract people's interest.

Natural extinction has been a part of Earth's history since life began. It is not only a natural process, but it is an essential one as well. The species that exist today do so because others have become extinct in the past. Mammals, for example, lived during the time of the dinosaurs but only as small, not very successful animals. They probably did not exceed a foot or so in length. Dinosaurs were very successful and could outcompete the mammals. The extinction of the dinosaurs, however, gave these little mammals a chance to take over empty habitats and become the successful animals they are today. What concerns scientists today is unnatural extinction caused by catastrophic destruction of habitats, which results in many species being unable to survive.

The following statistics do not constitute even the tip of the iceberg:

- In the early nineteenth century between thirty and forty million American bison lived in the continental United States. Steadily hunted over the years, there are now none surviving in the wild. There are only twenty-five thousand living in private reserves.[1]

- The elephant populations of Kenya alone are estimated to have been reduced by two-thirds in only eight years.[2]

- In 1970, the rhinoceros population was thought to total about seventy thousand animals; today only eleven thousand are estimated to exist in the wild. The Sumatran Rhino has the longest evolutionary history of the rhinoceros family, having evolved very little in the past forty million years. Today, fewer than seven hundred animals remain.[3]

- Between 1967 and 1972 the United Kingdom received 1.2 million Mediterranean Spur-thighed Tortoises from Morocco alone, as part of the exotic pet trade. 80 percent of these died in the first year of captivity.[4]

- The brilliant red Cock of the Rock, an inhabitant of the northern Andes, is imported to the United States and Europe as part of the exotic pet trade. It is thought that fifty are killed for every one that arrives safely.[5]

- Manatees, gentle aquatic plant-eaters, were once plentiful in US waters but were decimated by hunting. Only about twelve hundred manatees still remain in US waters today.[6]

- In China today there are many fewer giant pandas than there used to be because the bamboo forests where they live have been cut down to make farmland. When their habitat is destroyed, they cannot find anywhere else to live. They are in danger of dying out.[7]

- Whales have been hunted for centuries, to such an extent that there may not be enough individuals left in some species for successful reproduction. These mammals, among the largest on Earth, are in danger of extinction.[8] In a decade-long survey off Antarctica, scientists found only 453 blue whales in an area where they had expected to find perhaps ten times as many.[9]

- In a certain part of the rain forest in Brazil live approximately seventy-five little monkeys called golden lion tamarins. They are all that is left in the wild of this species because so much of its forest home has been cut down.[10]

- Agriculture, industry, and urbanization are destroying entire ecological systems in what is, by the time scale of biology, a blink of the eye.[11]

- Natural scientists fear that in the next thirty years an average of one hundred plant and animal species could become extinct every day.[12]

* * *

Life on Earth is dependent on the diversity of life. Diversity of life is dependent on the differences in organisms. Each person is different from another, and that is diversity. A human is different from an eagle, and that also is diversity. Diversity provides life its future by providing biological stability to this Earth. Some even suggest that life itself created and controls the environment necessary for continued life. Extinction of species reduces diversity. As more and more species become extinct, quality of life begins to suffer and eventually life itself. Every species that exists on Earth is really an experiment. Will it survive and for how long? The human species has a relatively short history. The future success of humans depends on decisions that must be made by humans in the next few years.

Organisms live in a habitat or "home." All species multiply in and adapt their habitats until they run up against some limiting factor. All habitats, no matter how large or small, have a limit on the number of individuals and the number of species that they can support. They reach the carrying capacity of their habitat, and their population stabilizes within certain limits. Carrying capacity is often used to describe the number of organisms that can be supported in a habitat. Organisms are limited by available food, water, shelter, or other things they need to exist. A habitat has limited amounts of these that it can provide. Over time habitats can change, and some species will become extinct. This is a natural occurrence. Humans have developed the ability to change consciously their habitat, thus amending carrying capacity for themselves and for other species.

These amendments often occur with no conscious thought of the consequences on other species or even on humans.

Humans are able to make use of many areas of the Earth as habitat. Some say that the habitat of humans is the whole Earth. But the Earth has its limits too. What is the carrying capacity of the Earth for humans? Some suggest that it may be as few as 2.5 billion people. Today, the Earth's population stands at some 5 billion but is expanding exponentially. That simply means it doubles in less and less time. For example, it took millions of years for the population to reach its first billion people. It will take only eleven years to go from five billion to six billion people. Scientists believe that the Earth's population may level off at about ten billion people in the not-too-distant future. However, if you look at different populations of humans on the Earth you will see that not all are growing. Some populations are actually fairly stable. These populations are generally in developed countries where poverty is not pervasive. Poor countries, in contrast, have tremendous growing populations. This is not all that unusual. More individuals in a family means the work to gather or grow food can be distributed and there are more to care for the very young and the very old. Developed countries generally provide for family welfare through a better standard of living. It has been suggested that conservation of the natural resources of poor countries can only be successful if those countries are developed first. Development does not have to be development as we see it in the industrialized areas of the western world. It does mean that basic support-systems that allow humans to live in some security from disease, hunger, war, homelessness, and poverty must be provided.

In the history of the human species we find in ancient and primary cultures the ethics for conservation. This conservation ethic is expressed in the archetypes of all the world's religions and cultures. This was brought home to me recently when I asked colleagues how some cultures can live without destroying the place where they live.

Shortly after discussing these questions, I read a story about a conservationist who was called to an island to determine why the wildlife that the native people hunted was becoming scarce. The people were quite concerned since these animals were their livelihood. The conservationist, rather quickly, determined that the culture of the people was enough to conserve the animals but that an outside pressure was causing the wildlife to disappear. A multinational logging company was cutting the forest down, destroying the homes of the wildlife. The most important thing about this story is that the culture of the people actually conserved the wildlife and left alone things which might have remained stable as they had for many years.

Time and isolation of populations have caused the natural protection of the environment to be suppressed in some cultures. Western culture is one that has suppressed this natural protection of the environment. The suppression of the conservation ethic originated long ago when the farmers in the Mediterranean were conquered by the herders and hunters of nearby regions. The idea that human beings are a part of nature was replaced by the idea of humankind conquering and controlling all. That philosophy became a part of the religions of the day and continues even now.

As these western religions spread and conquered "primitive" people, natural conservation was suppressed. Today, many people recognize the loss of the primitive ethic and feel that it is important to reestablish that thinking in western society. What the conservation ethic really involves is a reverence for life and a feeling of oneness with all nature, a recognition that "life" is not defined only as human life. The conservation ethic does not mean we place the same emphasis on all forms of life, but it does mean that we respect and understand all of life.

> Nature can never again make a new kind of elephant, or anteater, or whale, not as long as man is around with a rifle and a steam shovel.[13]

The American Indians of the plains knew this ethic. While they killed buffalo for food and other uses, they killed only what was needed and through their hunting ceremonies asked permission and forgiveness of the buffalo before the hunt began. They had a reverence for life that served to protect not only all other creatures but themselves as well. We find this philosophy a common thread in most of the peoples we label primitive.

Reverence for life comes from our knowledge that all life, no matter how diverse, is really one. We have a kinship with our own family, the family in another city, the snake in the grass, the rat in the barn, the elephant being slaughtered in Africa, in fact, with all living species. Consider that humans are 99 percent genetically similar to pygmy chimpanzees and to a lesser percentage with all other forms of life. We do, indeed, have a kinship with the creatures of our Earth.

I experience this oneness when I am hiking in the wilderness or along a river near my home. There is a realization that I am somehow related to the plants and animals I encounter. After all, we are all made of the same elements produced shortly after the big bang of universal Creation.

Today, species survival is threatened by human overpopulation and human consumption of the Earth's natural resources. The projected number of humans has already been mentioned. These humans will need a place to live and food to eat. But consider that most of the arable land on the Earth has been cultivated. The land that remains is marginal, at best, for producing the crops that now make up the diets of the majority of humans. Farmers today are facing the problem of growing food for eighty-six million more people each year, with twenty-six billion tons less of topsoil each year. We are seeing clean water becoming increasingly hard to supply to all people. Disposal of wastes of all types is an increasing problem. This all results in destruction of the Earth's habitats. That destruction means species become extinct.

Western civilization has developed a socioeconomic system based on consumption. We are convinced through the mass media that there is a certain way to live. We must have certain appliances, a certain type of house, etc. Our entertainment likewise is controlled by consumerism. No matter what you are interested in doing as a hobby there is a consumer price to pay. You want to ride a bicycle? To do it right you must buy a certain type of bicycle, a helmet, riding clothes and join a club — all for a fee. How about walking? There are shoes to buy and walking clothes, and you might be convinced to join the Y so you can walk on its circular track. Someone has thought of something that you can buy to do anything, and vast sums of money are spent to convince you that this is the accepted way to do it. Cities are laid out so that you must own a car to live in them. Suburban malls are built for automobile access. Look at all the drive-in windows on businesses. We developed an entire interstate road system so we can use cars and spend tons of money to do so. The auto industry, oil companies, tire companies, and a host of others want no less. Using cars less and then using only those with good fuel economy will have significant impact. Using a car consumes more than fuel. There is the energy to produce the car itself, not to mention the tires, batteries, oil, etc. All of these things are done with little regard to the environment or even to human social structure.

Overpopulation of humans causes pressure on the habitats of the Earth, resulting in extinctions that reduce the diversity of life and threaten life itself. According to Anne and Paul Ehrlich, "Rising death rates (of species) and a falling quality of life will lead to a crumbling of post-industrial civilization. The end may come so gradually that the hour of its arrival may not be recognizable, but the familiar world of today will disappear within the life span of many people now alive."[14]

If we were to look at the Earth from afar, we would contemplate a scenario that would have humans interfering with ecosystems to the point of causing the demise of our own species. We forget that human life is not the only life. Humans could disappear from the Earth, and life would continue. There are those who feel that scenario would be best for the Earth. It would take a long time for the Earth to recover from the ill effects of human existence, but in time, the Earth will heal itself. Habitats and the plants and animals that live in them would reach a balance, not static but naturally changing as it has for millions of years before humans.

I believe that humans have the collective ability to ensure that we are a part of the Earth's future. It will not be easy and the price for pulling this collective ability together will be high, simply because of what we have done in the past. It will involve elimination of poverty. It will mean that all religions and cultures will merge into one that provides equality for humans regardless of where they live or their sex or their race. We do not have to wait for a catastrophe. In fact, the impetus to realize a problem exists may be in something as simple as spiraling food prices. 1988 was the first year in many that the US produced less food than it consumed.

Today we are faced with difficult decisions about preventing extinction. Some people and institutions are involved in preventing the extinction of individual species. Others protect habitat of endangered species. Still others protect habitat areas like rain forests or wetlands or coral reefs. Within our current system of world politics and economics is it possible to do it all? It is really unfortunate to realize that our social structure may prevent us from saving ourselves. It seems straightforward enough that entire ecosystems should be preserved. This also preserves large groups of species and thus species diversity. Preserving all ecosystems of the world would place a great hardship on many populations of humans. We must instead identify those ecosystems that must be preserved and those that can be conserved (used with care). It is possible to provide for human needs by carefully using resources within ecosystems that are important to many forms of life. It is possible to do so with respect to the Earth and foresight for the survival of life, but not if our goal is just to make money. This is why there must be a fundamental change in the way humans go about living. Life-style must be patterned after a good quality of life within the limits of the Earth's habitat and not patterned after an advertiser's dream.

> The first [reason for conservation], which is not usually put first, is really religious. There are some millions of people in the world who think that animals have a right to exist and be left alone, or at any rate that they should not be persecuted or made extinct as a species. Some people will believe this even when it is quite dangerous to themselves.
>
> This non-humanistic value of communities and species is the simplest of all to state: *they should be conserved because they exist and because this existence is itself but the present expression of a continuing historical process of immense antiquity and majesty.*[15]

M. L.

* * *

TAKING ACTION

1. Consider the place you have chosen to live. Is it near your job site, shopping, schools, or do you have to drive to do these things? It would even help if you lived close to a bus stop or train station so you could travel to work or shopping on mass transit.

2. Don't be persuaded by TV commercials to buy the latest fashions or the latest gadgets. These change all the time in order to make someone money. Closely examine the things that you own and honestly evaluate whether they still function. Everything you buy comes not only with a dollar cost but also an environmental cost.

3. Purchase food with the least amount of packaging possible. Select the apples and put them loose in a biodegradable bag. Bring the bag you used last week to the grocery store and reuse it.

4. Reduce your consumption of fast-food red meat. In order to supply the huge number of fast-food hamburgers, rain forests are being destroyed to graze cattle to provide a cheap source for meat.

5. Do not purchase products made from endangered species. They may be advertised as legally obtained but most of these products are "laundered." Even if legally obtained, their consumption creates a demand that will be met. The US is second in the world in its consumption of products made from endangered species.

6. Avoid the use of nonbiodegradable products. These are often found in packaging for food and other products.

7. Recycle as much waste as possible. While recycling is growing in popularity, it is only the second step. The first is to reduce consumption, then recycle.

8. Become active in your community. There may be local groups that you can join. Consider the Audubon Society or a zoological society.

9. Several national groups are also worthy of your support. World Wildlife Fund, the Nature Conservancy, and National Wildlife Federation are good choices.

10. Never overlook letting your legislative representative know that you are concerned about our environment.

— 13 —

Toxic Shock: The Pesticide Fix

Susan Hagood

Home pesticides are poisoning more than insects and weeds.
Sales brochures published by the manufacturers of lawn and garden pesticides mislead consumers into believing that their products are completely safe.

Bryan Jay Baskin, *Harrowsmith*

Pesticides are a fixture in modern America. As a nation, we reach for an insecticide, herbicide, rodenticide, fungicide, or other pesticide almost out of habit. In a country spoiled by quick fixes and time savers, this is hardly surprising. But we are paying the price.

"Can anyone believe that it is possible to lay down such a barrage of poisons on the surface of the earth without making it unfit for all life?"[1] When Rachel Carson asked that question in her landmark book *Silent Spring,* annual production of pesticides in the US totaled 6.4 million pounds (1960). In 1987, that figure had risen to more than one billion pounds of active ingredients (the specific ingredient of a pesticide product formulated to kill the target pest) and pesticide sales to nearly seven billion dollars.[2] Globally, more than four billion pounds of active ingredients are used.[3] As our use and dependence on pesticides have increased, so has the evidence that pesticides can be a curse as well as a blessing:

- Pesticides have been detected in the underground water of twenty-six states as a result of normal field use.[4] Groundwater is the main source of drinking water for 90 percent of rural Americans and for 50 percent of all Americans.[5]

- The number of "pests" now resistant to one or more pesticides is increasing. This has resulted in the development and use of more potent poisons to overcome resistance.

- Insecticides kill beneficial insects as well as the insects considered to be pests. Of the more than one million species of insects, it has been estimated that only 0.5 to 1.5 percent have even been "pests."[6] Annual costs to agriculture from bee kills by pesticides and the resulting reduced pollination of crops has been estimated to total $135 million annually.[7]

- Since the 1940s, crop losses to insects have nearly doubled in spite of a tenfold increase in the amount of insecticide used.[8]

- Although no national system tracks human pesticide poisonings, the World Resources Institute estimates the number of human poisonings per year at three hundred thousand — most are farmworkers poisoned in the fields.

- In 1986, the US Environmental Protection Agency rated pesticide pollution as the most urgent environmental problem facing this country.

Our naive acceptance of pesticides as a panacea may be jeopardizing our environment and our health.

Federal Pesticide Regulation

The Federal Insecticide, Fungicide, and Rodenticide Act, known as FIFRA, is the federal law governing pesticide use in this country. First passed in 1947, FIFRA gave the secretary of agriculture the authority to register pesticides to protect the public from products that failed to perform their intended function and from those which were acutely (immediately) toxic. FIFRA has been amended several times since 1947, with the most sweeping changes made in 1972. The 1972 amendments shifted its emphasis from consumer protection and product performance to public health and environmental protection.[9]

Unique among public health and environmental statutes, FIFRA mandates that the federal Environmental Protection Agency consider both the risks and the benefits of pesticide use. It recognizes that the use of pesticides is the only instance in which we intentionally release poisons into the environment, though with beneficial intent.

In order to be registered by the EPA for a specific use, a pesticide must be determined by EPA to be free from "unreasonable adverse effects," that is, "any unreasonable risk to man or the environment, taking into account the economic, social, and environmental costs and benefits of the use of any pesticide."[10]

In order for EPA to determine whether a pesticide will cause "unreasonable adverse effects," the manufacturer seeking to register a pesticide with the Agency, and thus gain legal permission to market the product, must conduct a series of tests and provide the results to EPA. The tests that the agency requires vary depending on the pesticide and the way in which it is to be used, but are generally aimed at determining the pesticide's effects on soil, water, wildlife, and humans.

Each pesticide product must bear an EPA-approved label that specifies the purpose of the product, the active and inert ingredients, the product's chemical name and classification, directions for use, storage, and disposal, information about the pesticide's toxicity, and the correct action to take if the product is accidentally swallowed or spilled. In addition, the label must bear information about the product's risks to humans, domestic and wild animals, and the environment. All labels contain the warning that "it is a violation of federal law to use this product in a manner inconsistent with its labeling."

In 1972 amendments, Congress directed EPA to instruct all manufacturers of active ingredients to retest their products for the whole range of health and environmental effects. Congress mandated that pesticides registered before the development of current health and safety standards must be retested using current methods and reregistered by EPA in order for them to remain in the marketplace.

Reregistration is a complex process that has been exceedingly slow. There are more than six hundred active ingredients that must be reregistered. Commitment to reregistration and environmental and public health has fluctuated between administrations and within the EPA itself. Drastic budget cuts by the Reagan administration slowed progress significantly.

In addition, the wealthy and politically powerful pesticide industry has used political pressure and litigation to delay and limit the generation of data. Chicago's Industrial Biotest Laboratories (IBT), contracted to conduct thousands of health-related tests for pesticide manufacturers, was found to have submitted fraudulent data to the EPA, further delaying the reregistration process. "In complying with requirements for toxicity testing, the extent of fraudulent and misleading data generation by in-house scientists and client laboratories has shown that much industry considers public safety of small concern."[11] For instance, the registration of Alachlor, the most commonly used agricultural herbicide, was largely supported by IBT studies; the herbicide is now classified by the EPA as a probable human carcinogen.

At this writing, seventeen years after amendments to FIFRA mandated that pesticides be reregistered, work is complete on less than ten end-use products; 194 of the 600 active ingredients have thus far been reviewed to determine what tests still need to be conducted by the manufacturer. The 600 active ingredients are in turn formulated into approximately 50,000 pesticide products. Thus, tens of thousands of pesticide products are marketed, purchased, and used by consumers in the absence of complete information about the chemical's ability to cause cancer, birth defects, sterility, chromosome damage, and disrupt fragile ecological systems. "Until EPA completes reregistration it cannot fully assure that the public and the environment are adequately protected against possible unreasonable risks of older pesticides."[12]

FIFRA was amended in 1988 to speed the reregistration process. The law now requires EPA to reregister within nine years all active ingredients registered before November, 1984. By 1997, if all goes well, human health and the environment will be better protected from pesticides. But in the interim, we are playing a dangerous game of catch-up.

The 1988 amendments will also relieve EPA of most of the costs of storing and disposing of banned pesticides by transferring these responsibilities largely to the manufacturers.

More Improvements Badly Needed

Although these amendments are surely steps in the right direction, they only scratch the surface of pesticide reform. Future improvements in the law must address issues essential to the protection of public health and the environment. According to Public Citizen, a consumer and environmental advocacy organization, FIFRA should be further amended to:

- Require strong standards to protect farmworkers and other pesticide applicators.

- Require that consumers and farmworkers are provided with full health and safety information about the products to which they are exposed.

- Ensure that citizens and states can sue the EPA and pesticide manufacturers when the law isn't enforced. FIFRA is the only major environmental statute that does not currently provide for citizen suits.

- Allow local governments the authority to post warnings and/or regulate pesticide use in their communities.

- Preserve states' rights to set stricter standards than the federal government for pesticide residues in food.

- Establish a strong groundwater protection program.

- Prohibit the export of pesticides that are banned or restricted in the US.

- Promote viable, nonchemical pest control alternatives.

- Eliminate registration loopholes that allow manufacturers to market pesticides before they have been fully tested.[13]

- Require that EPA direct pesticide manufacturers to include warnings on pesticide labels listing inert ingredients in the products that have been found to be hazardous. "Inerts" can be as toxic as the active ingredient itself. Of the twelve hundred substances known by the Environmental Protection Agency to be used as inert ingredients, only three hundred are considered safe. Over one hundred are of "toxicological concern"; not enough is known about the remaining eight hundred to classify their risks.[14]

The Public Generally Assumes Pesticides to Be Safe

Unknown to the majority of Americans, the availability of a pesticide on supermarket and garden center shelves, its use by lawn care companies, and its registration by EPA is neither an indication of EPA "approval" nor a guarantee of safety.

People who buy and apply pesticides around their homes or who hire professional applicators to apply pesticides for them are not told that the pesticides have not been tested for chronic health effects, in accordance with current standards. Moreover, the pesticide industry sometimes makes safety claims that EPA considers to be false or misleading. . . . [15]

Professional pesticide applicators such as lawn care and pest control companies . . . claim that the pesticides they use are safe, harmless, or EPA-approved. These claims could persuade the public to purchase a service they would not otherwise use, or discourage them from taking reasonable precautions to avoid exposure.[16]

The products they spray have obscure names like diazinon and Tupersan. The trucks they drive . . . are clean and white, with just enough green on the tanks to be attractive. They come in the morning, spray their chemicals and leave. . . . Lawn care is big business. . . . Nationwide, companies service six million to seven million lawns.

But missing from the clean green and white trucks is the Environmental Protection Agency's warning for Tupersan — "The area being treated must be vacated by unprotected persons. . . . " Never displayed is the diazinon warning to "Keep children and pets off treated areas until the following afternoon."

Does the absence of these warnings mean that . . . children and pets are dying each year due to exposure to lawn chemicals? Probably not, but the fact is, nobody knows. While we find out, the spraying continues.[17]

State Programs

Since FIFRA does not now adequately protect the public, some states are moving to fill the gap.

In Iowa, the Comprehensive Groundwater Protection Act, enacted in 1987, seeks to reduce contamination of underground water supplies from a variety of sources, including agricultural pesticides and fertilizers, underground fuel storage tanks, landfills, and others. Data collected by the state indicate that pesticides are leaching into groundwater from normal field use.

Iowa has initiated an impressive program to achieve a reduction in the use of pesticides and fertilizers, to increase conservation of soil and energy, and to maintain farm profitability by working with farmers to determine the best management practices for individual farms. In some instances, for example, the state recommends to farmers that they alternate corn crops with alfalfa. The alfalfa adds nitrogen to the soil that corn requires, thereby eliminating the need to use nitrogen fertilizer. Some farmers participating in the program have saved up to $14,000 a year in reduced expenditures on pesticides and fertilizer.

In 1988, Texas launched a "right-to-know" program to make information available to agricultural producers and fieldworkers on the potential hazards associated with the use of specific agricultural pesticides. The program also provides training for all agricultural workers in the proper use of pesticides. Three years earlier, the Texas Department of Agriculture implemented regulations that require neighbors of fields to be sprayed with pesticides be notified prior to the spraying and that minimum time periods be established during which farmworkers cannot be required to enter fields after spraying.

The Texas Department of Agriculture is also working with farmers and ranchers in developing and using farming techniques that are less dependent on the use of pesticides. The department's consumer-information programs help Texans choose the least toxic methods of reducing pest problems in the home, lawn, and garden and encourage them to use alternative techniques in preference to pesticides.

California, Wisconsin, Minnesota, Maine, Nebraska, and other states also are moving to protect their residents and environment where FIFRA does not.

Some Pesticides Have Been Banned

DDT, the pesticide most known to the public, was banned in 1972 because it was found to reduce reproductive success in some wildlife species, most notably birds of prey, and because many of the insect species DDT was used to control had developed resistance to the insecticide, rendering it ineffective. DDT was the first of a class of insecticides called chlorinated hydrocarbons, or organochlorines, developed during and after World War II. Its introduction signaled the start of the "chemical age" and the end of farmers' use of traditional pest control measures that work with nature rather than against it.

In a familiar and fortunately now infrequent scenario, DDT was taken in by tiny aquatic organisms. Small fish eating these organisms were eaten by bigger fish, who in turn were eaten by bald eagles, predators at the top of the food chain. The eagles received all the DDT that had accumulated beginning with that in the bodies of the microscopic plant and animal life. Female eagles failed to lay eggs or laid eggs that were so thin they were crushed by the weight of the incubating bird. The population declined.

In one study of the tendency of DDT to accumulate in the bodies of wildlife, soil in an area of DDT treatment contained 10 parts per million (ppm) of DDT. Earthworms taken from this soil were contaminated by 141 ppm DDT, while robins, which pick up the pesticide when they eat earthworms, had accumulated DDT to levels of 444 ppm in brain tissue.[18]

By 1969, researchers were reporting findings of DDT or its metabolites in the bodies of wildlife in Antarctica and from areas never sprayed.[19,20] And other problems were becoming apparent. For instance, most of California's agriculturally significant insect pests had developed resistance to DDT by 1975.[21] DDT killed not only the target pests but also their predators. Pests surviving the spraying were left to breed without the natural control of their numbers exerted in part by their predators. This led to greatly increased reproduction and a phenomenon called target-pest resurgence. In addition, insects that were not previously pests became so when their natural enemies were killed.

Although DDT was banned for most uses in 1972, "hotspots," exist where residue continues to be found at equal or even increased levels. Hall reports that "... DDT continues to have major impacts on wildlife."[22]

Beluga whales, inhabiting the St. Lawrence River in the province of Quebec, Canada, have been called the most contaminated mammals on Earth. Their tissues contain a witch's brew of pesticides and heavy metals including many of the organochlorines that have been severely restricted for years. Many of these products, including organochlorine insecticides "are still available to our fauna through atmospheric transport from other continents, or because the large quantities used in the past will remain in our environment, un-degraded, for decades."[23]

Just as has DDT, most of the other organochlorines used for so long — pentachlorophenol, chlordane, heptachlor, toxaphene, aldrin, dieldrin, endrin, lindane, and others — have been banned or severely restricted in the United States, although American manufacturers still produce and sell 30 percent of the chemicals deemed too hazardous in industrialized nations to third world countries.[24]

> The agro-chemical industry exports hazardous pesticides that have not been registered or whose use is banned or subject to severe safety restrictions in their country of manufacture, to developing countries where their use cannot adequately be controlled. As a result, highly toxic or persistent pesticides are used indiscriminately throughout the third world, causing massive poisoning of the rural population and widespread environmental contamination.[25]

Modern Insecticides

Organochlorine insecticides have been largely replaced by two groups of insecticides, the organophosphates and the carbamates. These classes of chemicals are short-lived in the environment relative to the organochlorines, but are more acutely toxic to vertebrates than the organochlorines.

The development of organophosphates as insecticides can be traced to World War II nerve gas experimentation. Both the organophosphates and the carbamates kill by hampering the action of the cholinesterase enzymes of the nervous system. In cases of acute poisoning, the victim may experience symptoms that include difficulty in breathing, muscle twitching, decreased heart rate, loss of reflexes, paralysis, and convulsions. Effects of exposure are cumulative; exposure even to a minute amount, occurring after repeated exposures, may inhibit cholinesterase enough to be fatal.

Caught in the Crossfire

Organizations like Defenders of Wildlife have increasingly become concerned that our dependence on pesticides is having an unintentional and inexcusable toll on wildlife. "When agriculture and public health services switched from the organochlorine to the organophosphate and carbamate insecticides, human and animal pesticide poisoning increased worldwide."[26] This reflects the greater toxicity of these insecticides as well as their widespread and intensive use. Wild animals are too often caught in the cross fire of our war against "pests."

If not harmed by direct exposure to pesticides, wildlife populations can be negatively affected by the changes that pesticides cause in their environment. For instance, insecticides may kill large numbers of insects on which many species of birds depend for food. Butterflies, important plant pollinators, are extremely sensitive to insecticides. The labels of lawn care products containing one common insecticide, chlorpyrifos (Dursban), which is also used in agriculture, on golf courses, and in mosquito control programs, illustrate just how poisonous these substances can be:

> May be absorbed through the skin. May be injurious to eyes and skin.... Avoid breathing vapors and spray mist. Avoid spraying food crops. Keep away from food, feedstuffs, and domestic water supplies. ...This product is highly toxic to bees exposed to direct treatment or residues on plants.... (Chlorpyrifos) is highly toxic to fish, birds and other wildlife. Keep out of lakes, streams, ponds, tidal marshes and estuaries. Shrimp and crabs may be killed at application rates recommended on the label. Do not apply where these are important resources. Do not apply where runoff is likely to occur. Do not apply when weather conditions favor drift from areas treated.[27]

Although it is widely known that organophosphate and carbamate pesticides are killing wildlife,[28,29,30,31,32,33] it is very difficult to determine the extent of the mortality and the pesticides most involved. An animal poisoned by a pesticide often hides at the onset of poisoning symptoms. Dead animals are carried off by scavengers or quickly decay. The chances of wildlife mortality being noticed in agricultural use, which often occurs in relatively isolated areas, are especially small. Despite these difficulties, enough wild animals are being found to indicate that the magnitude of mortality is serious.

In its Special Review of granular carbofuran, EPA noted that members of at least fifteen unstable or declining species or closely related species have been killed by granular carbofuran. It expressed concern about the impacts of carbofuran on the already declining populations of birds such as the American goldfinch, the song sparrow, the rufous-sided towhee, the red-shouldered hawk, the loggerhead shrike, and northern harriers.[34]

In the spring of 1989, the Agency proposed canceling all uses of carbofuran because of its toxicity to birds.[35] The manufacturer and many segments of the agricultural industry vehemently objected. At this writing, it is not known whether EPA will persevere in canceling this highly toxic insecticide. Congress has already stepped in to slow the process. And FIFRA as currently written allows users of carbofuran to object to EPA's proposal and request hearings that could delay a cancellation for years.

As EPA slowly moves toward cancellation of just one insecticide, evidence that carbofuran is only one of many wildlife-killing pesticides continues to build. Fenthion, phorate, dicrotophos, diazinon (a common lawn and garden insecticide), and others are killing wildlife, reducing wild populations, degrading biological diversity, and weakening the biological systems upon which all of us depend.

Although most attention about the effects of pesticides on wildlife focuses on insecticides, other pesticides also negatively impact wildlife. Herbicides — weedkillers — second only to insecticides in the amounts used in this country, also take their toll.

Conifer forests, many federally or state owned, are routinely sprayed with herbicides like 2,4-D and glyphosate to kill plants that compete with young conifers for light, water, and soil nutrients. Heavy doses are used to kill woody brush — per acre amounts are typically double the amount used in agriculture.[36]

Although laboratory tests have indicated that rats dosed with glyphosate (known commercially as Roundup) eliminate all traces within five days, wildlife in treated forests is exposed to the herbicide repeatedly. A study conducted by Monsanto, Roundup's manufacturer, revealed that residues of glyphosate remained in wildlife fifty-five days after aerial spraying.[37] And when hunting seasons coincide with spray seasons, "a hunter who brings home contaminated venison for the freezer may unwittingly expose her or his family to repeated doses of brushkiller over a long period," since residues of both glyphosate and 2,4-D are stable when frozen.[38]

Humans can be directly exposed to these herbicides by consumption of forest foods. G. Payne reported that berries in sprayed areas have carried 2,4-D loads up to forty times EPA's limit for residues of 2,4-D on these fruits.[39] As a result of public concern about forest spraying, the Minnesota Department of Natural Resources has agreed to begin measuring residue levels in forest wildlife and food, and in the interim post-sprayed areas with signs that "warn passers-by to refrain from eating berries or other vegetation on the site."[40]

There is not in this country a system for tracking wildlife poisonings to determine what pesticides are killing wildlife, and which species are most affected. It is therefore impossible to estimate the toll our dependence on pesticides is taking on wildlife and our environment. And to the extent that the health of wildlife populations serves as an indicator of environmental and in turn human health, we must be concerned about the impacts of pesticides on wildlife not only for its own sake but for our own.

The federal Endangered Species Act requires every federal agency, including EPA, to ensure that any action it carries out or authorizes will not jeopardize the continued existence of any endangered species or destroy or adversely modify its critical habitat.

In 1984, EPA commissioned a study to examine how effectively it was implementing the Endangered Species Act in its pesticide actions. The resulting report was generally critical of EPA actions and found that members of a number of endangered species — bald eagle, manatee, brown pelican, gray bat, California condor — had been killed by pesticides.[41]

The reasons for reducing our dependence on pesticides are compelling: increasing resistance in target species, increased crop losses, contamination of surface and groundwater, pesticide residues in food, destruction of wildlife, disruption of biological systems, and the widespread and mistaken belief that pesticides are safe and that if a little is good, then more must be better.

On an Individual Level

By reaching for a pesticide without considering its risks, we do a disservice to ourselves, our neighborhoods, and the environment. "Environmental contamination with highly potent carcinogenic pesticides has reached alarming and pervasive proportions. Contamination of ground- and surface waters has become commonplace. Much comes from agricultural use, but increasingly we find that the most intensely contaminated areas are residential."[42] S. S. Epstein and S. Briggs note that the National Academy of Sciences has reported that home lawns may average ten pounds of pesticide applications per acre, while farmers rarely use more than two pounds.[43]

A recent review of pesticides concluded in part that of the forty pesticides which make up more than 95 percent of all pesticides used on residential lawns by lawn-care companies, more than a quarter are suspected human carcinogens and more than half have been shown to cause long-term health effects in lab animals or humans.[44]

Any reduction in our own use of pesticides can only help ourselves and the environment. We can reduce or eliminate our use of pesticides by learning to work with nature rather than against it, reserving chemicals as a method of last resort and using the least toxic products. Such an approach is generally known as integrated pest management or IPM, defined in former President Carter's 1979 environmental message:

> IPM uses a systems approach to reduce pest damage to tolerable levels through a variety of techniques, including natural predators and parasites, genetically resistant hosts, environmental modifications and, when necessary and appropriate, chemical pesticides. IPM strategies generally rely first upon biological defenses against pests before chemically altering the environment.[45]

The amount of information available about using IPM to reduce the use of pesticides and increase the protection of human health and the environment is growing. It is the responsibility of each of us to use IPM techniques in order to lessen our abuse of natural systems and our exposure to toxic substances. A list of sources of detailed information about using IPM techniques in lawn and garden management follows this chapter.

"One of the best kept secrets in the increasingly chemicalized lawn care industry is the fact that it is perfectly feasible to maintain healthy, attractive lawns with little or no use of pesticides."[46] By using grass species suited to the local environment and the uses to which the lawn is put, aerating the soil to reduce compaction, maintaining appropriate fertility and water levels, and cutting the grass to the correct height at proper intervals, pest populations rarely reach problem levels. In general, plants which are stressed by one or more factors (e.g., too much or too little water, mowing to very low levels, heavy build-up of thatch) are more vulnerable to serious infestation of weeds or invertebrate pests.

Lawn care companies often use pesticide and fertilizer mixtures on a fixed schedule without an evaluation of the pest problems in a particular lawn. They have largely abandoned soil aeration and other cultural techniques in favor of quick and easy herbicide treatments.[47] This approach does not correct the underlying causes of pest infestations. The pests return and with them the lawn care companies with more pesticides. "Excessive use of herbicides eventually throws the lawn ecosystem far enough out of balance that other pest problems develop, leading to more pesticide use and further increases in cost."[48]

There has been a great deal of effort placed in recent years in identifying and developing biological controls — the use of natural enemies such as predators, parasites, or disease — to control pest populations. Insect predators, such as ladybird beetles, green lacewings, and many wasps (some of which are parasites rather than predators) are important means to keeping pest insects under control. The eggs or larvae of many of these insects are available commercially for assistance in controlling such pests as aphids, mealy bugs, and spider mites.

Birds are very important insect predators. By refraining from using insecticides, which can both harm birds and reduce their food supply, and by maintaining trees and shrubs to provide food and nesting sites, the benefits of insect predation by birds are maximized. And bats are important predators of night flying insects. For instance, a single gray bat can eat up to three thousand insects a night.

As a Nation

The pesticide dilemma is that every attempt to take one control action causes numerous unintended effects. Since the 1940s this dilemma has often lead to a treadmill effect: the more we use certain chemicals, the more of them we have to use, and the worse the problem becomes. Human health has been put at risk, untoward ecological consequences have occurred, and costs have often gone out of control. Yet, used carefully and judiciously, pesticides can improve crop production and enhance public health.... The key to success is recognizing that pests and pest control take place in a larger system.[49]

As a nation, we must demand federal and state agriculture programs that give preference to low-input or sustainable agriculture systems in which the need for pesticides is reduced as a result of changes in cropping and tillage systems.

The use of cultural pest control techniques, such as crop rotation (which interrupts the cycle of pest populations), timing planting to miss peak pest populations, and various tillage practices, has given way to large-scale, chemical intensive production of agricultural crops. Pest control research, funded in large measure by the agricultural chemical industry, focuses largely on new pesticides and new applications aimed at keeping American farmers on the "pesticide treadmill."

(Agribusiness) funnel monies in the form of grants to our land grant university system for research. There is a built-in bias for land grant universities to develop technologies that are chemical and capital intensive. Because agribusiness plays such a large role in financing research at the universities, it is difficult for the universities to seek out and develop lower input strategies. We have a generation of university and extension specialists that are well trained in a chemical and capital intensive agriculture, but they are not well trained in looking at other forms of agriculture production.[50]

... In the 1960s large agribusiness establishments flourished. They furnished hats to the extension agents. You'd go to the meetings and you'd wonder who's working for who.... [51]

Financial institutions contribute to the pesticide treadmill by requiring farmers to commit to use of chemical-intensive farming practices in order to qualify for loans. The bias toward chemical solutions to pest problems is strengthened by current federal commodity price support programs that encourage farmers to maximize production of the same crops on the same acres year after year. Without crop rotation, the populations of pests of specific crops, such as the corn rootworm, are not disrupted and can become perennial problems. Rotating corn with other crops such as soybeans, for example, reduces the rootworm problem and the need for insecticides but is discouraged by some government subsidy programs.

In the face of maximized production, commodity prices drop, lessening farm profits and forcing farmers to seek even greater production by clearing more land and using more chemicals. In this system, only commodity exporters and chemical companies are assured a profit.

We cannot continue down our current path of ever escalating pesticide use. Our efforts to poison nature into submission are backfiring. We are learning that by poisoning one part of an ecosystem we too often change the balance and the function of the rest.

There is today reason to be cautiously optimistic that food and fiber production in this country will eventually become less dependent on chemicals. But it will require Americans to actively oppose this dependence in the face of the uncertain effects of chemicals on human health and the knowledge that we are harming the environment on which we all depend through their injudicious use. Terry Gips has noted that every time we shop, we "vote" with our dollars.[52] Without demanding food produced without pesticides or in low-input systems, we help to perpetuate the current system of pesticide dependence.

For the sake of wildlife, the environment, and in turn for our own sakes, it is time to stop paying the price of convenience and begin instead to enjoy the benefits of sane pest management.

S. H.

* * *

TAKING ACTION

1. Substitute natural products for moth balls. Commercial moth ball products emit hazardous fumes and contain hazardous contents. Natural moth repellants are available in various stores and through catalogs. Most often they contain cedar chips or shavings, or are simply small blocks of cedar. However, if you want to make your own repellant, combine one-half pound each of rosemary and mint, one-quarter pound of thyme, and two tablespoons of cloves. Place a portion of this mixture in a cloth, tie it at the top, and place it with your stored clothes. (Source: North American Conference on Religion and Ecology.)

2. Cosmetic products may actually harm us. Pesticides have been found in some brands of shampoos, and baby powder frequently contains asbestos. Just about any toxic product can be replaced with

nontoxic substances. For example use cornstarch instead of baby powder. (Source: "An Activist's Guide to a Better Earth," *Omni*, September 1989)

3. Following is a list of substitutes for products that are hazardous.

rodent poison	seal all holes with fine grade steel wool, use mouse traps.
insect repellent	two teaspoons of liquid soap per gallon of water — use pure soap.
garden herbicides, insecticides, fungicides	many nontoxic garden insecticides are now available — check with your local garden store.
drain cleaners	commercial bacteria is now available for keeping drains open, or, use boiling water, plunger, metal snake.
oven cleaners	steel wool and washing soda with small amount of water.
toilet cleaners	scrub with brush using powdered soap and scouring powder of baking soda, borax, or table salt.
silver polishes	rub with paste of baking soda and water.
furniture polishes	damp cloth — and rub with soft dry cloth.
general cleansers	mix two teaspoons borax and one teaspoon soda in one quart water. Store in spray bottle.
window cleaners	vinegar and water
laundry bleach	one-half cup borax per wash load
dyes	use vegetable dyes such as onion skins, teas, marigolds
motor oil, brake and transmission fluid	(dispose of at recycling center)
antifreeze	place directly in sewer
car batteries	(take to recycling center)
old, lead paints	use water-based (latex) paint, do not use aerosol sprays

(Source: Most suggestions are from Greenpeace Action giveaway, "Everyone's Guide to Toxins in the Home.")

4. Use organic pest control methods on your lawn and garden — get rid of pesticides. If we don't put poisons into the land and water, we won't have to confront them at a later date when we eat and drink. Several publications are available for guidance. One of the best is *The Encyclopedia of Natural Insect and Disease Control* (Rodale Press, Emmaus, PA.)

5. Treated wood. Wood that has been preserved by inorganic arsenic, creosote, and pentachlorophenol should be used only in areas in which the wood will not come in contact with the ground (but *not* inside the house), and only then when wood will not come into contact with public drinking water and where it could not become a component of food and animal feed. For example, do no use in a vegetable garden or in containers for storing silage or food for animals. If treated wood is cut, the cutter should wear a mask and goggles. It also should never be burned. Whenever this wood is purchased, the seller should give the purchaser directions from the EPA on how the product should be handled. The best choice is a selection of red cedar or cypress; both are rot resistant and require no toxic "preservatives."

For additional information on these subjects, contact the following:

Bio-Integral Resource Center
P.O. Box 7414
Berkeley, CA 94707

Institute for Alternative Agriculture
9200 Edmonston Road, Suite 117
Greenbelt, MD 20770

International Alliance for
   Sustainable Agriculture
Newman Center
University of Minnesota
1701 University Ave., SE
Minneapolis, MN 55455

National Coalition Against
   the Misuse of Pesticides
530 7th Street, SE
Washington, DC 20003

Northwest Coalition for
   Alternatives to Pesticides
P.O. Box 1393
Eugene, OR 97440

Public Citizen
215 Pennsylvania Ave., SE
Washington, DC 20003

Rachel Carson Council
8940 Jones Mill Road
Chevy Chase, MD 20815

— 14 —

Wetlands:
America's Endangered Habitat

J. S. Garton

> For want of a better name, we call them "wetlands." They are a
> mingling of land and water in myriad forms: estuaries, fresh and
> saltwater marshes, cypress swamps, prairie potholes, bogs and
> fens, oxbow lakes, wet meadows, and deep floodplain forests.
> They range from sunlit ponds on treeless prairie to brooding
> swamps of bald cypress and tupelo, from cordgrass marshes
> swept by Atlantic storm tides to alkaline sinks in the Great Basin.
> And all these wetlands are more richly productive of life than
> either land or water alone.
>
> John Madson, *The Nature Conservancy News*

Less than a hundred years after Coronado failed to find the fabled
seven cities of gold, English settlers on North America's Atlantic
coast laid claim to the richest gold mine in history. But unlike the
shining yellow towers of Coronado's dreams, this gold lay in full view.
It was the pure gold of vast forests, sparkling waters, rich soils, abundant wildlife and fishes, clear air, rolling grasslands, and millions of
acres of wetlands — marches, bogs, sloughs, sinks, swamps, potholes,
wet meadows, oxbows, and estuaries.

When the English first planted themselves in this new land, some
215 million acres of wetlands covered what later became the lower
forty-eight states. In one piece, it would have been a marsh the size
of Colorado, New Mexico, and Nevada, or one-tenth of the country's
land surface, excluding Alaska and Hawaii.

In those times, wetlands were everywhere. They lay pooled among rocky coasts and in broad tidal bays. They paralleled lakes, rivers, streams, and creeks. Great hardwood forests grew in some, as did hay grasses and blueberries. In the northern plains, wetlands occupied thousands of scrapes left by departing glaciers or lay in spongy, spring-fed mountain watering holes. Even in the deserts, wetland seeps defied the best attempts of the sun and winds to finish them off.

But wetlands carried with them a false reputation. Settlers mistakenly thought they were wastelands, homes for disease and pestilence; wetlands stood in the way of progress. High on the list of pioneer priorities, then, was the determination to drain or fill or do whatever necessary to get rid of wetlands.

Those early Americans and their descendants did a good job. In the mid-1970s, the US Fish and Wildlife Service (USFWS) found that more than half (54 percent) of the original wetland acres in the lower forty-eight states were gone, and that they were being destroyed at an average of 458,000 acres each year. At that rate, every two years, wetland acreage greater than the size of Rhode Island is lost; in ten years, a New Jersey-sized area is gone. Today, approximately ninety-seven million wetland acres survive.

Iowa now has only 1 percent of its natural marshes remaining, less than twenty-seven thousand acres. Californians have managed to destroy 91 percent of their wetland area. In Nebraska's Rainwater Basin, nine out of ten wetlands have been converted to agricultural uses; of the ninety-four thousand original acres of marshland there, only 10 percent survived into 1981. And so it has gone across the rest of the country.

To make it worse, government at all levels often devised incentives for wetland conversion. Even as late as 1989, a Department of the Interior report, "The Impact of Federal Programs on Wetlands," showed that despite new laws and policy changes, there still are several federal programs and policies that *encourage* the destruction of wetlands.

The image of wetlands as useless, wasted land is powerful; changing it continues to be difficult. The old question about a tree falling in a forest with no one to hear it has its parallels to our perception of wetlands. If no one hears a tree fall, does it make a sound? If wetlands exist without direct, visible benefit to the person inquiring, do they really have value?

The answer in both cases is yes, but demonstrating it is another matter. Flood prevention is one example. Persons living downstream from a wetland area don't see it slowing and holding flood water, or watch it removing silt. Those people probably aren't aware that a wetland even exists nearby. They just know that despite unusually heavy rains upstream, they don't have to evacuate their homes or clean up flood damage.

Near Boston, the US Army Corps of Engineers concluded in the early 1970s that wetlands protection was the least-cost solution to flood prevention; the perpetual protection of 8,500 acres of upstream wetlands would prevent flood damages costing an average of $17 million each year. Other studies show that floods may be lessened up to 80 percent in watersheds that have many wetlands compared to those with few wetlands, and that in a North Dakota area, pothole wetlands store almost 75 percent of the total rainfall runoff. Clearly, wetlands along rivers and streams and as part of watershed systems offer unappreciated natural flood protection worth billions of dollars of damage prevention each year.

Preventing or slowing soil erosion, providing a water supply, and recharging groundwater are other unsung roles wetlands play. A detailed 1982 soil survey showed US farms losing 3.1 billion tons of topsoil each year. Or, as reported in *State of the World* 1988, "For every ton of grain they produced, American farmers were losing six tons of their topsoil." (Even though $1 billion is spent in soil conservation projects each year by the US Department of Agriculture (USDA) and American farmers, more than 2 billion tons of soil above "tolerable" levels still are washed or blown away.)

Preserving wetlands will not solve all soil erosion problems. But wetland vegetation along river banks and other waters does reduce erosion, as well as slowing flood flows. Wetland tree species like willows, alders, cottonwoods, ashes, poplars, maples, and elms have kept some river banks from suffering erosion for one hundred to two hundred years. Along the Atlantic and Gulf Coasts, shoreline erosion has been checked by wetland areas of smooth cordgrass or mangrove swamps.

The USFWS reports that in Wisconsin, "Watersheds with 40 percent coverage by lakes and wetlands had 90 percent less sediment in water than watersheds with no lakes or wetlands." Obviously, natural and restored wetland systems are one important tool in reducing topsoil and water quality losses.

Wetlands also are potential areas for groundwater supply. In Massachusetts, at least sixty cities or towns have their supply wells in or next to wetlands. Close to half of that state's wetlands have been identified as potential drinking water sources. And in times of drought, wetlands also may provide water and food supplies for livestock.

Some cities have found wetlands useful for natural treatment of sewage. Tinicum Marsh, a 320-acre freshwater tidal marsh south of Philadelphia, is the best known example. Three treatment plants discharge treated sewage into Tinicum; in a day's time, marsh plants remove 4.9 tons of phosphorus, 4.3 tons of ammonia, and 138 pounds of nitrate.

The Alcovy River Swamp is a bottomland forested wetland in Georgia. Its twenty-three hundred acres filter impurities from a heavily polluted river; the value of this wetland for water pollution control has been estimated at $1 million annually.

Constructed wetlands are becoming more common as low-cost sewage treatment facilities. Right now, thirty-one towns in the US and Canada use artificial marshes to treat their sewage. The primary advantage seems to be financial; construction of a wetlands treatment system is thought to cost from one-tenth to one-half that of conventional treatment plants, and they are less expensive to operate. Such systems also provide habitat for wildlife and other benefits to the environment, like release of oxygen.

Though wetlands provide billions of dollars worth of benefits each year, the water quality, flood protection, and water supply potentials of wetland systems usually are not figured into any economic scheme. In a way, that's understandable. How many people sit around trying to calculate all the possible benefits of *not* having a broken leg or *not* losing their eyesight? Only after a leg is broken or one goes blind does a person begin to appreciate the value of the lost ability.

Wetlands suffer from the same shortage of foresight — only after wetlands are gone does it become obvious how much value should have been given them.

Most Americans — be they business leaders, educators, private citizens, policymakers, opinion leaders, or members of the media — lack knowledge, understanding, and appreciation of the many roles played by wetlands. Yet wetlands are one of this nation's richest naturally-occurring resources. As habitat, wetland ecosystems are extremely productive, providing abundant food, shelter, and nesting areas for all kinds of wildlife.

Wetland plants seem to be better than average at converting the sun's energy to plant material. In fact, wetlands are so productive, they've been called the farmlands of the aquatic environment because of the large amounts of plant and animal foods they produce.

It's not just the amount of vegetation that makes a wetland productive, it's the diversity. Wetland areas often support more than a hundred different kinds of plants. And no two wetlands are exactly alike. The insects, birds, amphibians, reptiles, mammals, microorganisms, invertebrates, and other life forms associated with one kind of wetland will be very different from those found in another.

A flooded cornfield can support only a small number of different kinds of birds, mammals, or insects. But a wetland made up of mudflats, permanent shallow pools, wet meadows, and trees is a different story. That is an ecosystem, full of complex relationships between predator and prey, decay and growth, life and death — everchanging, yet stable.

Coastal wetlands are hatcheries for millions of fish, shrimp, crabs, and clams. It has been estimated that around two-thirds of the major US commercial fishers directly depend on estuaries or salt marshes. Most freshwater fishes are thought to be wetland-dependent, too, because they either feed or spawn, or their young grow to adulthood in wetlands.

Muskrats, beaver, otter, mink, raccoon, and many smaller mammals live in wetlands. In northeastern Pennsylvania, wetlands provide refuge to black bears, while caribou use the wetlands of Alaska's North Slope as summer range and calving grounds. Turtles, snakes, alligators, frogs, and salamanders also are commonly associated with wetland habitat. Numbers can be astounding. In a small gum swamp in Georgia (less than one hundred feet wide), sixteen hundred salamanders and thirty-eight hundred frogs and toads were counted.

To many migratory birds, wetlands mean survival. There are some shorebird species that winter at the tip of South America, but nest high up in the Arctic Circle. These wading birds build up their fat reserves, fly nonstop for one to two thousand miles, land at a wetland area rich in food supplies, rest, build up their fat supplies, and repeat the process until they reach their breeding grounds. For them, the existence of "staging" wetlands is absolutely critical. They don't have energy to search out wetland areas when it's time to land. They "know" where particular wetlands exist that have an abundance of food and shelter. For shorebirds like these, it is essential that specific staging wetlands be protected all along their migration routes, from South America to Central America, Mexico, the US and Canada. If one of the staging wetlands is lost, one or more shorebird species could become extinct.

Cheyenne Bottoms Wildlife Area, a marsh and upland of almost twenty thousand acres in the heart of Kansas, has been identified as the most important wetland in the US for migratory shorebirds. In spring, 45 percent of all North American shorebirds migrating to far northern breeding grounds pass through Cheyenne Bottoms. Five shorebird species — the long-billed dowitcher; white-rumped, Baird's, and stilt sandpipers; and Wilson's phalarope — might die out forever if the Bottoms was destroyed because more than 90 percent of their populations funnel through the wetland before moving on to their nesting sites.

The existence of Cheyenne Bottoms probably was not as critical fifty years ago as it is today. But from 1955 to 1978, 40 percent of all wetlands in Kansas were wiped out, making Cheyenne Bottoms practically the only adequate wetland left for long distance shorebird fliers in the Central Flyway. Key wetlands in other flyways serve as staging areas too, but none have the numbers of shorebirds that Cheyenne Bottoms supports.

For ducks, geese, and other migratory birds who fly much shorter distances between rests, the existence of specific wetlands along their migration routes is less important than quality wetland habitat throughout. Especially important are the wetlands at the extremes of their migratory cycles. Ducks and geese primarily winter along the southern coast of the US, in the bays and backwaters of open-river systems, and in California's Central Valley. Peter Steinhart reports in *Audubon* that "California winters 60 percent of the ducks and geese of the Pacific Flyway, a fifth of the entire continent's waterfowl population."

Ducks breed in the northern plains of the US, Canada, and Alaska. Fifteen duck species nest in the Dakotas pothole country, but mallards, pintails, and blue-winged teal depend most heavily on that habitat. And if it isn't there, neither will the ducks nor the young they might have produced.

Other birdlife, like red-winged blackbirds, seem inseparable from marsh habitat, but killdeer, warblers, herons, egrets, pelicans, and a host of others make their homes in wetlands as well. At Cheyenne Bottoms, more than 320 different kinds of birds have been seen, three-fourths of all the kinds of birds in Kansas!

Shorebirds, waterfowl, and even some songbirds require wetland habitat to survive. Some bird species spend all their lives in wetland environments, while others only nest, feed, or overwinter in them. Loss of wetland areas means certain loss of bird numbers; in some cases, it could spell extinction.

There is no question that wetlands provide valuable benefits to the public in the form of naturally-occurring flood prevention and control, water quality, potential water supply, and groundwater recharge. More important, wetlands are ecosystems, a web of inter-dependent life that both feeds and fuels a continuing cycle of life processes, from the production of food and oxygen to the break-down of vegetation and human-made pollutants. As the specter of the greenhouse effect looms larger, the oxygen released by wetland plants may become one of humankind's greatest hopes.

Wetland ecosystems are America's endangered habitat. They are valuable beyond mere dollars and cents, beyond human dreams of new houses, highways, and factories. Wetlands are part of the thread and fabric of the natural systems of our planet. Their health is our health. Their destruction, in time, becomes ours. Knowing this, why are wetlands still under siege, what are the primary threats, and what can be done?

Our attitudes toward nature and wetlands go back a long way. In religious texts such as Genesis, human beings were given "dominion" over nature, a term often misinterpreted to mean exploitation. As long as humankind pronounced itself "better" than the rest of nature, it gave itself the excuse and the "right" to use all of nature's resources to serve its own desires without regard to the effect on other creatures. The view of humans as a *part* of nature was to be vigorously rejected, because it implied a responsibility to all inhabitants of Earth.

But the system of beliefs practiced by most native North Americans recognized that responsibility. The Native Americans saw themselves and nature in a brotherhood. Chief Seattle's letter in reply to a presidential request to sell his tribe's land sums it up well:

> We know the sap which courses through the trees as we know the blood that courses through our veins. We are part of the earth and it is part of us. The perfumed flowers are our sisters. The bear, the deer, the great eagle, these are our brothers. The rocky crests, the juices in the meadow, the body heat of the pony, and man, all belong to the same family.
>
> The shining water that moves in the streams and rivers is not just water, but the blood of our ancestors.... This we know: the earth does not belong to man, man belongs to the earth. All things are connected like the blood that unites us all. Man did not weave the web of life, he is merely a strand in it. Whatever he does to the web, he does to himself.

This ecological view of their place in the world may help explain why North America was so rich in natural resources when first settled by the Europeans, despite centuries of occupation by its original inhabitants. For Europeans, natural resources were the means to gain wealth; for the Indians, natural resources *were* the wealth.

Today, wetlands destruction persists because our society still looks at these ecosystems as a means to an end. We do not see what is there; our eyes see only what will happen to our bank accounts. We don't enjoy the life that is; our pleasure comes from bending it to our design. Cultural attitudes and behavior are the number one threat to wetlands — and the rest of our environment as well.

But number two on the list is agriculture. The American agriculture system is recognized worldwide for the amount of food it produces. Still, production has not come without cost. There may be no other industry in this country that has inflicted so much damage on the environment as agriculture. Massive habitat destruction is an obvious example, but large-scale soil losses to wind and water erosion can be traced to modern agricultural practices.

Besides pesticide and fertilizer contamination of water supplies, depletion of streams, rivers, and underground aquifers by mining groundwater for irrigation is a serious problem in many states. Seventy-nine percent of the loss of freshwater wetlands in the US can be laid at the door of agriculture.

In the Prairie Pothole Region, an area of some three hundred thousand square miles in central Canada and north central US, at least half of all North American ducks are produced each year, though it provides only 10 percent of the waterfowl breeding area. But much of this wetland habitat has been drained for agriculture.

Pond excavation in pothole wetlands and the plowing of range-land to create more cropland also threaten pothole wetlands. In 1976, nearly fifty-six thousand ponds in eastern South Dakota were dug — 77 percent were in wetland basins or streams. Pothole habitat loss has had a dramatic impact. Population numbers of some duck species are at all time lows. In part, declines are the result of prolonged droughts in the Canadian prairies, but much is due to alteration of wetland breeding grounds.

The drought of 1988 only made a bad situation worse. From 10 million birds in 1956, the northern pintail duck population has gone to 2.6 million in 1988. Blue-winged teal numbers were so few, the US Fish and Wildlife Service (USFWS) recommended that the 1988 early fall hunting season be eliminated. Just 10 of 181 marked female mallards in North Dakota hatched broods in 1988. (In normal years, most female mallards nest, and many renest.)

Wetland drainage and conversion to cropland affects more than waterfowl breeding areas. Four million acres of wetlands once graced California's Central Valley. Only 160,000 remain. As a result, Peter Steinhart reports that, "California's wintering duck population has plummeted from seven million birds in 1980 to two million in 1985.... Over most of the state, the great flocks of waterfowl are gone." He continues:

> Most of the original great blue heron rookeries in the valley are gone. There were once white pelican colonies all up and down the valley; today there are none. The tule elk, a small, swamp-loving species, survives only on refuges.... As the wetlands go, so do the phalaropes, grebes, sandpipers, egrets, herons, and rails. And so too do the fisheries.

Overcrowding of limited breeding and wintering grounds increases the likelihood of epidemics of avian cholera and botulism. "At times refuge personnel must go out and stack corpses like cordwood and burn them," Steinhart reports.

In addition to converting millions of acres of wetland habitat to cropland, agriculture has also affected private and public wetlands by chemical contamination of waters. Perhaps the most famous area is the Kesterson National Wildlife Refuge in California. Kesterson is a Bureau of Reclamation project. Begun in 1965, the plan was to take drainage water from irrigated fields that was too salty to be reused and carry it by ditch to San Francisco Bay. In 1983, it was clear that something was seriously wrong, and in 1984, 20 percent of the nests of certain species contained embryos with missing eyes, and deformed beaks, legs, and wings. There were dead embryos in 40 percent of the nests. Unfortunately, Kesterson receives drainage water from many sources other than the ditch, and some of it also contains contaminants like selenium, arsenic, and boron. Fixing the problem could be impossible.

With no solution in sight, the USFWS has stationed people at the refuge to fire guns in the air, so that migratory birds will not land and become poisoned. Currently, twenty-one wetlands in thirteen states are being investigated for toxic contamination.

A different kind of chemical situation in the pothole region threatens waterbird populations already stressed by drought and habitat loss. Aerial spraying of pesticides onto cropland drifts onto nearby wetlands, killing some waterfowl outright and making others more susceptible to natural stresses. Three days after a plane sprayed a sunflower crop with a legal amount of the insecticide ethyl parathion, a USFWS biologist found only 4 living ducklings from a group of 104 released in the potholes before spraying.

Perhaps as deadly to the survival of duck populations in pothole country is the devastation some of the newer insecticides cause to the ducks' food supplies of aquatic invertebrates. Invertebrates provide essential protein to laying hens and ducklings, and are a major food source for many shorebird species, too.

Unfortunately, eleven of the most frequently used insecticides in Canada and the US are classified as "highly toxic" to invertebrates or birds. Even worse, most are sprayed aerially. A study in the *Journal of Economic Entomology* showed that an average of 54 percent of aerially applied insecticides drift off the intended target, compared to an average of 3 to 5 percent drift from ground spraying.

So whether wetland areas become contaminated by runoff of agricultural chemicals or direct application of pesticides, the damage to the plant and animal populations of wetland ecosystems is equally devastating.

There is yet another threat facing wetlands that comes from our agricultural system — water depletion. Diversion of water for irrigation has caused two national Wildlife Refuges in Nevada to dry up, and threatens the remaining wetlands in the state's Lahontan Valley, on its western edge. A quarter of a million migrant waterfowl stop in the Lahontan wetlands, including some twelve thousand tundra swans and at times, 90 percent of the snow geese in Nevada. Large flocks of pelicans, up to thirty thousand birds, feed in the marshes.

In Kansas, groundwater use for irrigation has dried up many streams and creeks, and a large part of the Arkansas River. The Arkansas River is the major source of water for Cheyenne Bottoms, but the river stopped flowing at the wildlife area's diversion dam during the summer of 1988 and only began to flow again after the unusually wet summer of 1990.

Given all the ways agriculture can affect wetlands, it shouldn't be surprising that 79 percent of the destruction of freshwater wetlands can be traced to farming. In truth, it has long been a policy of our government to encourage farmers to drain wetlands.

Technology generally is several steps ahead of our understanding of its effects. Or, as publicist W. H. Ferry recently put it, "Our technology has outstripped our political imagination." When the chemical age dawned after World War II, fertilizers, pesticides, and herbicides came to the agricultural scene with a vengeance. Food production increased tremendously. Yet the relatively short span of twenty years of environmental effects were so dramatic they prompted scientist Rachel Carson to publish *Silent Spring*.

Center-pivot irrigation systems were the children of the 1950s, drawing water from enormous underground sources faster than it could be recharged. In the space of one generation, streams in Kansas, eastern Colorado, and many other states that flowed during the dust bowl years have been sucked dry; future generations have had their options reduced, perhaps for the life of this planet.

So while the finger of accusation may be pointed at farmers, it should be remembered that much of our system of agricultural practices can be traced to an alliance between government, banks, land grant institutions, and the chemical and agribusiness industry. Public demand for cheap food, regardless of environmental or social consequences, is an additional factor in determining the way America farms. Individual farmers can and should choose to change, but if wetlands are to be protected from further agricultural inroads, the primary attack will have to be aimed at the alliance of outside interests, which is fed by an uninformed public.

Agriculture is not the only wetland villain. The US Army Corps of Engineers has had a hand in wetland losses, too, especially wetlands associated with rivers and streams. The Corps has done considerable ecological damage even though originally it was assigned the job of improving the nation's navigation facilities. Soon flood control, regulation of hydraulic mining, water pollution, waterway development, irrigation, recreation, and hydroelectric power development were added to its responsibilities.

As of 1973, the Corps announced in its own publication that it had completed more than 4,000 civil works projects, built more than 19,000 miles of waterways, constructed some 350 reservoirs, built more than 9,000 miles of levees and flood walls as well as channelized 7,500 miles of rivers and streams. As of 1971, there was only one major stream in Delaware that the Corps had not channelized at least in part, and they had authorization to work on it.

It is difficult to estimate the loss in wetland habitat caused by the Corps' activities, but one place in desperate trouble today is the coastal area of Louisiana: sixty square miles of its coast disappears every year, or one wetland every fourteen minutes!

The Corps built hundreds of miles of levees and waterways to keep the Mississippi River from flooding. The flood-control structures have destroyed the ecological balance in the Mississippi delta wetlands, preventing fresh river water and sediment from feeding the marshes. Today, the river carries a yearly load of 183 million tons of sediment over the continental shelf and dumps it in the ocean — that's soil equivalent to twenty thousand dump truck loads per hour. Louisiana's coastal wetland ecosystems are home to two-thirds of all the wintering waterfowl in the Mississippi Flyway but scientists predict that four of Louisiana's coastal counties will be almost entirely under water by the middle of the twenty-first century without action to reverse the erosion.

While the Corps is not the only participant at fault in Louisiana, the devastation is typical of many Corps projects. In Tennessee, the Corps had been attempting to finish a project begun in 1960. Despite opposition from many federal and state agencies and organizations, as well as 90 percent of the people owning land adjacent to the project, the Corps insisted that the project is necessary. Already, ninety thousand acres of bottomland hardwoods have been destroyed — the remaining seventy thousand acres of hardwood wetlands will go if the project is completed. These wetlands have been labeled as critical by the North American Waterfowl Management Plan because they provide essential habitat for the five hundred thousand ducks wintering in Tennessee. In 1990, the Corps finally bowed to public pressure and said they won't continue with the project.

Since the 1930s, increased awareness of their values resulted in some efforts to save wetland areas. But while federal duck-stamp money was buying wetlands, farmers were paid federal money to drain them. And while the USDA was paying farmers to take land out of production, the Bureau of Reclamation was diverting water from wetland areas to open the arid west to crop production. River wetland systems that once provided flood protection were drained; then the Corps built levees and straightened rivers to try to reestablish control over runoff.

Yet another problem is differences in the definition of wetlands. Being able to identify a wetland may be a little like trying to define "good" art — you can't explain it, but you know it when you see it!

A wetland doesn't have to have water in it all the time to be considered a wetland. In times of drought, a wetland may be dry for more than a year, yet it still remains a wetland, and its true boundaries don't change. Permanently flooded deepwater areas (generally those deeper than six feet) are *not* wetlands because the primary habitat is water, instead of the vegetation and soils of a wetland.

Finding a consistent definition that includes a method for identifying a wetland's borders throughout the seasons is especially important in agricultural areas, where farmers often plow and plant wetland areas in dry years; good rains may later restore water levels, but the function of the wetland, the reason it is valuable, might be lost forever.

The Final Report of the National Wetlands Policy Forum (1988) says that while only two major definitions of wetlands are used at the federal level, "over fifty are employed in the nation's many regulatory, research, survey, and other wetland programs." That helps explain why so many governmental programs work at cross-purposes when it comes to wetland protection or management. Fortunately, several agencies reached agreement in early 1989 on the identification and definition of wetlands. This is an important step toward improved wetland protection, but it must be matched by a commitment.

Under section 404 of the Clean Water Act of 1972, the Corps has the responsibility to issue permits for activities that drain or fill wetlands, subject to input from numerous agencies, organizations, and individuals. The General Accounting Office said that the Corps often fails to adopt recommendations of other agencies, does not seek out permit violations, does not follow up on reports of suspected violations, rarely suspends or revokes the permits of violators, and does not enforce civil or criminal remedies, relying instead on voluntary corrections of the violations. Recommendations made by the GAO to improve the Corps' performance are awaiting Congressional enactment.

Standing in the way of widespread changes is this fact: excluding Alaska, sixty-five million of the nearly ninety-seven million existing wetland acres left in the US are privately owned. Despite greater awareness of the values of wetlands, many farmers and government employees are guided by the past. They continue to think of wetlands as "bad," and use what means they can to continue eliminating wetlands.

In an effort to discourage conversion of wetlands on private property, the Food Security Act of 1985 included major conservation measures. The "Swampbuster" provision withholds farm subsidies from landowners who convert wetlands to cropland. Unfortunately, the program is slightly flawed because it still allows farmers to drain wetlands as long as they don't grow certain crops in the dried area. The 1990 Farm Bill would make *draining* the wetlands illegal rather than crop planting. The Swampbuster program also suffers from lack of enforcement by the US Department of Agriculture (USDA). The Wildlife Management Institute reports that from 1985 through February 1988, only five landowners lost benefits because they drained the cropped wetlands. But within a year of that date, 107 farmers had been penalized $452,585 for violations. Still, with the large number of wetland acres in private hands, many more incentives will have to be developed to halt wetland loss.

And for a time, hope shone brightly on the horizon. The National Wetlands Policy Forum — an independent panel of government, business and environmental leaders, academics, farmers, and ranchers — was convened at the request of the Environmental Protection Agency in the summer of 1987. In November 1988 they released their report, *Protecting America's Wetlands: An Action Agenda,* which pointed out the basic flaw in current wetland programs — the absence of a clear, coherent goal.

President Bush provided them a cue when in the October issue of *Sports Afield* he announced his own policy on wetlands: "My position on wetlands is straightforward: All existing wetlands, no matter how small, should be preserved." Upon recommendation of the forum, the EPA in January 1989 adopted as a national policy the goal "to achieve *no overall net loss* of the nation's remaining wetlands base, as defined by acreage and function; and to restore and create wetlands, where feasible, to increase the quality and quantity of the nation's wetlands resource base."

No net loss! Those words were music to the ears of wetlands advocates. By declaring its support for the goal, the EPA broke new ground in this nation's treatment of natural resources. It set up seven objectives to meet the goal: wetland planning activities that include preparation of State Wetlands Conservation Plans, improvements to Section 404 enforcement and guidelines, adequate mitigation (replacement) for unavoidable losses, education and awareness programs, better assessment of cumulative impacts of wetland loss and degradation, and wetland restoration initiatives.

Unfortunately, pressure from the oil industry and the state of Alaska have caused the President to backpedal from his commitment to preserve "all existing wetlands." White House Staff watered down an agreement between the EPA and the Corps of Engineers that now will allow development to proceed without appropriate mitigation in areas where a large portion of the land is wetland, or when projects cause "insignificant" environmental damage. The loopholes in the "no net loss" program are primarily aimed at allowing the oil industry to develop Alaskan wilderness, especially the Arctic National Wildlife Refuge.

On other fronts, momentum for change is building. In December 1989, President Bush signed the North American Wetlands Conservation Act, which will fund wetlands conservation in the US, Canada, and Mexico. Legislation that would guarantee water to wetlands and refuges in California's Central Valley and allow acquisition of unprotected wetlands has passed one committee in the House, but still faces several hurdles before becoming law. Also, the United States is a member of the Ramsar Convention, an international treaty that identifies key wetlands in countries around the world and recognizes them as "Wetlands of International Importance."

A second system of protection was initiated privately by the International Association of Fish and Wildlife Agencies in cooperation with the World Wildlife Fund and the Academy of Natural Sciences of Philadelphia. This is the Western Hemisphere Shorebird Reserve Network, now administered by an international council of government and private organization representatives, and its purpose is to recognize the chains of wetlands in the western hemisphere that are essential to migrating shorebirds and secure protection for them.

The Stillwater Hemisphere Reserve in Nevada's Lahontan Valley was dedicated in the summer of 1988 and the Cheyenne Bottoms Shorebird Reserve in the spring of 1990. While neither of the international programs have real teeth, they do help reinforce awareness of the value of wetlands outside of narrow local, state, and national boundaries.

Many private organizations like Ducks Unlimited, National Audubon Society, the Nature Conservancy, and others own and manage wetland areas themselves. The National Wildlife Federation, National Resources Defense Council, Sierra Club, and Environmental Defense Fund are just a few of the other groups that have worked to insure that wetlands protection policies are enacted and enforced.

Still, there is one entity of vast potential that has barely been tapped — the power of the average citizen who cares and acts. History abounds with examples of a single person making a difference.

We are the last hope of wetlands. If we do nothing, more wetlands will die. We must ask ourselves hard questions: what is it that we really value? Are we wise enough to say no to ourselves, to say yes to life?

J. S. G.

* * *

TAKING ACTION

1. Decide what you want to do. Are you concerned about wetlands in your community or country, or are you hoping to influence national actions? Evaluate the time and energy you have to give and choose a project to match.

2. Get the facts. Learn everything you can about the area of your concern. The best wetland advocates have strong feelings about their projects, but they let facts and good information do the talking. Check sources in your library, contact your state department of environment, or contact a national environmental organization such as the Audubon Society, the Nature Conservancy, or the National Wildlife Federation as well as local and regional environmental groups for information.

3. Develop a program about wetlands to present to schools, organizations, and youth groups. Take people to visit wetlands — it's hard to get them to care from an armchair.

4. Write letters to newspaper and magazine editors, heads of conservation organizations, governor of your state, Congressional and legislative delegations, CEOs, and any other leaders who may be involved in some part of your project. Urge them to adopt actions and attitudes that protect wetlands.

5. Get acquainted with officials of wildlife and natural resource agencies. Let them know of your concern and willingness to help.

6. Attend public hearings on wetland projects; testify in the legislature.

7. Join a local conservation or environmental organization and work with others to change attitudes and laws, to interest others in wetland issues, to get people out experiencing nature.

8. Invite university staff, USFWS staff, or state conservation officials to present workshops on city planning and wetland protection, Wetland identification, map reading, and vegetation recognition to local organizations.

9. Many of us are not just "average citizens." We wear other hats. We can expand concern for wetlands into other parts of our lives. For example, if you are a

Teacher:

a. Incorporate examples of natural resources in the classroom. Math teachers use real problems from nature. In history, look at the effects of events on natural resources, etc.

b. Encourage hands-on experience. Bring nature into the classroom; take students outside. Volunteer to sponsor a nature club.

c. Evaluate teaching — what values and ethics do students get from your classes.

Wetland Owner:

a. Protect wetland habitat. Don't drain, fill, or contaminate wetland ecosystems.

b. Consider establishing a permanent conservation easement or deed restrictions that will preserve the wetland in perpetuity. Consider selling the wetland to a state agency or a private organization that will preserve it.

c. Alter farming practices — stop aerial spraying of pesticides, leave a habitat buffer zone around the wetland, manage the area for improved wildlife habitat, work to reduce the use of chemicals, make irrigation practices as efficient as possible, and begin a transition to dryland farming.

d. Educate neighbors about wetland values and protection.

Developer or Landscape Architect:

a. Look before you leap. Don't plan projects in wetland or floodplain areas.

b. If your development is near a wetland, don't build up to its edge — use the wetland as open space to enhance development.

    c. Leave wildlife corridors along streams and creeks from one development area to another; consider the impact of your development on watersheds and other ecosystems; don't isolate small patches of habitat.

Public Official:

    a. Commit your office to wetland protection.

    b. Make sure you and your agency keep both the spirit and the letter of any programs you administer.

    c. Inform the public of wetland values and the need for protection and restoration.

Banker:

    a. Don't finance projects that develop or destroy wetland areas.

    b. Make charitable contributions to groups and programs that preserve wetland areas.

Shareholder in Corporations:

    a. Examine what the companies in which you own stock are doing to wetland habitat and natural resources.

    b. Urge companies to adopt policies that protect natural resources.

    c. Invest in companies that are environmentally sensitive.

— 15 —

Animal Rights: a More Compassionate Life-style

Ingrid E. Newkirk

The underlying reason why beings other than humans need to be taken into account is that, like human beings, they too are sensitive to happiness and suffering. We should therefore be wary of justifying the right of any species to survive solely on the basis of its usefulness to human beings.

The Venerable Lungrig Namgyal, *The Assisi Declarations*

To synopsize what is written in Ecclesiastes 3:19 and in Chief Seattle's warning to the white man, when humans exploit and abuse non-humans they will suffer greatly for their arrogance. The harm we do to those with whom we must share this fragile Earth will return to harm our own quality of life, or worse.

In the book *Animal Liberation,* author Peter Singer wrote that for most humans the most direct form of contact with nonhuman animals comes at meal time: we eat them. Sadly, many people still think animal-based "foods" are necessary.

The myth that we need a lot of protein, as provided by such a diet, is responsible for osteoporosis, cancers of the colon and breast, and diabetes, among other killers. The protein myth was a result of animal experiments, specifically studies using rats — creatures who need almost one thousand times more protein that we do! Relying on such false information shortens the lives of tens of thousands of human beings each year. The fact is that animal products have three nutritional disadvantages: they contain too much protein, too much fat, and no fiber at all.

The truth is that a meat-based diet is destructive in many ways. For one thing, it kills the Earth. In Central and South America, the meat industry is involved in the wholesale destruction of the irreplaceable and invaluable rain forest, which is casually cleared, then planted with grazing grasses to rear cattle destined to become the cheap American hamburger. Worldwide, a forested area larger than Denmark — home to billions of birds, mammals, reptiles, and insects necessary to the world's biological diversity — vanishes every six months. For every acre converted for other purposes, seven acres of forest are converted for grazing pastures; two hundred million acres of once highly productive forest land are now reduced to grazing land.

The debate over land use for cattle grazing versus rain forest preservation is quite often violent. On December 22, 1988, Francisco Mendes, a rain-forest advocate and protector, was gunned down in Brazil and members of a family involved in cattle ranching have been charged with his murder. "At stake is the Brazilian rain forest.... This great, vast, beautiful place is being destroyed so quickly that some scientists say it will be rendered useless in less than twenty years."[1] Mendes organized peasants in order to protect the rain forest in the western Amazon. "But Mendes and his union were like David fighting the developer's Goliath in this wild and lawless land. Mendes is now just one of a thousand people said to have been killed in the last ten years by gunmen hired by ruthless land owners."[2]

On January 26, 1989, only minutes after CNN Headline News reported on the memorial services held for "Chico" Mendes, they aired a story of wild horses recently killed in the state of Nevada because the horses allegedly "interfered" with cattle ranching.

More than five billion tons of US topsoil are eroded yearly because of animal agriculture. Today, the average depth of topsoil has fallen from three feet to six inches.

It takes more than thirty calories of feed and fodder energy to produce a single calorie of food energy in the form of beef and more than 1,480 quarts of oil per American per year to provide a meat diet.

Feedlots and slaughterhouses are major polluters of rivers and streams, filling them with poisonous residues and animal waste. Billions of gallons of water are used to process animal bodies, and groundwater depletion for grazing has caused increasingly intractable water problems.

In the Third World, private and government money has gone into developing cash crops for export, while food production for the poor majority is neglected. Displaced peasants, either forced off the land or persuaded to sell their small plots to rich exporters, can no longer grow food to feed themselves or their families. Livestock production requires much more land, energy, and water use than are necessary to produce an equivalent amount of plant food. On a vegetarian diet, the world can support a population many times its present size. On a meat-based diet the current world population could not be sustained.

In 1984, 40 percent of the world's grain harvest was fed to animals going to slaughter. If the same grain was fed directly to human beings, there would be more than enough to feed the world.

The decimation of the rain forest by fast-food companies reduces rainfall in Africa, for each tree left standing can process forty gallons of moisture daily into the atmosphere. There is enough for everyone's need, but not for everyone's greed.

The production of beef kills other species, all of which are a part of the very important web we call biological diversity. In rainforest areas, the destruction of habitat has endangered the survival of species, causing certain ones to become extinct. In the US coyotes and wolves would not be poisoned and shot if people didn't eat steak and lamb chops. Cattle ranching has always competed with wildlife territory for land; additional wildlife territory is taken for crops, of which 78 percent is fed to "food animals" (e.g., chickens, pigs, turkey, and cattle).

The possible side effects of eating beef that has been produced with growth hormones and other drugs has been discussed extensively by John Robbins in his book *Diet for a New America*. But that issue was brought to wider public attention when the European Community banned the importation of US beef which has been subject to hormone implants. Not only have animal growth hormones been attributed to side effects in humans, but, "Hormones are used to get unnatural, quick growth to make animals conform to a factory-farming system," said Andrew Kimbrell, policy director of the Foundation on Economic Trends in Washington. "We urge a more natural setting."[3]

> I believe that animals have rights which, although different from our own, are just as inalienable. I believe animals have the right not to have pain, fear of physical deprivation inflicted on them by us. Even if they are on the way to the slaughterhouse, animals have the right to food and water and shelter if it is needed. They have the right not to be brutalized in any way as food resources, for entertainment or any other purpose.[4]
>
> Roger Caras

The second myth is the necessity of animal experiments. The Draize Test, for example, has been used since 1944 as the standard test for substances that might get into the human eye. Liquid, flake, granule, and powdered substances are placed into the eyes of rabbits, and then the eyes' progressive deterioration is recorded. The Draize test is responsible for the suffering and death of millions of rabbits each year in the United States, but does not prevent or help cure human injury.

During the test, one hundred milligrams or so of a concentrated solution are dropped into the eyes of six to nine conscious albino rabbits, who are often immobilized in stocks from which only their heads protrude. Their eyes often are held open with clips at the lid, and many rabbits break their necks or backs struggling to escape. The damage to the rabbits' eyes is then recorded at specific intervals over an average period of seventy-two hours, with the test sometimes lasting seven to eighteen days. Reactions to the irritants can include swelling of the eyelid, inflammation of the iris, ulceration, hemorrhaging, and blindness. Pain-relieving drugs usually are not administered. When pressed, experimenters claim their use would interfere with test results. When anesthesia is given, the relief is only temporary.

The Draize test is used to test nearly every established major brand of cosmetic and household product on the market, ranging from the "mildest" baby shampoo to the most caustic oven cleaner. Every time a company changes its ingredients or advertises a "new" or "improved" product, you can be almost certain that it retested the substance on animals.

The federal Food, Drug and Cosmetics Act does *not* require cosmetics manufacturers to test their products for safety and does *not* require animal tests. The Food and Drug Administration (FDA) recommends, however, that companies substantiate the safety of their products, or else attach a warning label to potentially hazardous products. Many companies therefore continue to perform the Draize test, mainly because their legal departments and insurance companies suggest they do the tests to cover themselves if they are sued. But the fact that animal tests have been done on a product does not mean the product has been altered to make it less harmful if misused. The term "safety" testing is very much a misnomer.

Noted toxicologists and health professionals agree that the Draize test is crude and imprecise mainly because the eyes of humans and rabbits are very different. The test is not analogous to the human-exposure scenario because it is strictly observational: No treatment is ever administered nor are any antidotes ever sought.

The opinion of a growing number of health professionals is reflected by noted ophthalmologist Stephen Kaufman, M.D., of New York University Medical Center: "I have no use for Draize test data because the rabbit eye differs from the human eye.... I know of no case in which an ophthalmologist used Draize data to assist in the care of the patient."[5]

Animal tests protect companies, not consumers. Knowing that a rabbit goes blind seventy-two hours after being dosed with dandruff shampoo doesn't help us. We already know not to pour caustic substances into our eyes and leave them there — the pain tells us that. We also know how dangerous various ingredients are, and we can run computer assays of mixtures of these ingredients to predict irritation levels. Human volunteers are already used by some companies to test for skin irritation; these tests provide much more accurate information than animal-based tests. To treat accidental poisoning victims, physicians can use data collected by hospitals from previous poisoning cases — data that is readily applicable to treating human injury.

Those who are interested in a more compassionate life-style will also consider the need for other types of animal experimentation.

For some experiments there is no need to consider a nonanimal "alternative" because the study is irrelevant, redundant, trivial, or all three. Many experiments are repetitive simply because the experimenter does not have an adequate familiarity with the literature in his or her field, or because experimental details are only slightly modified from previous experiments. This is particularly true for graduate students who may need to complete a project simply to earn a degree in behavioral and psychological experimentation. It is also often the case in basic research, where the only motivations are curiosity and a desire to have an article published, a grant funded, or a promotion awarded with little, if any, consideration given to the suffering of the animals or the actual value of applicability of the experiment.

For scientific, health, ethical, and economic reasons, nonanimal testing methods must be chosen over animal experiments, and more funding must be diverted in order to apply what we already know to human problems. For example, the opening of drug and alcoholic treatment centers is money far better spent than to continue existing "experiments" that create addictions in monkeys and rabbits. Citizens can help by contacting their legislators, voicing their concerns to academic and scientific organizations involved in animal testing, and by refusing to support companies that perform animal tests.

It is not as important that the reader know the specific nature of the alternatives as it is to know for certain that alternatives do, in fact, exist.

Alternative Methods: Healing without Hurting

Despite the claims of some animal experimenters, many, many alternatives to using animals exist. The following list of alternatives applies to many types of animal experimentation.

Some alternatives are:

Clinical and epidemiological studies. The single most important alternative is the study of human disease in individuals and in specific populations. Virtually everything of importance we have ever learned about the origins, transmission, symptoms, and treatment of human disease has come from these two fields. Clinical surveys use human volunteers, clinical case studies, autopsy reports, and statistical analysis linked with clinical observation of disease. This permits far more accurate observation and use of actual environmental factors related to human disease than is possible with artificially-induced disease in unnaturally confined (therefore immune-system stressed) animals.

Tissue and cell cultures. Single cells from human tissues can be grown outside the body after separation from their original tissue or organ. Each generation of these cells breeds identical cells almost without limit, thus providing a constant supply of identical test materials that can be kept free of contamination for years. This level of accuracy is impossible with living, changing animals. These tests are extremely useful for carcinogenicity, toxicity, and irritancy testing.

Organ cultures. Groups of cells from a single organ are grown in a feeding medium. The normal structure of the organ is retained, and the reactions and effects of substances upon a complete organ can be tested with results similar to those in an intact body. These cultures can be used in biochemistry, cancer research, genetics, immunology, microbiology, pharmacology, physiology, radiation, toxicology, virus research, and in the production of vaccines.

Bacteria cultures and protozoan studies. Many species of bacteria react in the same way to toxins, mutagens, and irritants as humans do. Protozoa and bacteria reproduce extremely rapidly and are easily controlled, stored, and maintained at a very low cost. Because animal tests are costly and time-consuming, only a fraction of the vast number of new products ready for market each year is tested at all, resulting in products entering the market prematurely, or in products for which continued use over several generations has not been assessed. Bacteria cultures and protozoan studies can be used in cancer, birth defect, aging, and heart disease research, in water pollution studies, and in insulin, anti-virus, and vaccine development.

Quantum pharmacology. This science utilizes mechanics, an understanding of molecular structure, and computerization to seek an explanation of the behavior of drugs on the basis of molecular properties.

Mathematical and computer models. Mathematical models can be used to make direct predictions of the functions of human systems. Computer models, by means of simulation, provide information that cannot be gained from experiments using living creatures. They are used in studies of a variety of anatomical systems, organ functions, in studying heart attacks, in nerve cell and neuro-muscular research, and in pollution studies. Computer models of the human circulatory and respiratory systems are now used as teaching devices in medical schools. HUMTRN (pronounced Hyoom-train) is a "living," ever-changing computer data bank that provides access to ten million bits of information about how a human body will react to any given substance. It can be programmed to simulate eating, breathing, perspiring, and aging.[6]

Genetic engineering. Genetic engineering is now being used to provide insulin of a much purer type than was available from using animals. Genetically-engineered insulin eliminates many harmful effects of conventionally produced animal insulin. Growth hormone and interferon can also be produced through genetic engineering.

Gas chromatography and mass spectrometry. These methods are used in the molecular analysis of such bodily fluids as blood, urine, and gastric fluids. Solutions are separated through vaporization into their basic elements and then identified by mass. These methods have proven very successful in vitamin and drug research, and in determining the type and amount of drugs taken in the case of an overdose.

The Ames test. Invented by Dr. Bruce Ames of the University of California at Berkeley, this in-vitro test checks substances for carcinogenicity by using strains of the salmonella bacteria, which produce cancer in human and other mammals. The test takes two to three days and costs a few hundred dollars, rather than the two to three years and $150,000 required for typical animal tests.

The CAM test. In the chorioallantoic membrane (CAM) test, a few drops of a potentially toxic substance in a saline solution are placed on the membrane of a chicken egg. By measuring the degree to which the blood vessels break down, scientists can determine the toxicity of the tested material. Although it would be preferable to use no animal products whatsoever, it is better to use eggs than sentient animals. The CAM test is intended for use by cosmetic and household product manufacturers as an alternative to the Draize test, but egg membranes have also been used to culture viruses and vaccines.[7] Egg tests have proven effective when animal tests have yielded conflicting results.

Placenta. The human placenta, which is usually discarded after the birth of a child, can be used for practicing techniques of micro-vascular surgery and for testing toxic side effects of chemicals, drugs, and pollutants. It provides a medium far superior to animal tissues because it is human, and it's entirely without cost.

Mechanical models. Sophisticated mechanical models are used as subjects for safety testing, such as in car-crash studies and tests of fireproof fabrics, and as teaching devices. Complex models are now available for use in medical and surgical training, and can provide reactions to many different drugs. A simulator has been created that includes a heart circulatory system, lungs, and a respiratory sys-tem, along with a means of testing responses to drugs and kidney functions.

Audiovisual guides and aids. Film, closed-circuit television, and videotape offer the advantage of allowing repeated viewing, play-back, and holding on a specific area of a demonstration as well as allowing the viewer to see procedures on human patients rather than on animals.

> It isn't necessary to torture and kill animals to show people how much money you have — you can buy a nice cloth coat and pin money to it.[8]
>
> Bob Barker

The seductive fur ads we see in magazines and commercials portray fur as a symbol of elegance. But these ads fail to show how most of the original owners of these coats met their gruesome deaths. Approximately thirty-four million furbearing animals — raccoons, coyotes, bobcats, lynx, beavers, and others — are killed each year by trappers in the United States.[9] Another six million to ten million animals are raised on fur "farms." Despite the fur industry's attempts to downplay the role of trapping in fur "production," it is estimated that 74 percent of all fur garments come from trapped animals.[10]

There are various types of traps, but the leg-hold trap is the most widely used. This simple but sadistic device has been banned in more than fifty countries, as well as in Florida, Rhode Island, and New Jersey.[11] When an animal steps on the leg-hold trap spring, the trap's jaws slam on the animal's limb. Dr. Robert E. Cape ex-plains that "if the trap is properly anchored, the captured animal will struggle to get loose, mutilating the foot and causing deep, painful lacerations. Or the animal will attempt escape by chewing off or twisting off the trapped extremity. There's no way anyone could convince me that isn't painful. Ten to twelve hours after be-ing captured, the animal is still in pain." After a prolonged time, he explains, trapped animals "will suffer from exhaustion, since they expend such a great amount of energy in attempting to escape. With exhaustion, the animal suffers from exposure, frostbite, shock, and eventually death."[12]

Up to one out of every four trapped animals does escape by chewing off his or her own feet. If these animals do not die from blood loss, fever, or gangrene, they may be killed by predators. Victims of water-set traps, including beavers and muskrats, can take up to twenty agonizing minutes to drown. Now that more and more people are learning about the barbarity of trapping, it should come as no surprise that a Yale University study reports that 79 percent of the general population opposes the use of the leg-hold trap.[13]

For animals who manage to remain alive in the traps, further torture awaits them when the trappers return. To kill the animals without damaging their fur, trappers usually beat or stomp their victims to death. A common stomping method is for the trapper to stand on the animal's rib cage, concentrating his weight near the heart. He then reaches down, takes the animal's hind legs in his hands, and yanks.[14]

Every year, approximately five million dogs, cats, raptors, and other animals, including endangered species, are crippled or killed by traps. Trappers call these animals "trash" because they have no economic value.[15]

Contrary to industry propaganda, there is no ecologically sound reason to trap animals for wildlife management. When left alone animal populations can and do regulate their own numbers. Trapping disrupts wildlife populations by killing healthy animals needed to keep their species strong, and populations are further damaged when the parents of young animals are killed.

Working alongside the commercial and private trappers are individuals paid with our tax dollars to trap and kill predators. These government hunters slaughter thousands of coyotes, mountain lions, bobcats, and other predators considered a threat by livestock ranchers, who often let their flocks and herds roam unattended on public lands that are part of the animals' habitat.

Trapping will become an obsolete business when people stop purchasing fur products. Help discourage trapping by discouraging the wearing of fur. Tell people you see wearing fur the facts about trapping — many people incorrectly assume animals are killed humanely. Write or call businesses that sell furs or that give furs as a contest prize and ask them to consider the animals and stop promoting cruelty. Ask your legislators to support trapping bans. Teach others that trapping is a cruel and destructive practice that stems from greed, not glamour.

I must interpret the life about me as I interpret the life that is my own. My life is full of meaning to me. The life around me must be full of significance to itself.[16]

Dr. Albert Schweitzer

Another myth that needs to be addressed is the belief that greyhounds, used for racing, are always trained on artificial lures. On the contrary, whenever you go to the track, it is possible that the dogs you see as contestants in the races have been trained with live lures. The greyhound industry would have the public believe otherwise because what happens to the live lures would outrage enough race-goers to possibly make considerable differences in the profits.

Following is testimony given before the Maryland Senate Rules Committee, March 11, 1986, by Robert Baker, Field Investigator with the Humane Society of the United States:

Racing dogs are trained in an event known as "coursing," in which young greyhounds are released to chase down a live jackrabbit within a fence enclosed field. Once caught, the quarry is usually mutilated by the dogs and left to die from its injuries. So that young dogs do not get discouraged, some trainers will break one of the rabbit's legs so that it can more easily be caught.... The next phase of training for many dogs is the "whirl-a-gig," which is a pole upon which a small live animal is suspended.... The pole moves around a small circular track. This teaches the dog to run in a circular path in chase of the dangling animal and somewhat simulates a race track situation. As an incentive, they are eventually allowed to "catch up" and attack the live animal bait. If the lure is still alive after the dogs catch and maim it, the small animal will be used again on a new set of dogs.[17]

As various state legislatures consider the question of allowing greyhound racing in their states, they must deal with the use of live lures as a part of the whole picture in spite of what the promoters say. The promoters of races argued, when lobbying the Kansas legislature, that live lures were no longer used. But when the enabling legislation was being drawn up in the state legislature in 1987, the proponents vigorously opposed an amendment that would ban live lures.

The next time you consider attending greyhound races, remember what kind of training the dogs may have experienced. Gandhi once said that the greatness of a nation and its moral progress can be measured by the way its animals are treated. Now you know a little more about several issues, and the moral choice is yours.

I. E. N.

* * *

TAKING ACTION

1. Don't buy exotic pets. One of the most inhumane fads is owning exotic animals. Such "fashionable" creatures are not meant to be domesticated, and we are not equipped to properly care for them. Bobcats and bears, to name only two, do not make good "house pets." In addition, incredible numbers of imported animals and birds die in shipment to this country. They are taken from their habitat, not properly cared for in the shipping process, and are highly stressed. Don't ever consider another living creature a fad.

2. Spay and neuter animal companions. Allowing dogs and cats to roam or to reproduce unwanted litters leads to cruelty and needless suffering. Don't let cruelty, abuse, and neglect happen to innocent dogs and cats.

3. Help wildlife wherever you can. Do not use chemical pesticides or herbicides. In your backyard or on your balcony, put out bird-feeders, birdhouses, and birdbaths when weather is extremely hot or extremely cold. Water for birds in the winter is especially important as it is essential to their digestion. Forestry departments in some universities offer "wildlife bundles" — a variety of trees, shrubs, and plants that provide food and shelter to wildlife in the winter months. These are available at a minimal cost and you'll have the pleasure of many colorful visitors.

4. Do not buy souvenirs, jewelry, or clothing made from such animal products as ivory, furs, reptile skins, and tortoiseshell.

5. Report animal cruelty either to the local humane society or to the police department. Look out for animals in extreme temperatures confined without proper shelter and water, and take action or help them.

6. Eat lower on the food chain. Substitute tasty vegetables, fruits, legumes, grains, and nuts for meat. According to current medical information it is far healthier for you as well. It also reduces high costs to the environment and cruel practices in factory farming.

7. Do not support dog races, horse races, rodeos, animal circuses, roadside zoos, or any other form of entertainment in which animals may be victims of cruelty.

8. Don't buy fur coats.

9. Please pay attention to the weather, and remember your pet. If

it is over 80 degrees Fahrenheit outside, do not leave your pet in a car. Always see that the pet has water and shade in the summer; in the winter, check the chill index — it makes a difference. Likewise see that your outdoor pet has plenty of protection from extremely cold weather and winds.

10. Please brake for animals! Countless numbers of animals die each year because drivers are unwilling to stop on roads and streets for a passing animal. Drivers often assume that it's up to the animal to get out of the way, but animals don't reason the same way humans are capable of reasoning. Many times an animal becomes confused or paralyzed with fear. Be compassionate, give them the benefit of the doubt. Stop your car and save their lives.

WASTE NOT, WANT NOT

— 16 —

Controlling Energy Use

Andrew Rudin

How we choose to produce and use energy will deeply affect the quality of our environment and the legacy we pass on to future generations. Heavy dependence on fossil fuels is responsible for air pollution in our cites, acid rain that is damaging our forests, and ecologically destructive oil drilling in Arctic and coastal regions. Fossil fuels are also responsible for about half the greenhouse gases that are warming the earth. The United States now adds over a billion tons of climate-altering carbon to the atmosphere each year.

Unless the US energy trends are redirected in the next decade, a host of environmental problems will become increasingly unmanageable. Energy decisions in the next four years can continue our wasteful use of fossil fuels and nuclear power, or they can move the nation towards an environmentally attractive and sustainable economy that is based on improved energy efficiency and clean renewable energy sources.

Blueprint for the Environment

We are learning that our use of energy has a considerable impact on the environment. The fate of our great grandchildren will depend on decisions that we are making today.

Instead of becoming a more energy-efficient society, America seems to be going in the opposite direction. The number of electronic appliances per household is accelerating. The sales of packaged air-conditioning systems set a new record of four million in 1988.

Americans have become addicted to energy. This is most apparent with gasoline and electricity. Efforts to curb the growth of cars

222

and the use of electricity in homes have been largely ineffective. The rate of growth of cars in America is now twice that of people. The Motor Vehicle Manufacturers Association revealed that Americans drove 2.8 percent more in 1989 than the year before. The average fuel efficiency of new cars dropped for the first time since 1983, about 0.4 miles per gallon. In spite of energy-efficient appliances, insulation programs, free energy surveys, and lots of other conservation technology, the average annual residential electric consumption in New York City increased 16 percent in the past six years.

We describe ourselves as energy gluttons. Yet, with the intent of protecting life-style, President Bush is creating, as this book goes to press, the greatest buildup of troops since World War II to defend the Saudi oil fields. The purposes of this chapter are first to discuss the values inherent in the life-styles that use less energy and second to present some concrete ways to reduce energy use in our homes. (The energy-saving suggestions are found in the "Taking Action" section.)

A Low-Energy Experiment

If you want to sample a low-energy life-style and understand the level of our reliance on energy, try an experiment for a few days. Turn off the gas, oil, and electricity coming into your home, and don't use the family car. Do you find that you are addicted to energy use? Do you suffer "cold turkey" withdrawal pains? Do you get any sense of how third world families function?

What happens to your family's attitudes without the normally available energy? What about your social attitudes? Do you have to rely on your neighbors more? Does going to the mall make sense? What takes the mall's place? This simple experiment may melt your ice cream, but it will also show that energy makes life easier in many respects.

At the same time, however, energy may be making America weak in body and mind. The car has stopped our walking around the neighborhood and calculators have dissolved mathematical skills. We may soon realize that artificial intelligence cannot compete with wisdom.

On a social level, it is interesting to see what happens when a community is forced to go without electricity and fuel. In the midst of your next utility blackout or community disaster (bad weather, flood, tornado, evacuation, etc.), watch what happens to social interaction. Sometimes the inconvenience is overwhelming. At other times, it is clear that distance between people is removed. The resulting social relationships can last for years, long after the memory of the disaster is passed.

On an even larger level, nations define themselves by energy. The big ones are called superpowers. And superpowers, such as the United States and Russia, have applied tons of energy in their attempts to solve international conflicts. But massive energy releases seem to have stopped working for the big nations. In both Vietnam and Afghanistan, sheer firepower could not compete with the wills of the people.

In addition, we are becoming aware that our high-energy diet is difficult to support. It is expensive. The massive build-up of armed forces in Saudi Arabia is costing America between 10 and 20 million dollars a day. Car exhaust is increasing the warming of the Earth's atmosphere. Air-conditioning refrigerants are depleting the ozone high in the sky, and rain made acid from coal-fired electric generating plants is killing forest and pond life.

My crystal ball says that the participants in America's energy party are going to have a wicked hangover. To avoid the headache, I suggest that we examine the positive aspects of low-energy life-styles. We must unsell ourselves, pull the plug, and become unaddicted to energy. Withdrawal from our speedy life-styles will either be voluntary or imposed by outside forces. Either way, we are going to slow down. It's just more pleasant to ease into the transition voluntarily.

Energy and Society

The late Earl Cook of Texas A&M University's geology department wrote a book called *Energy, Man and Society*. Professor Cook explains that high-energy societies are urban and materialistic. Power results from either personal wealth, managerial status, or election to a high office. Money lending is popular, and the society runs on credit and debt. Consumption is stimulated by advertising. Family and community are subordinated to the state. Overconsumption of food is counteracted by diet programs.

By contrast, low-energy societies place more importance on the family and community. The family is the main factor in determining social status and control. Time is more cyclical. Occupations are more agricultural. Social roles are more clearly defined, more conformist, and less innovative. Older people are more respected, but there are shorter life spans. Money lending is discouraged, and even portrayed as evil.

There are good and bad points to both types of societies. However, to wean people from high energy use, we should focus on the good personal and social aspects of not using energy.

High-Energy Life-styles

In comparison to America, West Germany and Japan use half the energy to produce similar goods and services. Does this have any connection with our tariffs on their lower-cost products?

America is dizzy with speed, and the pace of life is getting faster. There is more and more information to absorb, more things to do, more places to go than ever before. Mom and Dad seem to always be on the go, if they are both still married. Many, if not most, American employees live more than a day's walk from work.

We are raising our children around automobiles. Shopping malls are social meccas for our kids, and malls attracts drivers with free and abundant parking. They have all but killed the local independent merchants. Some Girl Scout troops hold camp-outs in malls, replacing the smell of pine and smokey campfires with the smell of stale popcorn and leather.

Our homes are dominated by television, and television is dominated by ads. Watch what happens to the family during a blackout.

Low-Energy Life-styles

What is a low-energy life-style? It's as difficult for us to achieve it as it is for a drunk to be sober or an addict to be straight. Our speedy lives involve abundant communication and transportation — both of which depend on reliable quantities of energy. Does the energy we use relate to modern problems? If we slowed down, would our divorce rate (51 percent) decline?

Less mobility could strengthen our families as we stopped packing our elders away in nursing homes and relying on kids to entertain themselves. Less television might rekindle conversation.

There are many wonderful low-energy activities with commonly accepted, positive attributes. Several examples are art, conversation, education, prayer, and thought. All of such pursuits use no electricity, gas, or oil. Average Americans prefer many aspects of low-energy life-styles. We prefer firelight, candlelight, and romantic slow rowboating around a pond. We prefer the company of family and friends.

Most adults even desire energy conservation. In a 1986 annual survey by *Professional Builder* magazine, 56 percent of new home buyers were willing to pay an extra $1,000 for energy-efficient features in new homes.

Why then are we so attached to high-energy life-styles — driving everywhere, spending countless hours in front of the television, overheating, overeating, and overlighting? The answer is that we have been sold onto that life-style.

Energy in the Past

One way to understand trends in energy is to consider how energy was used in your grandparent's house. To get you started thinking this way, let me tell you about my grandmother. She was born in Sweden in 1869, ten years after Colonel Drake first struck oil in Pennsylvania.

In the early 1950s, I visited Grandma in Rutland, Vermont. My mother and father took my brother and me there, mostly for holidays. She had no car. Room in the unheated garage was taken up mostly by a loom. She would sit out there for hours weaving rags into beautiful carpets.

She heated with coal and cooked with kerosene and wood. Life revolved around the kitchen. I remember endless conversations about every topic you could think of. Once in a while, someone would go downstairs to shovel coal into the furnace to heat a mostly uninsulated house. Leaving the kitchen for bed, I would snuggle into flannel sheets in the bedroom on the second floor.

Today, we call her strategy by fancy names. We say she used the "warm room" concept by living mostly in the kitchen. We say she used "direct control" of energy because each shovelful was proportional to heat loss and heat gain. We say that she "recycled" used clothing into rugs.

In comparison to modern life in the 1980s, Grandma's home had texture and depth. There was a lot of family conversation and play; there was no television or stereo or neighborhood mall. There was a sort of timelessness to our visits. The smells and laughter were so warm.

The energy she used was clearly visible — shovels of coal, armloads of wood, and bottles of kerosene. Nowadays, energy is invisible — hidden in wires and pipes. The only visible sign of energy use is frequently the invoice. Times have changed.

Selling Energetic Life-styles

America has been sold into life-styles full of electronic distance. We spend extraordinary and increasing amounts of time in front of video screens — television at home and monitors at work.

Each of us sees hundreds of advertisements each day. We see them in magazines and newspapers, on television and billboards. We hear them on radio. Since Americans are already well-off in comparison to third world countries, we are sold and told to consume things we don't need.

For each ad we see, for each item we purchase, and for each mile we drive, energy is used. Currently, about $400 is spent on advertising for every American each year. ($109 billion total in 1987.)

Some aspects of energy are almost poetic. In one sense, practically everything is energy — electrons swinging around nuclei with mostly nothing in between. Light can be defined fundamentally as either particles of energy or waves of energy.

A key characteristic of energy use is that it is measurable. Very accurate meters count kilowatt-hours of electricity, gallons of gasoline and oil, and cubic feet of gas. Individually, we can easily measure whether a particular strategy for reducing energy use works or not. Local utility companies are accurate scorekeepers. And nationally, the Department of Energy measures the amount of energy consumed by the entire nation, and our consumption is increasing.

Measuring energy use has many implications. First, national strategies of energy conservation can be evaluated. For example, we know that the Residential Conservation Service (RCS) operated by utility companies was not very effective. The RCS program was mandated for all larger utilities by the National Energy Act, which was passed in the Carter administration.

Second, the effectiveness of products can be demonstrated. We know that simple time clocks and clock thermostats can be as effective, or even more effective, than complicated, expensive, temperature-control systems.

Third, and most important, your individual progress can be documented. If you read your meters and keep track of your gallons, you can quickly determine what works and what doesn't. Conservation is a matter of simple experiments and scorekeeping.

Here's an example. If a 176-pound person climbs upstairs sixteen feet to the next floor in ten seconds, the amount of power generated will be 390 watts. Harnessing that power would light up about four 100-watt bulbs.

In other words, we can quantify the work done because energy is measurable. Some people have calculated that the amount of power that one American uses is equal to having about two hundred servants.

Motivating Energy Conservation

What motivates conservation? First, since we are addicted to it, the fear of running out of energy is probably a prime motivation to conserve it. It is fairly clear, however, that we are not going to run out of it in the near future.

Second, there is financial motivation. If you use less energy, you will spend less money. When costs were high in the 1970s there was more concern about energy. Energy costs are increasing, but price jumps similar to those of the 1970s have yet to occur again. Smaller increases due to gasoline tax increases and oil import fees are likely.

Third, energy conservation happens when it makes our lives more convenient. For example, mass transit in and around the cities becomes popular as urban parking spaces become rare and expensive. Fluorescent lights are considered when it becomes inconvenient to frequently change short-lived incandescent bulbs.

Fourth, there is the link between energy use and environmental degradation. People who watch the television or read are now learning about the link between energy use and global warming, acid rain, and ozone depletion. The motivation to preserve and conserve will become more popular as environmental concerns grow. However, in the short term, a warming trend will stimulate sales of air-conditioning equipment.

Fifth, and finally, there is the link between high-energy use and life-style. My hope is that the negative values associated with high-energy use will become visible, making a conserving life-style popular.

What specifically can be done by average Americans?

America uses more petroleum for transportation (64 percent, up from 51 percent in 1973) than any other use. Cars don't waste energy, people do. Fuel-efficiency standards are not the determinant for efficient transportation in America. The rate of population growth for automobiles is twice that for people in spite of a more than threefold increase in gasoline prices since 1970.

Drivers are driving more. The average American driver drove about 11,800 miles in 1988, up more than 18 percent since 1970. Reagan's administration rolled back automobile efficiency standards, and forty-one states adopted higher than fifty-five mile per hour speed limits in 1988. With such an explosion of automobiles and traveling, it matters less how many miles per gallon cars consume. It matters more how much we drive.

Bluntly, an old, huge Lincoln Continental that is driven three miles a week uses less gas than a tiny Honda civic driven by a commuter three hundred miles a week. It's not what you have, as much as how you use it.

Recently, cars have taken over our lives. Almost every other prime-time TV ad promotes new automobiles. We have our drive-thrus and drive-tos.

Living at Home

Energy conservation in our homes comes from a combination of two factors — changes we make to the structure and changes we make in our life-style. To determine how much conservation came from each factor, similar townhouses were studied in a development in New Jersey (Sonneregger, Princeton, September 1977). Energy bills were analyzed for 205 buildings and separated into two categories — those with occupants that moved out with others moving in, and those occupants who stayed.

When a family moved out of a home, and another family moved in, the pattern of energy use usually changed dramatically. One conclusion of this study was that to a large extent, it isn't necessarily the structure that is inefficient, but rather certain occupants.

In families with relatively low energy costs, there usually is one person who accepts the responsibility for energy. This may be the husband or wife. Without anyone accepting the responsibility, it is less possible to have a successful program. Who has this responsibility in your family?

You need to know your home's energy use efficiency. Success in energy cost reduction is generally more noticeable in wasteful buildings. Are you wasting your time by trying to make an efficient building more efficient?

Energy is measurable. The utilities keep fairly accurate records of electric and gas use, and can supply computer printouts showing a history of energy use. Fuel oil dealers also can supply similar information. Ask them for information on your energy use if you have not kept past records and wish to make a comparison.

Suggestions for what we can do to end our glutton-like use of energy follow in the "Taking Action" section of this chapter. There are a number of suggestions — encouragements — that are guidelines for those who are concerned and willing to contribute to ending the ecological degradation of overconsumption. If we don't willingly begin to conserve our resources, there will come a time when we are required by law to do so, and that is never pleasant.

A. R.

* * *

TAKING ACTION

1. Lower your thermostat; use clock thermostats and minimum/maximum thermometers. Clock thermostats can reduce the tem-

perature during the day and night automatically. There are several inexpensive but sophisticated commercial models that have a true seven-day programmability.

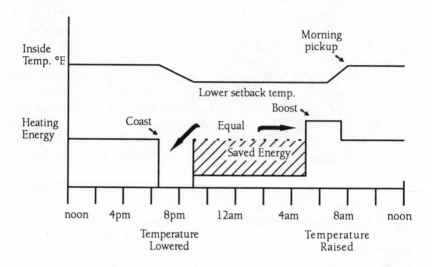

2. The most cost-efficient and ecologically sound thing to do is to save gas by not driving. This means consolidating trips, shopping at stores close to home — within walking distance or on a bus route, car pooling, and using mass transit.

3. Keep a record of every purchase of gasoline. Divide the miles driven between purchases by the number of gallons purchased. Experiment with tire pressure, not using air conditioning, and avoiding fast stops and starts. Does your car get more miles per gallon? Total the number of gallons purchased each month. Then vary your habits. Watch the change in gallons purchased each month.

4. Carry a sign in your car that says, "Your Car Pollutes My Air." When you are behind a car with a smoky exhaust, place the sign upright on your dashboard and honk.

5. Keep your car tuned. Follow the maintenance procedures recommended by the manufacturer. It will have greater resale value, use less gasoline, and burn gasoline with less pollution.

6. Get good bikes for your family. There are incredible bikes for sale now — fifteen-speed, light and inexpensive. Your kids will have greater freedom, develop healthier bodies, and will learn not to demand use of the family auto for every trip.

7. Attain and maintain efficient heating and cooling systems. The simplest maintenance procedure is changing filters in systems and keeping the lint filter clean on your automatic clothes dryer.

8. Saving air-conditioning electricity.

- When you do not need the air-conditioning system, turn it off.

- When possible, cool with fans instead of air conditioners.

- Keep filters and coils clean.

- When you are going to purchase a new cooling system, consult the ratings in *Consumer Reports* magazine. Purchase ones that require the least electricity for the cooling capacity you need.

9. Adjust lighting controls. One of the easiest ways to lower light bills involves adjusting or adding lighting timed switches for the shortest number of operating hours. When one hour is trimmed from the schedule on a 24-hour time clock, 365 hours of operating time are saved each year.

10. Replace burned-out lamps (light bulbs) with efficient lamps. Exchange your current bulbs for lower-wattage fluorescent bulbs that will save energy. Initially more expensive than traditional bulbs, they will save you money in the long run by saving energy. When a lamp burns out, it makes no economic sense to replace it with a standard, inefficient lamp. One source for energy-cost efficient lighting is the Energy Federation (508) 875-4921.

11. Reduce water temperatures. Temperature of the domestic hot water in your home should be 110 degrees F. or less if you use city water that is chlorinated. Well water that is not chlorinated should be 130 degrees F. in order to kill any Legionella bacteria. A hot shower is 109 degrees and warm water for washing hands is about 95 degrees.

12. Wrap an insulation blanket around your water heater. Install pipe insulation on the first few feet of hot water pipe coming from the water heater.

13. Install water saving showerheads. Sources are the One Stop Energy Shop (800) 537-4004; and Seventh Generation (800) 456-1177.

14. Buy more efficient appliances. Before purchasing a new appliance, determine which brand and model number uses the least energy and has the greatest value. Check *Consumer Reports* magazine.

15. Consider alternatives to typical traveling vacations. Camping is different from motel hopping. Travel by AMTRAK whenever you can. Reclaim your neighborhood by walking through it frequently. Walking is healthier than riding in a car.

16. Keep track of your energy use. Lower energy use will make America a more secure, healthier, and robust country. Individuals, friends, and communities will become more unified, regain economic strength, and have more control over their own destiny.

17. *Demand* of your US members of Congress and the Administration that they divert money from existing sources (such as those used to fund the defense of oil in the Middle East) to research and development that will make available to the public the solar, wind, and biomass techniques of renewable energy!

— 17 —

The City of Portland: Setting a Good Example

Earl Blumenauer, Commissioner of Public Works, Portland, Oregon

Disregard of natural processes in the city is, always has been, and always will be both costly and dangerous.
Anne Whiston Spirn, *The Granite Garden*

As an Oregonian and as an elected official since 1972, I have been privileged to be involved with a variety of interesting environmental issues. In 1971, Oregon adopted the first "bottle bill," and now over 90 percent of the glass, aluminum, and plastic deposit containers are returned. Oregon was also the first state to ban aerosol products utilizing chlorofluorocarbons (CFCs) as a propellant. These were difficult and controversial issues. No meaningful environmental legislation was ever adopted by acclamation, and usually it requires us to change existing practices. We Oregonians care deeply about the environment and are willing to make changes in order to protect it.

Polystyrene foam products are gaining national attention because of damaging environmental effects. We use these products for five minutes, but they last forever as litter or in our landfills. The foam waste generated by one major fast-food chain would fill one of the World Trade Center Towers in New York City each week. This epitomizes the problems associated with our "throw-away society." American cities face reduction in landfill capacity, concerns about garbage incineration, and threats from toxic waste. Portland's foam bans, together with efforts to deal with plastic in the waste stream,

233

encourage different ways to think about solid waste and single-use packaging.

Portland became involved with the polystyrene foam issue in July 1988 through unanimous approval of a ban on city purchase of any polystyrene foam products manufactured with chlorofluorocarbons (CFCs) and any foam products of a readily disposable nature. The ban also applied to vendors who lease city space and activities, such as park festivals, which require a city permit.

Beginning in January 1990, Portland prohibited a total of two thousand restaurants and retail food vendors from serving prepared food in polystyrene foam products. The city's decision was made after months of research and input from industry representatives, concerned citizens, restauranteurs, and environmental groups.

In taking action, the city council indicated its concerns with several major aspects of polystyrene foam including *chlorofluorocarbons* or *CFCs*. There is general agreement that certain chlorofluorocarbons are very damaging to the Earth's ozone layer, which protects the Earth from the sun's radiation. Although manufacturers of food-service products have indicated that they are already voluntarily phasing out the use of CFCs, questions remain. The major substitute blowing agent used, HCFC-22, still depletes ozone (although at a reduced rate), and the atmospheric effects of other alternatives are not well known.

Maximizing the life of landfills is a major issue facing cities across the country. It has taken ten years to site a new landfill to serve the Portland metropolitan area. Waste reduction measures are thus very important.

Common sense and state law define waste management practices in order of priority to be: reduce, reuse, recycle, incinerate, and landfill. The partial foam ban will reduce waste that poses a problem for our landfills and will lead to the wider use of biodegradable paper products, which can be composted in an industrial compost facility currently planned in Portland, and washable reusable dishes.

Polystyrene foam is not biodegradable and, being 97 percent air, takes up a lot of volume relative to its weight. In Portland's waste stream, plastics have been measured at roughly 7 percent by weight and projections indicate significant growth in the future. While the city recognized that other food containers contribute to landfill problems, the foam ban is an important part of an incremental approach. The council will consider other steps in the future.

Recycling is also a critical component of solid waste management. The city of Portland implemented a multi-material recycling collection program in 1987. Currently, 26 percent of Portland households participate in monthly, curbside recycling of newspaper, glass bottles, tin cans, corrugated cardboard, aluminum, ferrous metals, non-ferrous metals, and used motor oil. Our goal for 1991 is 40 percent.

Oregon law defines "recyclable materials" as those that can be collected and recycled at a cost less than collection and disposal. Foam containers do not meet this test currently and don't appear able to do so in the foreseeable future. Any foam collected must be sorted, cleaned, processed, and made into new (non-food container) products.

While industry does recycle its plastic industrial waste, recycling of plastic waste discarded by consumers, including polystyrene foam products, has only recently been intensively pursued. During the summer of 1989, some demonstration programs to collect used polystyrene food containers were developed by the plastic industry and major retail users at a few Portland restaurants. Customer participation rates were not high. It remains unclear how takeout containers can effectively be recycled.

Industry is eager to show that polystyrene foam can be recycled. We welcome that and look forward to working with them to make plastic recycling more effective. Meanwhile, since the Portland ban is partial only, there is plenty of polystyrene foam in the community (such as food containers at nonprofit establishments, packing material, boating supplies, etc.) as well as other plastic items that can be recycled in demonstration programs.

Finally, in Oregon, we care about maintaining the natural beauty of our state and preserving wildlife. Because foam products are not biodegradable, they are a major contribution to litter. Polystyrene litter is highly durable, buoyant, and nonbiodegradable, and therefore persists and detracts from the appearance of an area longer than many other types of litter.

While government action is important, individual citizens can make a difference by reducing their use of polystyrene foam and other plastics. Specific citizen action suggestions follow in "Taking Action."

I am hopeful that the actions of Portland, other local communities, and individual citizens will send a strong message to industry that we encourage its ingenuity to deal with the social and environmental consequences of products and their packaging and the need to find better solutions to solid waste problems.

E. B.

* * *

TAKING ACTION

1. Recycle as much as you can to help reduce the general volume of waste going into landfills and to reduce industry's reliance on virgin material to produce their products. Collection of newspaper, glass, tin cans, corrugated cardboard, aluminum, ferrous metals, non-ferrous metals, and used motor oil is fairly common. Recycling programs for plastics are not widespread. Many communities have drop-off centers for these materials and community groups such as scouts and other service organizations often sponsor collection efforts. A growing number of communities now offer curbside collection. Ask your garbage hauler or call your local government for information.

2. Increase your use of durable, washable dishes and reduce your reliance on disposables as much as possible. Don't buy polystyrene foam items such as plates and cups.

3. Use cloth diapers or diaper services.

4. Buy products such as eggs, oils, condiments in recyclable or biodegradable containers. Save plastic containers you do buy and use them to store household items or for other purposes. Or find out if recycling is available in your area.

5. Patronize restaurants that do not use polystyrene-foam packaging or plastic packaging. Many restaurants use washable dishes for food eaten on the premises and biodegradable paper packaging for takeout items. They should be applauded for their environmental consciousness.

6. Don't buy items with excessive packaging such as individually wrapped cheese slices or fruit pieces wrapped in cellophane. Consider buying in bulk.

7. Reuse brown paper bags as garbage can liners instead of plastic. Use waxed paper to wrap sandwiches instead of plastic wrap.

8. Contact environmental organizations that care about the problems associated with plastics and nonbiodegradable packaging. These groups often are involved in lobbying for local and state government action. To be successful, these groups need citizens to write letters and call elected officials. Testify at public hearings.

MONEY TALKS

— 18 —

The Bottom Line

The Reverend Thomas Berry

> It is impossible, admittedly, to give an accurate economic value
> to the goodness of good work, much less to the goodness of an
> unspoiled woodland or prairie or desert, or to the goodness of
> pure sunlight or water or air. And yet, we are required to make
> an economy that honors such goods and is conversant with them.
> An economy that ignores them such as our present one does,
> "builds a Hell in Heaven's despite."
>
> Dr. Calvin DeWitt

The absurdity of contemporary economics is its effort to impose a
human industrial economy on the organic functioning of the Earth.
That this is a supreme and deadly arrogance is becoming ever more
evident. Now we find ourselves caught in a impasse from which there
is no evident escape. We appeared to succeed so well in the early days
that we took no notice of the price we would one day have to pay
for our folly.

The tragedy is that even now when our scientists are telling us
quite plainly of the disintegrating processes taking place throughout
the planet, few of our political, economic, educational, or religious
leaders seem to understand just what we are being told. Nor have
our scientists ceased from their support of this terrifying industrial
process. Nor have our subservient communications media shown any
consistent interest in these issues.

The difficulty is simply that human economics is not integrated
into the ever-renewing economics of the natural world. This is the
only sustainable economics. The proper role of the human is to in-
tegrate its own life processes into the life processes of the natural

237

238 / *Money Talks*

world. The human was brought into being by the natural world and can only be sustained by that same world. The first obligation of any economic system is to see that the Earth system itself is sustained in its abundance and fertility. The well-being of the Earth is a condition for the well-being of the human.

Also, as regards management, the Earth is the supreme model of any managerial process. Human management can only be a slight addendum to the managerial processes whereby the Earth goes through its cycle of the seasons, the processes whereby it governs the vast hydrological cycle, the manner in which it relates the vast variety of living forms to each other from the lowly single-celled bacteria to the massive shaping of the blue whale at sea. Throughout the entire planet we witness a total participatory process.

The deep pathology of our present economics can be seen in the cutting down of the tropical rain forests for timber and other uses. The benefits received are ridiculous in relation to the deleterious consequences for the total functioning of the life-systems of the planet. Also in relation to the life-sustaining resources present in the forests. Absurd, too, when we consider the vast pharmaceutical resources of these rain forests. An economic absurdity, a resource-use absurdity, an aesthetic, religious, moral absurdity.

Among the glaring deficiencies of contemporary economics is the absence of such terms as "gross Earth produce" and "Earth deficit," as though these were irrelevant to the entire range of economics. National and international products and deficits are noted. The narrow range of so-called classical economics can be seen in such terms as "wealth of nations." The entire study of economics is cast in terms of national or international economies.

The great advance is supposedly our coming into a comprehensive sense of international or global economy. This term "global economy" is a falsification since what is really meant is a global "human" economy. There is not the slightest reference to a truly global or planetary economy, which would refer to the comprehensive economy of the planet Earth itself. Economists have had to depend on the ecologists to think through these questions of a global economy.

Only now through the efforts of organizations such as the Worldwatch Institute, the World Resources Institute, and the Conservation Foundation have we come to an audit of the resources of the planet in any comprehensive manner or to any significant evaluation of what is happening in the larger realms of our industrial economics. But even now when we have these various reports on the state of the Earth, little of this enters into the discussion of our economists. Even less is taught in our schools of business administration.

The linguistic deficiency can be seen in reference to the various types of debt. There is the national debt of over $3 trillion, the foreign debt of some $380 billion. There is the third world debt due to the US of some hundreds of billions that is unlikely ever to be paid. Add to these the annual budgetary deficit of some $140 billion. Why is there no reference to the debt due to the Earth? The Earth is the ultimate guarantee of all debts. When the Earth goes into deficit a thousand alarms should ring throughout the entire range of our industrial, commercial, and financial establishments. It should be the first thing taught in the schools of business administration.

We are constantly told that the governing issue is the bottom line, meaning profit and loss in money values. But there are two bottom lines below this monetary bottom line. There is the bottom line of the effects on society, effects that until recently have been ascribed to externalities not entered into the accounting process. "Externalities" itself is a strange term, meaning those things irrelevant to the commercial-industrial world. Then there is the bottom line of what is happening to the natural world. This, too, is considered irrelevant to the economic process. Any effort to insist that these effects are in some manner measurable and should at least enter into consideration is resented by our present economic establishment.

Strangely enough the survival of the Earth as a necessary condition for any sound economic process is never considered. Nor is there any thought given to the proper purpose of the entire complex of commercial, industrial, financial, and managerial progress: to enhance the human mode of being in its properly human fulfillment. The presence of any such moral considerations within the sphere of economics is said by Milton Friedman to be a distortion of the economic process. He has, strangely, had his way.

Now we look about in dismay not simply at the consequences to the imaginative, emotional, and spiritual fulfillment of our lives but at the catastrophic consequences of this attitude on economics itself. From a planet that was enormously fruitful and abundant it is becoming destitute, an economic wasteland.

Even more strange, when confronted with this impasse we are told that the human community cannot survive except with this ever greater industrial production. Industry is providing jobs. With jobs people make money and with money they buy the things they make with their jobs. But the jobs are precisely what is ruining the planet. We are burning the timbers of the house that protects us from freezing in the cold. We are destroying the ship that keeps us afloat. We are eating our seed grain.

There are other ways for survival and for survival at a much higher level of human fulfillment. These are being identified and carried out by a multitude of new movements. They are best seen in the bio-regional movements, in the new emphasis on organic agri-culture, in the movements for appropriate technologies, in the new ways of shaping cities to the local ecosystems, in the new efforts at energy production that do not harm the environment, in the new systems for waste disposal.

There exists also a new concern in the public media. While the media are for the most part co-opted by the industrial establishment, the media are beginning to attend to the impasse that is emerging throughout the industrial system. The industrial establishment it-self is becoming aware of the need for a more sustainable system of economics. Yet the present system is too deeply established to adapt easily to such a new relationship with the natural world.

We can only expect in the immediate future a rising conflict be-tween the entrepreneur and the ecologist, between those seeking to impose a humanly-contrived industrial system on the organic func-tioning of the natural world and those who see the need of humans to abandon their assault on the Earth community, the only sustainable community that we know of.

T. B.

* * *

— 19 —

Environmental Economics in Practice

Susan Meeker-Lowry

> There is only one economy. It is fifteen billion years old. Life,
> intelligence, beauty and excellence of every kind are produced
> in the Great Economy of the Universe. Human economies are
> simply skillful means of working within the Great Economy for
> the ongoing prosperity of Earth's life and being.
>
> Brian Swimme, *The Universe Is a Green Dragon*

What does "economics as if the Earth really mattered" mean? What
kinds of choices, what actions, does it imply? How do we *do* it? These
are hard questions. In order to answer them we need to do more than
think about issues such as resources and who owns the land, although
this is essential, of course. We also need to *feel* what it means to let the
Earth *really* matter — as individuals, inside, at a deep, personal level.

The need to do so is obvious. Even in places where there is beauty
as far as the eye can see, we are discovering toxic waste dumps
leaking into water supplies, cancerous and dying fish, trees being
killed by acid rain. Town planners are beginning to talk about limiting development and many are creating long-term development
plans. However, even with managed development, there is a finite
amount of land and other resources. If we say that the most important things in our lives are family, community, health, peace, and the
like, then we must take these things into consideration — serious
consideration — when making plans for any kind of development.

It is true that what is good for the Earth is also good for us.
The fact is that all goods and services are ultimately derived from

241

the Earth. That's the source. I believe, too, that when we act out of love and caring, we pay more attention, act more intentionally and become more open to participation and sharing than when we act out of fear or because of old, often unconscious, patterns. So what I ask is that we open ourselves in a new way to the Earth, to the cycles and patterns and relationships in nature, to see what we can possibly learn. Then we need to allow this learning to guide us as we work to create an economy "as if the Earth really mattered."

Opening to the Earth is a very personal, very individual matter. I believe we each have a unique gift, although we are often puzzled about exactly what it is — perhaps even fearful we don't have one. We think it has to be something grand like having a wonderful musical talent, so we overlook what is really special about ourselves. The way we comfort our children perhaps. Or the way we enter a room and add our special touch, or bring an energy or lightness or gaiety to a group. So it is with nature — and our relationship with it. As we open to our own uniqueness, we will begin to see what is special in other "ordinary" things.

As we begin to appreciate and honor the "special in the ordinary," our lives become more enjoyable and peaceful. We relax and trust more. We are freer to make decisions that truly reflect who we are and what we really value. It is a subtle process and it varies for each of us. Nevertheless, the process is real and through it we become stronger and clearer.

This has direct implications for creating an economy, and community, as if the Earth really mattered. We must be discriminating in order to see through illusions and promises that can't be fulfilled. The profit-driven market economy as we know it depends on our being driven by an almost unconscious but constant need to consume, to want more. We are pushed to advance to the next technological level simply because we *can,* not because it is wise or desirable in the long term. It does not require that we ask questions about sustainability, environmental quality, or human rights in order to continue. As a matter of fact, it often actually seems that the fewer questions or demands for responsibility we pose, the "better" the current economy performs.

I believe it is possible to provide good jobs, decent and affordable housing, and creative opportunities for people who do not require the exploitation of the Earth or other people. We do not now have expertise necessary to bring such immense changes about; however, that does not mean that it is impossible. Indeed, I feel it is essential that we *do* see the possibility; otherwise our future looks desperately bleak. Although changes will take time to bear fruit, it is important that we take the first steps today.

It is easy to despair over the plight in which we find ourselves these days. We do not have to look far to see hunger, poverty, injustice, and ecological devastation. It is becoming increasingly obvious to many that the traditional ways of dealing with jobs and housing do not work. At best, most of our programs are stop-gap measures that do not address the structural changes that need to take place. And even for these more traditional programs, tax dollars are stretched as are the funds of public and private agencies, no matter how well-intentioned. More people than ever are starting to realize that it is up to us, as concerned people, to create the opportunities we desire in our communities.

As an activist in the area of what is being called socially responsible investing, I have been witness to the growing awareness of investors that our money is a tool for creating change. It is literally an extension of who we are. What we choose to invest in speaks for us. If we invest in a company that builds nuclear weapons, *we* are building those weapons ourselves. If we invest in a company that exploits workers in the third world, *we* are exploiting those workers. Not someone else; not some manager in an ivory tower — *us!* With this awareness comes the desire to channel money into more positive directions. Investors are beginning to ask, "How can I support my local community with my investments? Is it possible to have my money working for positive changes closer to home?" As more of us ask these questions, the opportunities for this kind of financial expression increase. The process is beginning and growing even as you read these words.

Revolving loan funds (RLFs) are among the most promising and exciting vehicles currently available for connecting concerned investors with worthwhile projects. There are now over three dozen RLFs with over $45 million in combined assets. These funds exist for a variety of purposes and all provide an essential bridge between non-profit, community-based organizations and projects and concerned investors. They finance low- and moderate-income housing, cooperative and worker-owned businesses, community land trusts (rural and urban), limited equity co-ops and limited equity housing, appropriate agricultural development, even the creation of worker-owned co-ops in the third world.

Although there are variations from fund to fund, basically this is how they work: money from lenders is pooled and used to make loans. As the money is repaid, it is loaned again to other projects, hence the name "revolving loan fund." Lenders to the funds are individuals, organizations, religious institutions, and corporations. The research being conducted by some funds is showing that the vast majority of these loans are made by concerned individuals. Loans are made to projects without access to traditional sources of capital at below-market rates.

RLFs are committed to the values of cooperation, local control and ownership, appropriate community-controlled development, and economic justice. An important service they provide to borrowers is technical assistance that ranges from assistance in developing a business plan, to locating the best contractors for a job, to providing ongoing accounting and planning services. This technical assistance, combined with stringent (though human-based) screening initially, is the investor's greatest security. Loan applicants are expected to do their homework, just like anyone else. "They put us through the wringer. They have to make sure we don't lose money." Funds also use collateral, such as real estate, to back up loans. The end result is that these RLFs have a default rate of which most banks would be envious. Lenders have always been repaid on schedule as well.

Investment opportunities vary from fund to fund. Many allow investors to set their desired rate of return from 0 percent to a maximum, usually the money-market rate. Most also allow the investors to decide the terms of the loan (length, schedule of repayment, etc.). Some even allow the loans to be targeted toward specific areas or projects.

The largest and best known of the RLFs is the Institute for Community Economic's RLF based in Greenfield, Massachusetts. As a nonprofit organization, ICE was founded in 1967. Its RLF was established in 1979 to provide a bridge between its projects and individuals seeking ways of supporting community development work. Today, ICE is capitalized at over $7 million and has served as a model for many other RLFs currently in operation. ICE has made over two hundred loans, more than half of which have been repaid. They have had only one default of less than $2,000. Most of their loans are between $5,000 and $50,000 for an average of three years. Eighty-two percent have been for land and housing, 10 percent for businesses, and 8 percent for community service organizations such as soup kitchens or cultural centers. Eighty-seven percent of ICE's funds are loans from individuals and most of these loans are for less than $10,000. Terms are from one to three years and interest requested is between 3 percent and 6 percent.

What kinds of projects do loans to these funds actually support? Let's take a look:

- The Cooperative Fund of New England has made over eighty loans to co-ops and businesses such as Cherry Hill Cooperative Cannery in Vermont, which sells its own applesauce, "dillybeans," and other products as well as provides a community cannery for local growers doing their own canning.

- The New Hampshire Community Loan Fund has made several loans in the past three years to enable residents of mobile home parks to buy their parks and become home owners at last.

- The Institute for Community Economics enabled the United Wood-cutters Association in Mississippi, who were traditionally exploited by powerful timber and paper interests, to purchase timber harvesting rights.

My work over the past several years has shown me that many seeds for creating strong, diverse, local economies with foundations rooted in the basic values of cooperation, respect for diversity, attention to scale, sustainability, and integration with Earth's limitations exist and are being planted even as I write these words. Many have been around for quite some time. Others are new and have exciting implications. I believe the most successful of these will be those that incorporate an Earth awareness into their basic philosophies and into their projects. This will insure sustainability over time. Sustainability does not only mean that the project continues to be financially viable. Sustainability also means that the enterprise must not deplete the Earth, that it actually enhances the culture and environment over time, and supports the community in all ways by the relationships it fosters between itself and its "stakeholders" (workers, investors, consumers, community members, the Earth).

Given the planet's real limitations, we must take pains that our enterprises nourish rather than starve the future. Our work will be only enhanced by a greater understanding of our relationship with nature and the lessons the Earth teaches. Cooperative, respectful, diverse, balanced, and harmonious relationships are ultimately what keep ecosystems alive. We are responsible for this.

Currently, we are not very skillful at working within the "Great Economy of the Universe" as Brian Swimme puts it. We will become more skilled, I feel, as we open to our own uniqueness, to our special gifts, and as we begin offering them to others. Doors will open, and we will see that we do, indeed, have strength and power.

The specifics of creating a community-based economy include supporting the development of cooperatives of all sorts, worker-owned businesses, and small businesses; looking at creative ways of financing these ventures (social investors, revolving loan funds, local currencies, loan collateralization programs). Although it is not easy, some are even developing new credit unions and banks to finance and support small, local, responsive enterprises. We can initiate work exchange systems, barter networks, and other creative ways of sharing our talents and time that are not part of the traditional market economy.

Key to the success of these alternatives — many of which are growing at an incredible rate around the world — is the quality of relationships they allow in our communities. If our relationships encourage cooperation and respect rather than competition, if we can begin to eliminate exploitation of all sorts, if we take the issue of sustainability seriously, then we have a greater chance of succeeding, especially if we are open to the wonder, awe, and mystery of life on this planet. The beauty nourishes. Let us breathe it in! As the poet Mirabai asked hundreds of years ago, "Without the energy that lifts mountains, how am I to live?

S. M.-L.

* * *

TAKING ACTION

1. Monitor corporate America. Information on products that are manufactured by environmentally- and social-conscious companies can be obtained from the Council on Economic Priorities in New York. Its publication, *Shopping for a Better World,* lists products and companies as to their involvement in: charitable giving, women's advancement, minority advancement, defense contracts, animals' testing, social disclosure, community outreach, nuclear power, South Africa, and the environment. They can be contacted at 30 Irving Place, New York, NY, 10003, or by telephone at (800) 822-6435.

2. Invest with care. Many individuals are now becoming interested in investing in companies that take into consideration the environment and social justice. There are several social-conscious investment possibilities that have a good economic record. Check with an investment broker to gather additional information. The power to bring about change is very much rooted in the way we spend our money, including how we invest it. Contact: Social Investment Forum, 711 Atlantic Ave., Boston, MA 02111.

3. Be honest with yourself. Make the distinction between what you really need and what you want. Enormous natural resources are used to produce items that are, for most people in the world, a luxury. Buy what you need and avoid trends and faddish products that will be replaced by new trends and fads before the previous items can be worn out. Avoid impulse buying.

4. Be a watchdog. Whenever you hear of a company polluting the environment or participating in animal cruelty, boycott their products.

If department stores, catalog companies, and other retail sources sell ivory, articles taken from endangered species, or other products that have a destructive effect, don't buy from them but do write or call and tell them why. They will listen. Act on your own and tell others to do so as well.

5. Object to the governmental spending you feel excessive or unnecessary, be it local, state, or federal. Remember that politicians represent YOU. If they want to keep their job, they'll listen. But you must tell them you do not favor excessive spending habits.

6. Buy products that will last. And if you use an item infrequently, borrow it from family, friends, and neighbors.

7. Contact *Catalyst* (64 Main St., Montpelier, VT 05602) for information on our projects, our corporate research and related publications, or a copy of our newsletter.

THE ENVIRONMENT IS A MORAL ISSUE

— 20 —

The Religious Foundations
of Ecology

Calvin B. DeWitt

On earth God's work must truly be our own.
John F. Kennedy, Inaugural Address

More is known today about how the world works than at any time in history. We have accumulated immense knowledge of the requirements for sustaining life on Earth as well as of the processes that are destroying species, biotic communities, ecosystems, and life itself. From this knowledge has come a substantial theory and practice of soil conservation, biological conservation, and restoration ecology. Richly supported by comprehensive scientific and technical literature, cultivators and people who advise cultivators can be excellent keepers and renewers of land and life. This literature and expertise is ever expanding through the contributions of a highly-disciplined research establishment, historically unmatched in size and competence. And it continues to describe in detail the biospheric changes and environmental alterations that now envelop the globe. Yet, in the midst of such immense knowledge, we confront environmental degradation of a magnitude and extent never before experienced by our species. While knowing more about nature and conservation than people had at any other time in human history, we never have experienced greater environmental degradation and destruction.

What can one say in the presence of such apparent irony? Clearly, one can conclude that *mere* knowledge, no matter how comprehensive or extensive, is not sufficient to achieve and maintain a sustainable Earth. On the one hand, as environmental historian Donald Worster has observed, knowledge can show people "that nature [is] a thing of beauty and integrity, a set of laws that must be obeyed, an order that must be respected and protected." On the other hand, knowledge tells people "about a nature that [is] power inchoate... power waiting for human ingenuity to develop it, power that should not be left dormant." Since knowledge can be used to employ nature as "the means to whatever end men had in mind, whether it be wealth or war, pleasure or security, bondage or freedom," we find that the degradation that threatens us and Earth is rooted in knowledge itself. Without knowledge we could not have achieved the means for large-scale intensive use of the Earth; we could not have imposed our will upon the planet. Earth's degradation is rooted in knowledge, "in that complex and ambitious brain of Homo sapiens, in our unmatched capacity to experiment and explain, in our tendency to let reason outrun the constraints of love and stewardship and in our modern, nearly universal drive to achieve infinite power over our surroundings.[1]

Reflecting the insufficiency of knowledge ("science"), Huston Smith observed in 1958 that "science... makes major contributions to minor needs." By contrast, "Religion, whether or not it comes up with anything, is at least at work on the things that matter most."[2] And so it is that this chapter addresses religion — the structures and beliefs whereby human beings constrain, discipline, and orient themselves in ways that bring them life more fully. Religions move beyond the description of what is, past the question of what is possible, to what *ought to be*. In this time of global degradation, the merely descriptive and technical must be surpassed. It is necessary to rise above contributions of *mere* knowledge and *mere* science to those "things that matter most," and particularly to the requirements for living sustainably on a sustainable Earth. We need to move beyond describing the world, developing and applying instruments to it, and itemizing our use and abuse of it. Thus, the importance of considering religion.

Not that religion has always achieved wholeness — it has served not only to sustain life and environment but it also has wrought abuse of people and the environment as well. While recognizing and acknowledging the glaring deficiencies of religion at various times and places, religion has been and continues to be a strong shaper of society and environment. Some believe that religion is so strong a force that the roots of our current ecological crisis derive from religious teachings. Others detract from religion's importance by focusing "on what has shock value for the curiosity seeker... the strange, the bizarre, and the fantastic." In the words of philosopher

Huston Smith, "Such [bizarre] material is part of the religions of man. But to focus on it, lifting it out of context and waving it before the public drool, is, where not straight sacrilege, the crudest kind of vulgarization."[3]

Religion helps sustain civilization and the environment. But because religion may be captured by things that matter least, it may become an accomplice in Earth's destruction. Religion might yield to forces it attempts to challenge and constrain, thereby lessening its quality and becoming irrelevant. Given the current degradation of Earth, one is led to suspect that religion is not confronting the new reality of Earth and its degradation, that it is not helping to discipline the individual and control self-interest, that it may be a passive bystander or even a participant in Earth's destruction. The current quality of religion is thereby brought into question. Religion has accommodated to the pressures of the times, has drifted into irrelevancy, or both.

Elevating quality of religion includes rediscovery of long-standing beliefs that bring quality to living on a quality Earth. It also may include investigation into how adequately various religions deal with basic values and problems. Religion alive restores the ability of people and society to master themselves. It uncovers and revitalizes beliefs that bring respect for Earth's integrity, wholeness, and harmony — beliefs that prompt self-discipline, that reinstate individual and corporate responsibility toward each other and the Earth, that provide the constraints of stewardship. "Religion alive confronts the individual with the most momentous option this world can present. It calls the soul to the highest adventure it can undertake.... The call is to confront reality, to master the self."[4] The present reality is Earth's degradation at the hand of people and society. It results from an undisciplined pursuit of self.

In this age of invention and innovation we have come to believe that we know enough to create, in a geological moment, systems that are superior to self-sustaining ecological systems which have stood the test of geological time. In the spirit of such inventiveness one also might be persuaded to think it necessary to develop a new religion to address the pressing need for new ways of living. Without investigation of long-standing religions, we might assume that we are superior to those in the past, that we are the only ones in history to know the best way to live. Our record of arrogance toward the environment should give us pause as we consider the contributions of religion.

It is difficult to give recognition to religion or to religions with tenets different from one's own. Huston Smith helps us here as he observed:

We must listen first to our own faith.... But we must also listen to the faiths of others.... We must listen to them, first, because ... our times require it. The community today can be no single tradition; it is the planet. Daily the world grows smaller, leaving understanding the only bridge on which peace can find its home.... For understanding, at least in realms as inherently noble as the great faiths of mankind, brings respect, and respect prepares the way for a higher power, love — the only power that can quench the flames of fear, suspicion, and prejudice, and provide the means by which the peoples of this great earth can become one to one another.... But the reverse is equally true. Love brings understanding; the two are reciprocal. So we must listen in order to further the understanding the world so desperately needs.[5]

It now is necessary to explore those religious teachings of stewardship, care, and love that counter self-indulgence at the expense of others, thereby addressing the responsibility of people to care for and restore the Earth. It is to reach people's hearts, impressing upon them responsibility for the Earth. "The surest way to the heart of a people is through their religion,"[6] observed Huston Smith.

This chapter is a recognition that knowledge without stewardship is insufficient for sustainable living; that science without love is inadequate for maintaining a sustainable biosphere. It is a recognition that religion, as a system of values that lead us toward making choices for sustainability, not only has a place but provides a foundation upon which the ecological choices before us can be made.

Environmental Teachings of Five World Religions

Respect for the integrity, wholeness, and harmony of the Earth and its life is shared by the world's great religions. In 1986, an interfaith conference held in Assisi, Italy, brought together representatives from five of the world's major religions to discuss religion and nature. In a statement of solidarity, the Assisi Declaration established a clear relationship between the Buddhist, Christian, Hindu, Jewish, and Muslim beliefs and a call to stewardship. Following are excerpts representing each religious tradition:

Presenting the Buddhist perspective at Assisi, the Venerable Lungrig Namgyal, abbot of Gyuto Tantric College, India, quotes His Holiness the Dalai Lama: "As we all know, disregard for the Natural Inheritance of human beings has brought about the danger that now threatens the peace of the world as well as the chance to live of endangered species. Such destruction of the environment and the life depending upon it is a result of ignorance, greed and disregard for the richness of all living things.... We are the generation with the awareness of a great danger. We are the ones with the responsibility and the ability to take steps of concrete action, before it is too late."[7]

The Christian perspective, presented by Father Lanfrancho Serrini, Minister General of the Franciscan Order, affirms that "man's dominion cannot be understood as license to abuse, spoil, squander or destroy what God has made to manifest his glory.... Dominion cannot be anything else than a stewardship in symbiosis with all creatures.... Every human act of irresponsibility towards creatures is an abomination. According to its gravity, it is an offense against that divine wisdom which sustains and gives purpose to the interdependent harmony of the universe."[8]

Respect for harmony and integrity in nature is integral to the Hindu perspective and is evident in the declaration of His Excellency Dr. Karan Singh, President of the Virat Hindu Samaj: "The Hindu viewpoint on nature... is permeated by a reverence for life, and an awareness that the great forces of nature — the earth, the sky, the air, the water and fire — as well as various orders of life including plants and trees, forests and animals, are all bound to each other within the great rhythms of nature.... The Hindu tradition of reverence for nature and all forms of life, vegetable or animal, represents a powerful tradition which needs to be renurtured and reapplied in our contemporary context."[9]

In the words of His Excellency Dr. Abdullah Omar Nasseef, the Secretary General of the Muslim World League, "The essence of Islamic teaching is that the entire universe is God's creation.... For the Muslim, mankind's role on earth is that of a khalifa, vice-regent or trustees of God. We are God's stewards and agents on earth. We are not masters of this earth; it does not belong to us to do with it what we wish. Unity, trusteeship and accountability, that is tawheed, khalifia and akhrah, the three central concepts of Islam, are also the pillars of the environmental ethics of Islam.... Muslims need to return to this nexus of values. The notions of unity, trusteeship and accountability should not be reduced to matters of personal piety; they must guide all aspects of their life and work...."[10]

And the Jewish perspective, in the words of Rabbi Arthur Hertzberg, Vice-President of the World Jewish Congress: "Adam named all of God's creatures, he helped define their essence. Adam swore to live in harmony with those whom he had named. Thus, at the very beginning of time, man accepted responsibility, before God, for all of creation. Now, when the whole world is in peril, when the environment is in danger of being poisoned, and various species, both plant and animal, are becoming extinct, it is our Jewish responsibility to put the defense of the whole of nature at the very centre of concern."[11]

These five religions, as well as the Native American religious traditions, show caring respect for Earth and its creatures. Yet, the scope of this chapter restricts it to two predominate religions of the western hemisphere: Judaism and Christianity.

The Hebrew scriptures of Judaism have no word for "the environment." Neither do they have a word for "nature" or "the Creation." They do not provide for an objective environment set apart from human beings. This recognizes that we too are creatures and thus are *part,* and not *apart.* Thus, modern Jewish and Christian religions inherit the concept that everything comprises an orderly and harmonious whole — a whole that in later Jewish tradition and in the Christian scriptures is designated as "the Creation."

Therefore, out of concern that use of the term *nature* and *the environment* sometimes serve to distance and alienate people from reality, I often use the term "the Creation" throughout this chapter. To Jews and Christians, to all religious people, "the Creation" has a richness and depth that goes beyond "nature" and "the environment," and as such should be respected.

SEVEN DEGRADATIONS OF THE CREATION

In providing the ecological background for an assessment of religion and ecology, one must first be aware of the fact — as has been asserted in many examples throughout this book — that the Creation is being seriously degraded locally and globally. Nearly every year since 1980, the Au Sable Forums on religion and ecology, held at Au Sable Institute for Environmental Studies near Mancelona, Michigan, have documented the Creation's degradations, reflecting what some of the authors have said in previous chapters.

The global crisis of enveloping Earth can be summarized as seven degradations of Creation: (1) alteration of planetary circulations and exchange — exchanges of energy between sun and Earth are being altered with consequences for global warming and increased transmission of damaging ultraviolet radiation; (2) land degradation — cropland and food production capacity is being degraded by erosion, desertification, and salinization; (3) water quality degradation — both surface waters and groundwater are being polluted by agricultural chemicals and landfill leachates; (4) deforestation and habitat destruction — this is rampant across the world with nearly one hundred thousand square kilometers (twenty-five million acres) of tropical forests lost annually; (5) species extinctions and biotic alterations — animal and plant species are extinguished at three per day and bioengineered organisms are introduced into agricultural and natural ecosystems that have not shared in the millennia of coadaptation of native species with the environment; (6) wastes and global toxification — the seventy thousand chemicals produced by modern society have combined with tons of solid, liquid, and radioactive wastes that threaten nearly everyone; (7) human and cultural degradation — long-standing human cultures that have lived sustainably for centuries are rapidly degraded and extinguished by nonsustainable development.

RELIGIOUS TEACHINGS IN CHRISTENDOM

Christendom contributes to a secularizing progression of godlessness. In my address to the Au Sable Forum 1984, "Creation's Challenge to the Church," I reported the findings of Stephen Kellert, Associate Professor of Forestry at Yale University, indicating that knowledge of the creatures, respect for the Creation, and understanding of ecological relationship was inversely related to frequency of church attendance. My assessment at that time, and now, is that Christendom has progressively separated itself from the Creation. It has been stung in the past by its proclamations against ideas of science and has uncomfortably debated the theory of evolution. In the words of Robert Meye in 1985, "When the Church has appealed to the Old Testament, specifically with respect to creation of nature, it has repeatedly locked horns with contemporary science. So much so, in fact, that the careful study of the creation material and other related biblical materials, remains the domain of a few, dedicated scholars." Not only have the scholars been avoiding potential conflicts between theology and contemporary science, but so it would seem have those who bring the word in sermons, homilies, and songs. References to the Creation are diminishing over the years and decades. Most of the remaining references are about those aspects of the Creation that appear to be "safe" such as the grandeur of the heavens and the majesty of distant mountains. Christendom has progressively been losing its reference to the Creator and Creation. It also has retreated to the merely personal: personal health, personal sin, personal salvation. In this way it increasingly has reflected self-oriented values of society.

Thus, it would seem that western society has been experiencing a long-standing progression to godlessness. The planet has become godless in human minds and thinking; so also has its economy. Western religions have gone so far as to disregard God as Creator in the governance, life, and work of church and synagogue.

RETURNING TO CREATION'S CARE AND KEEPING

From a religions perspective, godlessness in society and creatorlessness in Christendom are among the causes of the ecological crisis. Also, from a religions perspective, the meaning of stewardship has been forgotten in a largely exploitive world.

The centrality of the Creator — In a biblical study, Robert Meye counters godlessness in society and Creatorlessness in Christendom by affirming the centrality of God as Creator as addressed in both Old and New Testaments. He emphasized that revelation of God as Creator is "the constant basis of biblical faith.... Whether expressed in creed or in psalm, the formal statement of belief, or in song of praise, God is known and worshipped as Creator and Sustainer of all creation."[12]

The meaning of stewardship — Stewardship is restrained and disciplined care for Earth and its creatures. David Ehrenfeld and Rabbi Bentley in their paper "Nature in the Jewish Tradition: The Source of Stewardship" (Au Sable Forum, 1982) observe that:

> For Jews it is the Sabbath and the idea of Sabbath that introduces restraint into stewardship.... On the Sabbath, the observant Jew does more than rest, pray and refrain from ordinary work. At least three other elements of Sabbath observance that are critical to stewardship: we create nothing, we destroy nothing, and we enjoy the bounty of the earth....
>
> Nothing is created, and this reminds us of God's supremacy as Creator and our own comparative inadequacy. Nothing is destroyed, and this reminds us that the creations of this world are not ours to ruin. We enjoy the bounty of the earth, and this reminds us that although our work, if properly done, will uncover for us far more of God's bounty than we would otherwise have enjoyed, nevertheless God and not human intervention is still the ultimate source of that bounty.[13]

Dyrness (Au Sable Forum, 1984) affirms the biblical message: "God has created the world as a place where righteousness and beauty will be established. But this involves a system of relationships, between God and his people, among people, and between people and the land, which is all included in the covenant God has established with the earth. There is every encouragement to use wise methods of stewardship.... When we respond in obedience, we will enjoy the fruit of the earth and the poor will be cared for. When we turn from God we can expect ecological disaster and social oppression."[14]

Working from the Hebrew scriptures, David Ehrenfeld and Rabbi Bentley (Au Sable Forum, 1982) remind us that "The theme of accountability runs strong in Judaism, and it is accountability that puts teeth in stewardship.... When stewardship is corrupted by power in the absence of restraint, it becomes tyranny and exploitation."[15]

The challenge to congregations — Given the biblical affirmation of the Creator and the responsibility of humankind and the church for the stewardship of the Creation, Fred Van Dyke (Au Sable Forum, 1985) concluded that "the center of the Church is thrust into the heart of the ecological crisis. And the center of the gospel's message lies at the very heart of the environmental problem. God calls men and women to abandon self-centered lives and self-centered value systems, and to recognize Him as Lord-Creator of the universe and ourselves as creatures in it."

THE HOUSEHOLD OF THE CHURCH

In his scriptural study of the idea of the *plan* or *economy* of God, Howard Snyder (Au Sable Forum, 1981) observes that "God's 'economy' is the plan he has worked out for the proper managing of his house — both the entire created order and his special household, the Church. Particularly in Ephesians 1:10, *oikonomia* signifies the plan of salvation, the economy of God. God is the divine economist, the creative Lord who from the foundation of the world has established a plan for the fullness of time. And this plan centers in Jesus Christ and the work of the Holy Spirit in and through the Church.... We must understand and recover the *biblical ecology of the Church* and be faithful to our stewardship mission in the world today. We must see the church as the community of God's people and household of God, commissioned by God to be 'a dwelling place of God in the Spirit' for making the wonderful grace and works of God known now to the whole range of principalities and powers in the world."[16]

WORKING TOWARD GLOBAL SHALOM

After observing that "in its contemporary technological ability to destroy and create life, humanity strives to replace God, in belief and practice (Au Sable Forum, 1982), Wesley Granberg-Michaelson went on to note that "the Church is that part of creation which has accepted God's redemption and salvation. Therefore, the church's life is to evidence signs of a restored relationship between humanity, the creation and God.... Isaiah's prophecy of the coming Messiah (Isa. 9:6) refers to him as the 'Prince of Shalom.' His rule will establish the shalom of God ... the peace which Christ promises to us, and the peace of Christ with which we greet each other, refers to God's shalom — the fulfillment of all creation. This becomes the hope and the vision of our tasks of earth-keeping ... restoring the harmony to the creation, and preserving its ecological balance, is the means for establishing true security."[17]

Priests of Creation — At the conclusion of his detailed history of Christian missions and missionary Earth-keeping, Dennis Testerman (Au Sable Forum, 1985) concluded that "we are called to be priests to Creation; ours is a ministry to *all* the earth." He noted that "this assertion may sound strange to the ears of some missions-minded Christians," but also observed that "its acceptance simply involved an extension of the traditional missionary role of the physician and healer to include all of God's creation."[18]

Eastern Christianity — In some aspects, Eastern Christianity provides examples of Creator awareness and awareness of the Creation itself. Bishop Paulos Gregorios of Delhi, India (Au Sable Forum, 1984) helped us see this more clearly through his fresh translation of John 1, Colossians 8, and Romans 8. "The whole creation stands on tippy-toes, with neck outstretched ... awaiting the redemption of the children of God." Particularly illuminating was his observation that western theologians pay too much attention to words. It is a perspective on ourselves that western hemisphere congregations will want to keep in mind.

Hebrew and Christian Teachings on the Creation

THE HEBREW SCRIPTURES

Analysis of the Torah (The Five Books of Moses), the Prophets (Nevi'im) and the Writings (Kethubim), which together comprise the Hebrew Bible and which are referred to as the Old Testament in the Christian Bible, yields the following:

1. The testimony of the Creation.

All Creation and all creatures praise the Lord — Everything that God has made praises their Creator (Ps. 148): Earth and people (Ps. 96:1, 8–9); fields and everything in them, trees of the wood (Ps. 96:11–13); fruit trees and cedars, wild animals and all cattle, small creatures and flying birds (Ps. 148:9–10); the heavens, the sun, moon and stars (Ps. 96:11; 97:6; 148:3–4); the sea and all that is in it (Ps. 96:11; 98:7); the world and its inhabitants, the floods and the hills (Ps. 98:7–9); lightning and hail, snow and clouds, stormy winds that do his bidding (Ps. 148:8); and all lands (Ps. 100:1–3); all flesh (Ps. 145:21); everything that has breath (Ps. 150:6); and all God's works (Ps. 103:22, 145:20). "From the rising of the sun unto the going down of the same, the name of the Lord is to be praised" (Ps. 113:3).

Reasons for this praise of God by the creatures — All creatures praise the Lord for God's wondrous works, each performed in wisdom (Ps. 104:24). They praise their Creator for steadfast love, for wonderful works to the sons of men (Ps. 107:21); for faithfulness and justness of the Lord's works (Ps. 111:7); for unsearchable greatness and mighty acts, for the glorious splendor of the Lord's majesty and abundant goodness (Ps. 145:3–7). They praise God for faithfulness, graciousness, sustaining love, providential care, justness in all the Lord's ways, and kindness of all doings (Ps. 145:13–17). "They will tell of the glory of your kingdom and speak of your might, so that all men may know of your mighty acts and the glorious splendor of your kingdom" (Ps. 145:11–12).

The voice of Creation's testimony — The heavens proclaim the Lord's righteousness, and all the people see the Lord's glory (Ps. 97:6). "The heavens tell the glory of God; the skies proclaim the work of His hands. Day after day they pour forth speech; and night after night they display God's knowledge. Their voice goes out into all the earth, their words to the ends of the world" (Ps. 19:1–2, 4).

2. The testimony of God in the scriptures

The scriptures include God's testimony on the Creation: "I am He; I am the first, and I am the last. My own hand hath laid the foundations of the earth, and my right hand spread out the heavens; when I summon them, they all stand up together" (Isa. 48:12–13). "I am the Lord who has made all things; who alone stretched out the heavens; who spread out the earth by myself " (Isa. 44:24). To this God's people reply, "You alone are the Lord. You made heavens, even the highest heavens and all their starry house, the earth, and all that is on it, the seas, and all that is in them. You give life to everything, and the multitudes of heaven worship you" (Neh. 9:6).

3. The qualities of the Creator

God's wisdom and knowledge as Creator — It is God who is the Creator of all (Gen. 1:1); the Lord by wisdom laid the Earth's foundations, by understanding the Creator established the heavens. By the Lord's knowledge the depths of the sea were divided, and clouds drop down the dew (Prov. 3:19–20). The Lord laid the foundations of the Earth and has ordained all things: the Earth, its dynamic atmosphere, its animals.

The Creator's righteousness, integrity, and love — The Lord's Creation pours forth righteousness (Isa. 45:5–8). The Lord loves righteousness and justice. The Earth is full of the loving kindness of Jehovah. By command of the Lord were the heavens made, and all the host of them by the breath of his mouth (Ps. 33:4–6). The heavens and the Earth are Jehovah's; the Lord has established the Earth and all it holds (Ps. 89).

The Creator's goodness and providence — The Creator's goodness, faithfulness, and steadfast love is displayed in his Creation (Ps. 136). The Lord's love reaches to the heavens; God's faithfulness reaches the skies. God preserves man and beast (Ps. 36:5–6). He makes springs to flow and provides water for the Earth and its creatures, the creatures wait upon God for their food and life; all were made in his wisdom; He deserves our devoted and thankful praise (Ps. 104:10–35). "When you send your Spirit, they are created, and you renew the face of the earth" (Ps. 104:30).

God's righteousness, lawfulness, and goodness — The Creation clearly shows the Creator's righteousness and lawfulness (Ps. 97:6). The Lord founded the Earth by wisdom and the heavens by understanding (Prov. 3:19). The Lord's marvelous work includes wonderful and orderly fashioning of human beings through embryological development to adulthood (Ps. 139:14–16) and creation of the marvelous hippopotamus, harmoniously integrated into its wetland habitat (Job 40:15–24). All of the Lord's work is right and is done in faithfulness. The Earth is full of Jehovah's loving kindness. By the word of Jehovah were the heavens made, and all the host of them by the breath of his mouth (Ps. 33:4–5).

The Earth and universe and all it contains are harmonious, declare justice and integrity, and demonstrate shalom. The Creation is good, it is very good (Gen. 1). The goodness is displayed in the handiwork of God in the heavens, in the Earth, and in his creatures (Ps. 19).

The goodness of Creation is so apparent that it is declared by the very existence of Creation itself, and through it God's power and divine majesty shine forth. The Lord rejoices in his works: in the springs of the valleys, in the great sea, in the wild goats and the hippopotamus (Ps. 104; 19:1; 97:6; Job 40:15–24). The "goodness" of the Creation is not confined to the narrow use of the term by human beings. Its goodness includes the glory of the storms which drive the waves of the sea and beat down the forests with their force (Ps. 29). It includes the provision of prey for the lions, and power for the crocodile (Ps. 104:21; Job 41:1–34).

4. Human impact on the Creation

However, the goodness of the Creation is restricted by the disintegrative and unjust actions of human beings. The degrading and polluting works of humankind impoverish the ability of the Creation to bring God praise (Gen. 1:11; 3:6–9; 4:8–9; 6:5–6; 11:3–6). The degradation and injustice brought by human beings against the integrity of the Creation is pervasive, affecting persons, creatures, homes, habitats, human and biotic communities, ecosystems, the biosphere, and outer space. Sin as we have come to understand the term in a narrow and personal sense is not adequate to describe the disintegrative actions of humanity against the integrity of Creation (Exod. 23:10–13; Lev. 25:2, 23–24; Isa. 5:8–10; Ps. 104:35). The authority to destroy the Creator's works is not ours (Job 40:19) but only that of the Creator — their author and maker (Ps. 29, 24; Gen. 6:13).

People willfully become like God, choosing to know good and evil (Gen. 3:5, 22); exhibiting arrogance and pride (Isa. 13:11); killing and putting out of the way relatives, prophets, wise men, and teachers who profess and seek what is right (Gen. 4:8–9). The thoughts of the human heart became evil (Gen. 6:5) pursuing things that God hates — arrogance, lying and false advertising, killing innocent victims, scheming and plotting, eagerly doing evil, falsifying information, and aggravating dissent (Prov. 6:16–19). People, in violation of the Lord's will, become drunk, exploit the flesh (Gen. 9:20–25; Eph. 5:15–19), and arrogantly build cities and towers (Gen. 11:3–6). In their arrogance, some prey upon the defenseless, entrapping them with legal loopholes and dirty tricks; they boast freely of the things they crave, praise others who pursue their own personal gain, and revile the Lord. The arrogant person says, "Nothing will shake me; I'll always be happy and never have trouble." His mouth is full of curses and lies and threats (Ps. 10:2–11).

God looks down from heaven on the children of humankind to see if anyone remains who understands and seeks God. But everyone has turned away (Ps. 53:2–3); there is no one righteous, not even one (Ps. 53:3); evil-doers frustrate the plans of the poor, but the Lord is their refuge (Ps. 14:2–3, 6). We all, like sheep, have gone astray; each of us has turned to our own way (Isa. 53:60).

5. The Creator's response

Thinking of the individual as the only important thing and doing everything out of self-interest destroys society. Wisdom and knowledge mislead when one thinks, "I *am,* and none else besides me" (Isa. 47:10b).

How do you know if you are appointed? Those appointed to warn society have a serious obligation to fulfill their task. If they sound the alarm but no one responds, the unresponsive society is at fault and will pay the consequences. But, if the ones appointed fail to sound the alarm they are at fault (Ezek. 33:1–6). It is unworthy and irresponsible for appointed watchers to be blind to what is happening, to lack knowledge, to use their position merely to satisfy their own appetites, to lead or mislead people without understanding, or to be preoccupied in seeking self-gain. "Come," each one cries, "let me get wine! Let us drink our fill of beer! And tomorrow will be like today, or even far better" (Isa. 56:10–12).

God hates arrogance and pride, evil behavior, and perverse speech (Prov. 8:12–13). God says, "I will punish the world for its evil, the wicked for their sins. I will put an end to the arrogance of the haughty and will humble the price of the ruthless (Isa. 13:11). The prayer of the upright is "Let slanderers not be established in the land; may disaster hunt down men of violence." The Lord secures justice for the poor and upholds the cause of the needy. "Surely the righteous will praise your name and the upright will live before you" (Ps. 140:11–13).

THE CHRISTIAN NEW TESTAMENT SCRIPTURES

Analysis of the New Testament, which together with the Old Testament comprises the Christian Bible, yields the following:

1. The testimony of the Creation.

God's sustaining care of Creation bears God witness to all nations, a witness seen through God's goodly provision of rains, fruitful seasons, foods, and gladness (Acts 14:16–17). Did the people of Earth not hear the heavens declare God's glory: Paul, in his letter to the Romans, quotes Psalm 19 when he states: "Of course they did: 'Their voice has gone out into all the earth, their words to the end of the world'" (Rom. 10:18). The Creation has testified to the Lord from the beginning until now and we are left with no excuse but to know God's power and majesty; "For since the creation of the world God's invisible qualities — God's eternal power and divine nature — clearly seen, understood from what has been made, so that men are without excuses " (Rom. 1:20 NIV).

2. The incarnate Christ as Creator.

Christ the incarnate God, the Word, creates the Earth and universe and does the "manual" work of molding, speaking, and forming (John 1:1–5; Col. 1:16–20). Christ is the One through Whom all creatures are made. "In the beginning was the Word, and the Word was with God, and the Word was God. The same was in the beginning with God. All things were made through Him; and without Him was not anything made that hath been made" (John 1:1–3). "He is the image of the invisible God, the firstborn over all Creation. For by Him all things were created: things in heaven and on earth, visible and invisible, whether thrones or powers or rulers or authorities; all things were created by Him and for Him. He is before all things, and in Him all things hold together" (Col. 1:15–17). "You are worthy, our Lord and God, to receive glory and honor and power, for you created all things, and by your will they were created and have their being" (Rev. 4:11).

3. Redemption of the Creation.

The message of redemption is clearly presented in the New Testament books of Romans and John. The translations of Paulos Mar Gregorios, Bishop of Delhi (Au Sable Forum, 1984), are the ones used here.

From Paul's letter to the Colossians we read: "He, Christ, the Beloved Son, is the manifest presence of the unmanifested God. He is the Elder Brother of all things created, for it was by him and in him that all things were created, whether here on earth in the sensible world or in the world beyond the horizon of our senses which we call heaven; even institutions like royal thrones, seats of the lords and rulers; all forms of authority. All things were created through him, by him, in him. But he himself is before all things; in him they consist and subsist; he is the head of the body, the Church.

"He is the New Beginning, the First-born from the dead; this way he becomes in all respects pre-eminent. For it was (God's) good pleasure that in Christ all fullness should dwell; it is through him and in him that all things are to be reconciled and re-harmonized. For he has removed the contradiction and made peace by his own blood. So all things in the visible earth and in the invisible heaven, should dwell together in him. That includes you, who were once alienated, enemies in your own minds to God's purposes; immersed in evil actions; but now you are bodily reconciled in his fleshly body which has tasted death. Christ intends to present you, holy, spotless and blameless, in God's presence, if you remain firm in the faith, rooted and grounded in him, unswerving from the hopes of the good news you have heard; the good news declared not only to men and women on earth, but to all created beings under heaven. It is the gospel, that I, Paul, have also been called to serve" (Col. 1:15–23).

And from Paul's letter to the Romans: "The created order awaits, with eager longing, with neck outstretched, the full manifestation of the children of God. The futility or emptiness to which the created order is now subject, is not something intrinsic to it. The creator made the creation contingent, in his ordering, upon hope; for the creation itself has something to look forward to — namely, to be freed from its present enslavement to dis-integration; the creation itself is to share in the freedom, in the glorious and undying goodness, of the children of God. For we know how the whole creation up till now groans together in agony, in a common pain. And not just the non-human created order; even we ourselves, as Christians, who have received the advanced gift of the Holy Spirit, are now groaning within ourselves; for we are also waiting — waiting for the transformation of our bodies and for the full experiencing of our adoption to the status of God's children. For it is by that waiting with hope that we are being saved today. We do not hope for something which we already see. Once one sees something, there is no point in going on hoping to see it. It is there. What we hope for is what we have not yet seen; awaiting its manifestation, in patient endurance" (Rom. 8:18–25). Thus, Christ the Creator of everything is the redeemer of the whole Creation, the reconciler of all things.

Requirements for Creation's Care and Keeping

THE HEBREW SCRIPTURES

The Torah, Prophets, Writings, and New Testament address several principles that bear on the relation between belief and ecology in Jewish and Christian religions. These are as follows:

1. *Acknowledge God as owner of all the Earth.* The Earth is the Lord's and everything it contains (Ps. 24:1; Exod. 9:29; Job 41:11). The Creator is owner of the Earth because God created and established it (Ps. 24:2; Gen. 1–2). The land must not be sold permanently since it belongs to the Lord and you are only my tenants (Lev. 25:23).

2. *Keep and preserve Earth as God keeps us.* Sinless people before the Fall were given the command to cultivate and guard, protect, and preserve (Hebrew *shamar*) the Creator's perfect garden (Gen. 2:15). Such people — "Earth-keepers" — are to keep (*shamar*) God's garden as they keep (*shamar*) God's law (Exod, 15:26) and God's commandments (Exod. 20:6). Earth-keepers are to keep (*shamar*) God's Earth as God blesses and keeps (*shamar*) the people of the Lord (Num 6:24). Earth-keepers are to keep the land as God forever keeps (*shamar*) the Lord's people from all harm and watches over their life, their coming and their going (Ps. 121:7).

Sinless people, before the Fall, are commanded to subdue and rule over the Earth and its creatures (Gen. 1:28). The requirements for exercising dominion and ruling over subjects by sinful people are found in Deuteronomy 17. The one who rules must be extremely well-versed in the law — the Torah — and must read it all the days of their life, and through it to learn to revere the Lord and follow its words and decrees (Deut. 17:18–19).

If ruling and dominion are self-serving and do not keep, guard, and protect the creation, the rule and dominion are lost and the land no longer provides for its people stewardship (Lev. 26:18–20). Ruling and dominion are lost altogether if they, in service of self-interest, neglect caring for the Creation (Isa. 56:10–12).

3. *Give the people, the land, and the creatures their Sabbath rests.* The Lord commands that there be a Sabbath of solemn rest for the land (Exod. 23:10, 11). One year in every seven should exclude sowing, pruning, and reaping (Exod. 23:10, 11). If God's commandments are observed and obeyed, the people will dwell in the land securely; the land will yield its fruit, the people will eat their fill, and the loss of one year of production will more than be made up by the productivity of the other six years. If God's law is observed and obeyed, then it will rain at the proper times and the land will yield

its increase, the trees of the field will yield their fruit, and people will eat bread to the full, and will dwell in the land securely (Lev. 25:18–22).

If these commandments are not obeyed, the land will be devastated, and the people will be driven off. Only afterwards, as long as it lies desolate, will it then enjoy its Sabbaths. Alone. As long as it lies desolate it will have rest, "the rest which it had not in your Sabbaths when you dwelt upon it" (Lev. 26:32–35).

4. *Respect Earth when participating in its blessings.* People must not disrupt Earth's providence as they take of its provisions. The prophet Ezekiel asks: "Is it not enough for you to feed on the good pasture? Must you also trample the rest of your pasture with your feet? Is it not enough for you to drink clear water? Must you also muddy the rest with your feet? Must my flock feed on what you have trampled and drink what you have muddied with your feet?" (Ezek. 34:18–19).

5. *Confess to God our abuses of Earth.* Confession of sins against the Creator is a requirement of the scriptures. A Hebrew proverb states: "He who conceals his sins does not prosper, but whoever confesses and renounces them finds mercy" (Prov. 28:13). Again: "Blessed is the man who always fears the Lord, but he who hardens his heart falls into trouble" (Prov. 28:14).

6. *Save the Creatures from extinction.* Faced with destruction of the Creation and its creatures because of the disruptive and abusive acts of human beings, Noah was commanded by the Creator to preserve every species from extinction by rescuing them from destruction and reestablishing them in their habitats (Gen. 6:11–9:17).

THE CHRISTIAN NEW TESTAMENT SCRIPTURES

1. *Acknowledge God as owner of all Earth.* The New Testament affirms the Hebrew scriptures (2 Tim. 3:26) and reiterates some of the Hebrew scriptures as the affirmation that the Earth is the Lord's (1 Cor. 10:26).

2. *Christ is the New Testament example of sinless dominion and rulership.* Perfect, sinless people are commanded to rule over the Creation, have dominion over Earth (Gen. 1:28), and guard (*shamar*) the garden (Gen. 2:15). Sinless people are those who are fully in harmony with God, who do not go their way, who know only good and not evil. The scriptures declare that all have sinned and fall short (Rom. 3:23, 1 John 1:8–10) with three exceptions: Adam before his sin, Eve before her sin, and Jesus Christ. Thus, the example Christ sets for exercise of dominion is crucial in the New Testament scriptures.

While Christ remains sinless (Heb. 4:15; 7:26–28), Adam and Eve disobeyed the Lord, lost their stewardship over the Garden of Eden, and were driven from it (Gen. 3). Only Christ lives his life without rebellion and sin, and is the only example of one exercising sinless dominion. Thus, dominion is defined in the scriptures by the life and actions of Christ, who "made himself nothing, taking the very nature of a servant (Phil. 2:7). From this we understand dominion by the perfect human being to be service, not oppressive rule. Human beings are asked to follow his example, to adopt "the mind of Christ (Phil. 2:1–5). It is Christ who teaches his followers to pray "Thy Kingdom come, Thy will be done on earth" (Matt. 6:10), and through this reminding them to so behave on Earth that heaven will not be a shock to them.

The gospel of John not only identifies Christ as the Creator, but also explains that Christ comes to Earth because God loves the cosmos (John 3:16). The one through whom all things were made and through whom all things hold together (John 1:1–5; Col. 1:15–20) out of God's love for the cosmos (John 3:16) is sent to set people right with the Creator, the Word, and the Redeemer (Rom. 3:21–31).

Conclusion

While knowing more about nature and conservation than any other time in human history, we never have experienced greater environmental degradation and destruction. Having discovered how nature works and what we are able to do, we have not been constrained by what we must do to protect and care for Creation's integrity. Unconstrained by what ought to be, we have proceeded to do whatever is possible, with degrading consequences for Earth and its creatures. The heritage of religions of constraint has been spurned. In the words of Donald Worster, "What traditionally had been regarded as vices, the dark energies of greed and envy were transformed into virtues and blessings to the race."[19] Long-standing religious teachings that bring a caring and sustaining stewardship to Earth have been set aside and neglected as people pursued a course of greed and disregard for the richness of all living things. Religious reverence for life and the Earth has been discarded in the haste to convert Creation's richness into products to be used and thrown away. Yet our religions have warned against the vices of greed and envy, and counselled us that we are not masters of the Earth, but responsible and accountable trustees, defenders of wholeness and integrity. But we have allowed the quality of religion to diminish as it increasingly got in the way of a new and pervasive ethic of self and self-interest, even to the point that self-interest sometimes became one of its tenets. We now have come to a time when it is necessary to re-nurture and reapply religious reverence for life, to show the degrading effects of greed on Earth's integrity, and to raise the quality of religion to the level that will enable people to live with caring integrity on a life-sustaining Earth.

The people of the Book profess that the Earth is the Lord's and all that it contains, that the entire universe is God's Creation, yet know that Earth is being seriously abused by the actions of humankind. The creatures whose salvation is told in Genesis 9 — the creatures saved by Noah's faithful and costly obedience to God's directive — once again are being threatened with destruction as they are displaced from house and home by those who grasp and take Creation's tangible wealth. Responsible stewardship of the planet is overshadowed and outdistanced by irresponsible avarice — by the drive to transform Creation's ecological and life-sustaining wealth into personal riches. Stewardship is seen by many as foolishness. Yet it is this foolishness that must now be taught and practiced.

Our hope is for restoration and continuation of a self-sustaining planet. It is a hope for a self-sustaining house; a place to dwell securely; an *oikos* where brokenness and decay are replaced with healing and restoration; where ecological sickness and death are replaced with ecological health and life. It is a hope that would let Earth do its self-sustaining work.

Earth is challenging people and institutions to see and respond to the degrading consequences of their actions. Individuals and congregations are among those being seriously challenged. Ecology is not a specialty; ecology is the business of all who claim Earth as home. To those who believe, ecology is the working out of faith in self and the world; it is the business of achieving and maintaining personal and biospheric integrity. To religion, it is the elevation of quality to such a degree that profession of integrity is incorporated into thinking, life, and living. Religion renewed and refreshed in love for the land and its creatures is religion made relevant to Earth's challenge. For people of the Book, religion renewed and refreshed in love for the Creator and God's Creation is religion that brings a caring keeping of the Creation. Religion of quality provides a critical foundation for assuring that the self is mastered and that ecological and technological knowledge is used for healing and restoration of Earth.

C. B. D.

* * *

TAKING ACTION

The review of the Hebrew and Christian Scriptures suggest a number of possible responses for religious institutions and congregations who are translating concern for the global problem into local practice. Among these are the following:

- Placing the Creation and its proper stewardship in the program of the congregations.

- Providing stewardship alternatives to "winning" and rising up the ladder of worldly power.

- Selecting Creation-aware song, hymns, and scriptural studies.

- Including references to the Creation that connect with congregational land and property and the immediate neighborhood.

- Selecting Creation and stewardship scriptural material for staff and student studies and devotionals.

- Planting a congregational sustainable-Earth garden.

- Adopting an endangered species and helping to save it from extinction.

- Helping to place the Creation and stewardship into the thinking and practice of society.

- Discussing the Creation without being distracted by the evolution debate.

- Making each church, synagogue, or congregation meeting place a Creation-awareness center.

Translating the global problem into local practice also can include:

- Making an inventory of congregational and area lands and developing a stewardship plan.

- Supporting the readers and priests of Creation.

- Making each congregation a Creation-awareness center.

- Fostering development of the knowledge of the Creation out-of-doors.

- Making each religious camp a model Creation-caring center.

- Conducting retreats and conferences on Creation-awareness themes.

- Holding conferences for clergy on the land and stewardship.

- Developing and using outdoor centers in stimulating the Christian colleges and seminaries to produce people who can provide leadership and service in Creation-awareness and Christian environmental stewardship.

- Fostering respect and support for those who reach out to save the Creation and its creatures.

- Developing strategies for exponential growth of Creation-awareness and the scriptural principles of stewardship and their proper practice.

— 21 —

The Wages of Greed

Judith S. Scherff

> We are about to commit ourselves once and for all time either to
> a planet rich in wonderment and beauty, or to a planet that is a
> mockery of itself, drenched in poisons, littered with metal junk
> heaps.... This is mankind's last chance on earth. From here on,
> the world will be a heaven or a hell of our own choosing.
>
> Roger A. Caras, *Last Chance on Earth:*
> *A Requiem for Wildlife*

On March 19, 1989, the *New York Times* published an article by
Senator Albert Gore entitled "An Ecological Kristallnacht. Listen."
(Kristallnacht is the name given to that night in 1938 during which
Nazis shattered glass while pillaging thousands of Jewish businesses
prior to the beginning of World War II. World political leaders,
with few exceptions, continued to listen to Hitler rather than pay
attention to events.)

Evidence that we are on the brink of an ecological holocaust is
as clear as the glass that shattered in Berlin, according to Gore. And
during those years and the years preceding, we ignored the warnings.
According to Gore, "Some, like Prime Minister Neville Chamberlain
in Munich, would rather adapt to the threat than confront it. This
time, they are protected not by an umbrella but by floppy hats and
sunglasses."[1]

We have treated our environmental prophets much like Winston
Churchill was treated when he warned of impending war — we have
hooted, booed, and dismissed them. But Churchill was right then,
and so was Rachel Carson, and so are present-day givers of warnings.

As Senator Gore explained, we are at an ecological Kristallnacht. It is 1938 all over again, and this time, the entire Earth is involved.

There is a common theme that unites these chapters, and that theme is human greed. Our value system has wreaked havoc upon our planet, and in a very few years. What Aldo Leopold called the "law of diminishing returns in progress" (a term he used in his book *Sand County Almanac,* 1949) is well-established in our world and running at full tilt.

We arrived at this point in time, at this environmental apocalypse, largely because of an attitude that the Earth has unlimited resources and those resources are to be used for whatever profit can be derived from them. As a result, we have taken too much, we have killed too many, we have abused it all.

There are those who don't want to hear this kind of talk. But when they protest, look beyond their rhetoric to their special interests. They will identify themselves by their actions, past and present. Have they been involved in ecological destruction?

What was once exploration, when our continent was first settled, has evolved into exploitation. And consideration for the laws of nature has been ignored. This attitude, at least in the United States, has hardly been more pervasive and destructive than in the eight years of the Reagan Administration. Those who were a part of that administration were noteworthy for their rapacious attitude toward the environment.

The Reagan policy was to include those who abuse the Earth in environmental decision-making.[2,3,4,5] The intent was to establish what appeared to be a strong economy without regard to the degradation these decisions were causing ecologically.[6] And we were told that the basis of this economic philosophy was the trickle-down theory, a theory in which, as it turns out, greed was an integral part.

And trickle down it did, through the Congress, through Wall Street, and all of its financial environs. It served as the basis for individuals in large corporations and small companies to do whatever they felt necessary to achieve profits well in excess of any they really needed. Financial gluttony overwhelmed any possible concern for the environment.

Certain members of Congress were equally insensitive to the environment. Just one example: seven major industries whose goal it was to weaken the Clean Air Act gave over $1 million to the campaign coffers of certain Senate and House members during the 1980 elections. The problem is not just that these industries offered the money; the problem is that the illustrious members of Congress took the money and voted accordingly.[7,8]

And we are all affected by the political action committees (PACs) who pass this money around. They pay members of Congress to vote, in this case, against environmentally sound policies. And the effects of their votes, also trickle down. The Public Interest Research Group has revealed, "Their influence reaches you when you bite into an apple treated with daminozide (or alar), a probable human carcinogen that cannot be washed or peeled off.... Their influences reaches you when you munch on cereal made from corn sprayed with Captan, proven to cause kidney tumors and birth defects in laboratory animals.... Their influence reaches you when you swallow aldicarb-contaminated water, suspected to cause immune system disorders in humans."[9]

The pesticide lobby is the source of this particular example. And the pesticide lobby is composed of a coalition of chemical manufacturers, food growers, and grocery companies. The Grocery Manufacturers Association, according to Ralph Nader, "gave $654,894 to members of the Senate Agriculture Committee and $607,051 to members of the House Agriculture Committee from 1981–1986."[10] They gave this money in order to weaken the pesticide law, a law which gives the "pesticides industry every available break while public health suffers at every turn."[11]

It would seem that large corporations with money to spend on Capitol Hill get their way going and coming. Not only have laws and regulations been established that have proven beneficial to the manufacturing and selling aspect of certain corporations (such as pesticides, off-shore oil drilling, etc.), which presumably increased their profits, but on the other hand, laws have been excessively lenient when it comes to some of these corporations paying taxes on those profits.

Philip Stern, in his book *The Best Congress Money Can Buy*, explains just how this situation works to the benefit of corporate America: "The U.S. tax law obliges tens of millions of average taxpayers to pay 10 to 30 percent of their incomes to the Internal Revenue Service every April. By contrast, 130 large corporations contrived, in one or more of the years 1982 through 1985, through adroit use of tax loopholes enacted by Congress, to escape without paying a penny of tax on their billions of dollars of profits."[12] Senator Paul Simon commented on this legalized inequality, "The astonishing result is that the janitor at General Electric pays more taxes than GE" — one of the zero-tax companies.[13]

These are examples of national leadership — national leadership that repeatedly displayed its contempt for the environment in favor of corporate profits by consistently making what amounts to obscene gestures towards the laws of nature and to those Americans who have no choice but to suffer the consequences of greedy policy. Earth first! reminds us of the eventual results of this political behavior: "There are no jobs on a dead planet."

Greed Trickles Down

This flagrant violation of respect for the individual and the balance of nature was mimicked throughout big business as it worked in conjunction with the government and took its lead from these examples. In some ways, we have seen the darkest side of capitalism. We have witnessed the accrual of money for the few at the expense of the whole. What's good for corporate America is not always what's good for all America, and that is being confirmed whenever we read headlines such as:

> "Year End Brings Billion-Dollar S & L Giveaway"
>
> " 'Junk Bond' Leader Is Indicted by US in Criminal Action"
>
> "How Trading Practice Gyps Futures Customers"
>
> "US Takes Over 20 Texas Banks: High Cost Seen"
>
> "Futures Scandal Likely to be Costly"

Greed has run rampant, and the news has reported such consequent actions as insider trading, junk-bond schemes, corporate raiding, stock manipulation, and savings and loan corruption. Of this trend, *Time* reported one individual as saying, "What is being done threatens the very basis of our capitalist system."[14]

It is the American taxpayer who ultimately pays for excessive greed. In *Time* magazine's cover story entitled "A Game of Greed," the author stated that it is the American taxpayer who will "wind up underwriting the buyouts to the tune of billions of dollars because interest payments on the giant borrowings are deductible as a business expense."[15] It is the American taxpayer who will bail out the savings and loan institutions. It is the American taxpayer who will suffer from the effects of polluted water, the diminishing number of species, a dwindling rain-forest ecosystem, green-house warming, and every other manifestation of environmental degradation. It is the American taxpayer who will pay for the clean-up of the environment, if political powers will even allow us that option, while the corporations guilty of these ills may pay nothing.

The average American has been gouged, just as the Earth has been gouged. It is the prevailing attitude of greed that allows developers, ranchers, petroleum barons, money manipulators, and others to feel no regard to the Earth as a survival system; to disregard wantonly the ecological requirements necessary for health. According to James Robertson and André Carothers, who wrote of this issue for *Greenpeace* magazine,

> It is clear that economics has divorced itself from moral and ethical considerations. Vast inequalities in wealth are ignored or justified by adherence to "free market" principles, and corporate criminals who steal millions of dollars or contribute to the health problems of entire communities are almost never brought to justice.
>
> In short, conventional economics now conflicts with social as well as ecological needs, with fairness and justice, with religious and spiritual values, and with common sense.[16]

And on local levels and with individuals, the trend continues. An article by Dan Dignam for *Tour & Travel News* reported that the development of a resort on St. Croix, held up for twenty-four months by environmentalists, was allowed by the US Virgin Island's District Court to commence breaking ground. He writes, "The Environmental groups say nearby Salt River Bay provides food for sea turtles, nesting for several endangered species of birds and is home to one of the last surviving mangrove populations — a tropical maritime tree — on the island." The developer, of course, says their project will not affect the area.[17]

This same developer owns other property on a nearby Caribbean island which, at this writing, rents for between $735 and $2,550 per unit, per night. How much of this Earth are we willing to sacrifice for excessive profits? We must ask that question over and over again. We must remember that question whenever we see the Earth being despoiled for profit at the expense of all of us and of all life. It is virtually certain that in order to achieve environmental integrity, we're all going to have to modify our life-style to a simpler level, to a less affluent level, because,

> It is largely the great affluence of our American people which determines the present ecological threat of extinction to this planet. It encourages the overconsumption of luxuries, and hence of all natural resources of which we have had luxurious amounts — water, oil, soil, wildlife. It contributes to the pollution of our air, with all the evil complications thereof, through transportation and manufacturing, through comfort and convenience. Worst of all, it contributes to perhaps our greatest national sin — *waste!*[18]

Those of us who feel as if we are looking at the situation from a distance outside of the power structure are not alone in our concern for what has happened and the fact that the middle-class American is getting stuck with the bill while at the same time our environmental assets are being diminished day by day. From within corporate America's own ranks came what might be considered a prophetic remark: "Do I sense Fear? Yes. At some point there is going to be a rebellion against greed."[19]

The Destructiveness of Greed

If we are ever to achieve an integrity in the Creation and in the intricate patterns of life that have been evolving over millions of years, we must create a sensitivity within human beings, inherent in which is a reverence for all life. It is necessary for our own survival.

How we treat our surroundings and other life will determine what, in the end, happens to us as a species. The destructive and the creative view of our relationship with other species is contrasted in the following printed segments, one from a newspaper and the other from a book. (The prairie dog is the subject of both statements.)

In the newspaper article, the writer states that prairie dogs are classed as vermin, and thus hounded mercilessly by most landowners, "but to sportsmen they are a classy long-range target."[20] The writer continues by acknowledging that their former territory has been drastically reduced. They are not loved by ranchers, and there have been efforts to eradicate them with widespread poisoning. He contends that the rough pasture created by the prairie dog habitat is hard on combines and other large farm equipment. The writer goes on:

> He squeezed the trigger and two dogs flew left and right, flung three feet away and cut almost in half by the fast-traveling 55-grain jacketed slug. The pair had been sitting one behind the other, and the bullet harvested both as it zipped across the top of the burrow.
>
> Switching to a .22 Hornet, the rifleman settled the crosshairs of the telescope sight on a prairie dog showing his head and shoulders 150 yards away. At the crack of the rifle, the prairie dog flew out of his burrow like a champagne cork from a bottle as the bullet plucked him from the hold and flung him a foot and a half away.
>
> Clearly, a couple of weeks in a prairie dog town would be a post-graduate course in riflery.... The little barking squirrel of the high plains is unquestionably "the world's best self-erecting target."
>
> And his hide makes a good pair of gloves, too.[21]

Another view of the prairie dog was expressed by Lewis Regenstein in his book *The Politics of Extinction*.

> The passing of the prairie dog will inevitably carry with it an entire ecosystem. It will bring about the disappearance of the critically endangered black-footed ferret... as well as jeopardize other life forms, such

as the burrowing owl, which are dependent on the vanishing habitat provided by the prairie dog.

Prairie dogs, and their evolutionary predecessors, have played a valuable role in the ecology of the western plains almost since these lush grasslands came into existence millions of years ago. Their digging and burrowing activities mix and enrich the soil, and dredge millions of tons of mineral-rich subsoil to the surface. This appears to be an important factor in the high mineral content of these grassland soils and their rich nutrients, which grow "hard wheats" and high-protein grasses.... [22]

The outlook for the prairie dog is not bright. Although these animals lived through the Ice Age and other massive climatic revolutions, they may not survive the human "civilization" that has been so recently inflicted upon them. They do not understand that, despite their harmlessness, man does not tolerate intruders upon "his" land.[23]

Two accounts. Two very different viewpoints of a species. Multiplied by millions of people and countless species, human population will survive — or not — depending upon which viewpoint prevails. We humans are a part of this whole system and we are dependent upon biological diversity of many other species just as important as the prairie dog. If they go, so do we. What is wrong with us that some of us cannot see this connection? That many humans seem incapable of feeling any reverence for other life may be the root problem that we face in all the world.

The Turning Point

Many point to the Old Testament as the source of their "right" to kill. But it is up to the clergy and everyone else who claims a religious foundation and association to act on the voluminous injunctions of environmental stewardship found in the Old and New Testaments. And stewardship requires much more from us than many are used to because attending church one hour a week is just that — attending church one hour a week. If we call ourselves Christian or Jewish or Buddhist or Muslim — if we believe we are religious by whatever name — then the activity to support that claim takes place between one service and the next in the community and in the world. This is what is referred to as stewardship.

Just as the sin of omission can be attributed to a major portion of organized religion and ordained clergy, the sin of pride can be attached to a few environmentalists. Most salaried employees of environmental organizations or research groups are dedicated individuals who welcome the assistance of any and all in their effort to make better this world. There are, however, always a few who spoil the soup. In this case, there have been occasions when self-appointed elitists have kept the general public at bay on environmental issues. As a result, their arrogance has only added to environmental problems. We are in no position to turn down the help of anyone. We need everybody we can get to join the eco-bandwagon.

We have a choice. We can voluntarily make changes or be forced into it. But we *will* have to change, because our human numbers are increasing while simultaneously non-renewable resources are rapidly decreasing.

> It's obvious that a lot of the minor — if terribly reassuring — luxuries of the heedless life will have to go, the extra air conditioners, fuel for the boat, unlimited trips in the big car. Surviving this long-term crisis, far more pervasive than any that has come before in human experience, is going to require ways of thinking that are entirely foreign to self-centered consumption.[24]

We can begin to become environmentalists through our selection of our next meal. Just one change in our life-style such as foregoing beef can have a positive effect on the rain-forests. You learned of the murder of a native Brazilian and of the killing of horses in Nevada because of cattle ranching. And although there are only approximately twenty-five hundred buffalo in the Yellowstone Park area, the hunting of this once nearly extinct species is now allowed again, and Montana hunters have gunned down a record number. Ranchers claim, among other excuses, that the bison deplete food needed by cattle.[25] From the information available concerning the production of beef, one may well conclude that cattle ranching takes far too much of a toll on the environment to remain at its current level. And so it becomes incumbent upon us to ask ourselves, each time we make a meal selection, if beef is worth the price to the whole of the environment.

Saints

The worst mistake we can possibly make is to think or guess or believe or imagine or conclude or rationalize that one individual cannot make a difference! One individual, acting on an issue, has made considerable difference time and time again. To say that one person really cannot make a mark is a worn-out excuse to abdicate responsibility.

The June–July 1988 issue of *National Wildlife* featured just such personal achievements and honored seven people in an article entitled "People Who Make a Difference." Among those seven is Ila Loetscher, then eighty-three years of age, who has given at least twenty years of her life to saving the ridley turtle along the Texas Gulf Coast. She made news again on February 16, 1989, when she and her group saved several sea turtles that had become comatose from the subfreezing temperatures that affected the Gulf area for several days.[26]

Also in that article is the story of Jan Garton, who wrote the chapter entitled "Wetlands: America's Endangered Habitat" for this book. In recognizing her achievements, the article credited her with "almost singlehandedly" ensuring the vitality of one of the nation's most important wetlands.[27]

These are just two of many silent heroes. The vast majority of men and women who have given years in time and much money to take on a single issue and to make it right again or, in some cases, die trying, are probably never recognized. But they know what they have accomplished for the benefit of a species, the effects they have had on certain issues, and the contributions to the health of the Earth and all of us who live here. There are saints on Earth as well as saints in Heaven.

Unfortunately, acts of charity towards the Creation and behavior that indicates a willingness to share the Earth are so rare, that we're often surprised when we actually witness them.

> When Christianity happens it is such a stranger we call it by a special name, we call it a saint. Dumbstruck by the phenomenon of Francis of Assisi, our only reaction is, "My God, it works." The Rule of sainthood will never change.[28]

We are going to gather the collective energy, determination, and indignation of a lot of people who, heretofore, have not been actively involved in the effort to redeem the land and air and water. We need people who will not tolerate the less-than-honest marketing tactics of polluters (from manufacturers to applicators), the politicians whose loyalty is to those who enlarge their bank accounts, the developers who have not the slightest concern for the environment they are about to bulldoze, and anyone who degrades the Earth by taking advantage of nonhuman species and by using Earth as their own personal trash dump.

To aid Mother Earth in our common struggle to survive and maintain a healthy ecosystem may not always be easy. It is possible that many of us will run up against opposition because what we are going to be required to do will involve putting an end to the abuse by the greedy. And when greed is challenged, we will be opposed. Looking at our opposition will reveal their special interests — we will see where they are coming from and what or who they are protecting at the expense of the whole.

Confrontations present a choice for those of us who will be striving to give aid to Mother Earth. We may temporarily be placed in a situation that will cause us to adopt personalities different from our true selves. This occasional position has been described quite accurately by Robert van den Bosch in his book *The Pesticide Conspiracy:*

> But sometimes the things we cherish are threatened, and then we must either take a stand or be overwhelmed in our passivity. Either way, we pay a price, for if we choose to fight effectively, we must make unpleasant character adjustments and divert time, energy, and thought from the things we would rather do. But if we remain indifferent, we stand to lose much of what we love, not to mention our self-respect.[29]

Earth is a living organism that we have abused and battered. We have bulldozed it, poisoned it, blown up parts of it, and killed portions of it. We have caused the blood of too many of its creatures to be shed out of no motivation other than greed. How much more of our destructiveness can our life-support system, our Mother Earth, tolerate? How many more species must we render extinct before the death knell tolls for human beings?

Like it or not, we will — each of us — determine the future of the earth and of ourselves either by action or inaction. We are responsible, and there's no getting around that. Whether or not we act on our responsibility will determine the future of life on earth.

J.S.S.

* * *

TAKING ACTION

1. Voter responsibility. To identify politicians as corrupt and to let it go at that or pass corruption off as something we can't do anything about relieves us of our responsibility. In choosing to forget that ultimately we are the government, we have allowed PACs to gain control of our government. However, we still have the form of power that is only one step ahead of money, and that is the vote. Voter pressure is more influential, if anything can be, than PAC money. Our representatives need to be reminded of this. So if we begin, individually and collectively, to convey our distress about corruption and environmental degradation, we will be accepting our responsibility as we practice stewardship for restoring health to ourselves and our planet.

2. You vote with your dollars. Before you spend money on shrimp, tuna, veal, or beef, remember what their production and marketing

entails and all that has been lost in the process. Whenever you hear that a company or corporation is involved in the process of degrading any part of the environment, do not support their activity with your dollars.

3. Clergy and religious leaders. You, too, must make choices. Will you educate your congregation to be stewards of the Creation or defer that responsibility on behalf of industrial and corporate dollars in the collection plate? You will offend the greedy if you declare that all of us must participate in the stewardship of the Creation. Many of you will have, in your congregations, those who represent companies and activities that degrade the Earth. You may well have to choose between the circumstances that affect the public and those that circuitously bring money into the collection plate.

4. Choose your area of action. None of us can do everything, but everyone can do something. Select those subjects in which you are most interested and learn about them. Read what you can. Tell people. Gather support. But do something!

5. You can act both globally and locally. You can make a difference in issues both internationally and at home.

6. Join environmental and animal welfare organizations. Because of their size, they can accomplish much. But they need your help. Select those in which you are most interested and become a member.

7. See that the environment is the subject of presentations at local clubs. Invite speakers or obtain information to pass to the members about the environment and what they can do. Start study groups in these organizations or in your church in order to discuss the many facets of environmental stewardship.

8. The "save-our-jobs" pleas of coal miners against the clean air act, shrimpers against the use of turtle-excluder devices, and of loggers against the preservation of some forests must be looked at from the balanced perspective of hundreds of thousands of people who have been required to change jobs. The "save-our-jobs" rhetoric implies that unless an individual continues to do exactly that job, he or she will never work again. That is not the case. The individuals involved simply may be required to do something else for a living. Meanwhile, environmental restoration will begin for the benefit of *everyone!*

9. Remember the issues: overpopulation, greenhouse effect, rain forests, animal cruelty, clean air, clean water, pesticides, sustainable

agriculture, wetlands, extinction, excessive trash, and environmental illnesses. Ultimately, you and I and every single individual are responsible for the outcome of each of these issues. Our hope lies in our ability to see that the Earth is no longer abused by accepting our undeniable responsibility as stewards of this magnificent Creation.

Appendix A

Companies that *do not* use animals for testing

An asterisk indicates a company whose products contain no animal ingredients.

ABEnterprises
Abracadabra, Inc.
Aditi Nutri-sentials
Advanced Design Laboratories
*AFM Enterprises
African Bio-Botanica Industries
Alba Botanica Cosmetics
Alexandra Avery Purely Natural
  Body Care
Alexandra de Markoff
Allen's Naturally
Almay Hypo-Allergenic
Alvin Last
*Amberwood
*American Merfluan
Amway
*Ananda Country Products
Andalina
Arbonne Intl.
Armstrong World Industries
*Aroma Vera Company
Atta Lavi
Aubrey Organics
*Aura Cacia, Inc.
Auroma Intl.
*Auromere-Ayurvedic Imports
Austin Diversified Products
Austin's
Autumn-Harp, Inc.

*Avanza
Aveda
Avon
Ayagutaq
*Aztec Secret
Babor Natural Cosmetics
*Baby Touch
Bare Escentuals
Basically Natural
*Baubiologie Hardware
Baudelaire
Beauty Naturally
Beauty Without Cruelty
Beehive Botanicals
Benetton Cosmetics
*Biogime Intl.
*Biokosma
Bo-Chem Co.
*Body Love
The Body Shop
The Body Shop, Inc.
Boerlind of Germany
Bonne Bell
Bonne Sante
Botanicus Retail
Breezy Balms
Bronson Pharmaceuticals
*Bug Off
Carlson Labs

Carma Labs
Carole's Cosmetics
Caswell-Massey
*Cernitin America
Charles of the Ritz
Chempoint Products
Chenti Products, Inc.
Christian Dior Perfumes
Clear Alternative
*Clearly Natural Products
Clientele
*Colour Quest
Columbia Cosmetics
  Manufacturing Company
Come To Your Senses
*Comfort Manufacturing Company
*Compassion Cosmetics
The Compassionate Consumer
Country Comfort
Crabtree & Evelyn
Creighton Labs
Critter Comfort
Cruelty Free Cosmetics Plus
DeLore Intl.
Dermatone Laboratories
Dessert Essence
*Dr. E. H. Bronner
Dr. Hauschka Cosmetics, Inc.
*Duncan Enterprises
Earth Science, Inc.
Ecco Bella
EcoSafe Laboratories
Ecover Products
Elizabeth Arden
Elizabeth Grady Face First
Espree Cosmetics
EvaJon Cosmetics
Everybody
Farmavita USA
Finelle Cosmetics
Fleur De Sante, Inc.
Flora Distributors
Focus 21 Intl.
*Forever New
Freeman Cosmetic
G. T. Intl.
General Nutrition

Germaine Monteil
Giovanni Cosmetics
Glowing Touch (Panacea II)
*Golden Lotus, Inc.
Golden Pride/Rawleigh
Grace Cosmetics (Pro-Ma)
*Granny's Old Fashioned Products
Gruene Kosmetik
Heavenly Soap
Hewitt Soap
Home Health Products
*Home Service Products Company
Houbigant
*Huish Chemical Co.
Humane Alternative Products
Humphrey's Pharmacal, Inc.
i Natural Cosmetics
Idagrae Products
Image Laboratories
Institute of Trichology
Integrated Health
International Rotex, Inc.
International Vitamin
Isadora
Jacki's Magic Lotion
James Austin
Jason Natural Products
Jean Naté
Jean-Pierre Sand
Jeanne Gatineau
Jeanne Rose Herbal Body Works
John F. Amico & Co.
John Paul Mitchell Systems
JOICO Laboratories
Jurlique Cosmetics
Kallima
Kenra Laboratories
Kimberly Sayer, Inc.
Kiss My Face
Kleen Brite Laboratories
KMS Research
*KSA Jojoba
*LaCrista
*L'anza Research Laboratories
La Prairie Incorporated
P. Leiner Nutritional Products
Levlad, Inc.

Life Tree Products
Lily of Colorado
Lily of the Desert
Livos Plant Chemistry
Lotus Light
Lowenkamp Int.
Luseaux Laboratories
Luzier Personalized Cosmetics
Magic Lotion
Magic of Aloe
Marie Lacoste Enterprises
Martha Hill Cosmetics
*Martin von Myering
Matrix Essentials
Max Factor
Metrin Laboratories
*Mia Rose Products
Michael's Health Products
*Microbalanced Products
Mira Linda Spa in the City
*Mountain Fresh Products
Mountain Ocean, Ltd.
Naturade Cosmetics
*Natural Organics, Inc.
Nature Basics
Nature Cosmetics, Inc.
Nature De France
Nature's Gate Herbal Cosmetics
Nature's Plus
Nectarine
New Age Creations/Herbal
  Bodyworks
*New Age Products
*Neway
Nexxus
*No Common Scents
North Country Soap
NuSkin Intl.
NuSun
Nutri-Metrics Intl.
Oriental Beauty Secrest
  (Panacea II)
Orjene Natural Cosmetics
Oxyfresh
Painlessly Beautiful
Patricia Allison Beauty Sorority
Paul Mazzotta

*Paul Penders USA
PetGuard
*Pets 'N People
Phoenix Laboratories
Prestige Fragrances
Princess Marcella Borghese
Pro-Line
Puritan's Pride
Queen Helene
Rachel Perry
Rainbow Concepts
Rainbow Research Corporation
Red Saffron
Redken Laboratories
Reviva Labs, Inc.
Revlon, Inc.
RR Industries
Royal Laboratories
Rusk
*Sappo Hill Soapworks
*Scarborough & Co.
Schiff
Sebastian Intl.
*The Shahin Soap Company
Shaklee U.S.
Shikai
Shirley Price Aromatherapy
Sierra Dawn
*Simplers Botanical Co.
*Sirena Tropical Soap Company
*The Soap Factory
Sombra Cosmetics
SoRik Intl.
Spare the Animals
Sparkle Glass Cleaner
St. Ives, Inc.
Studio Magic
Sukesha
Sunrise Land Products, Inc.
Sunshine Products Group
TerraNova
Tom's of Maine
Tonialg Cosmetics Intl.
Truly Moist
Tyra Skin Car
Ultima II
Ultra Beauty

Val-Chem
Velvet Products Company
Victoria Jackson
Visage Beaute
Viviane Woodard Cosmetics
Wachters' Organic Sea Products
Wala-Heilmittel, GmbH
*Warm Earth Cosmetics
Watkins

Weleda, Inc.
WiseWays Herbals
Wite-out Products
*Without Harm
Wysong
*Youthessence
Yves Rocher
Zia Cosmetics

Sources: *PETA Factsheet, Animal Experiments, #6* (revised February 22, 1990), *The PETA Guide to Compassionate Living*, p. 8. Reprinted by permission.

Appendix B

Companies that use animals for testing

An asterisk indicates those that have declared a moratorium on animal testing — encourage them to announce a permanent ban:

Alberto-Culver Co.
American Cyanamid Co.
Andrea Rabb
Aramis, Inc.
*Armour-Dial, Inc. (Dial Soap, Dial Shampoo, Dial Anti-Perspirant, Tone Soap, Man Power Deodorant and Anti-Perspirant, Liqua 4 Cleansing System, Bruce Floor Care Products, Magic Pre Wash)
BeautiControl Cosmetics
*Beecham Cosmetics
*Beiersdorf, Inc.
Boyle-Midway Division of American Home Products (Easy Off, Quick-Dip Silver Cleaner, Sani-Flush Toilet Bowl Cleaner, Black Flag, Wizard Air Fresheners and Deodorizer, Aero-Wax Floor, Woolite Cold Water Cleanser, Diaper Pure Laundry Aid)
Breck
Bristol-Myers Co. (Drano, Windex, Twinkle, Renuzit, Vanish, Endust, Mr. Muscle, Behold, Miracle White Laundry Detergent, Excedrin, Bufferin,

Ban Vitalis, Comtrex, Keri Lotion)
Carter-Wallace, Inc.
Chanel, Inc.
Cheesbrough-Ponds, Inc.
Church & Dwight
Clairol, Inc. (Herbal Essence Shampoo & Creme Rinse, I Like My Grey Shampoo, Condition Shampoo and Conditioners, Final Net)
Clarins of Paris
Clinique Laboratories, Inc.
Clorox Co. (Clorox Liquid Bleach, Clorox 2 All Fabric Bleach, Formula 409, Liquid-plumr Drain Opener, Soft Scrub Liquid Cleanser, Twice As Fresh Air Freshener, Tilex Mildew Stain Remover)
Colgate-Palmolive Co. (Cashmere Bouquet Soap, Vel Beauty Bar Soap, Irish Spring Soap, Axion Pre-Soak, Fab Laundry Detergent, Fresh Start Concentrated Laundry Detergent, Dynamo Liquid Laundry Detergent, Cold Power Laundry Detergent,

Ajax, Dermassage Dishwashing Liquid, Palmolive Dishwashing Liquid, Rapid Shave, Colgate Toothpastes, Colgate Instant Shave, Flourigard Anti-Cavity Dental Rinse, Wash'N Dry Towelettes)

Cosmair, Inc.

Coty

Dana Perfumes Corp.

Del Laboratories

Diversey Wyandotte Corp.

Dorothy Gray

Dow Chemical Co.

Drackett Products Co.

Economics Laboratory, Inc.

Eli Lilly & Co.

Estée Lauder, Inc.

Frances Denny

Gillette Co. (Right Guard, Soft & Dri Anti-Perspirants, Dry Idea Anti-Perspirants, Foamy & Trac II Shave Creams, The Hot One Shave Creams, Mink Difference, Silkience, Tame Creme Rinses, Earth Born, Heads Up Hair Grooms, Deep Magic Cleansing Lotions, Happy Face Washing Cream, Aapri Facial Scrub, Foot Guard Deodorant)

Givaudan Corp.

Helena Rubenstein

Helene Curtis Industries, Inc.

Jean Patou, Inc.

Jergens

Johnson & Johnson

S. C. Johnson & Son, Inc. (Brite, Future, Glo Coat, Klear, Klear Wood, Step Saver, Super Bravo, Beautiful, Johnson's Paste Wax, Super Kleen Floor, Glory Foam, Liquid Glory, Favor, Jubilee, Klean'n Shine, Pledge, Glade, Big Wally Foam Cleaner, Crew Disinfectant Bathroom Cleaner, Raid Insecticides, Off and Deep Woods Off, Agree Shampoo &

Conditioners, Edge Protective Shave, Enhance Shampoo & Conditioner, Rain Barrell Fabric Softener, Shout Stain Remover, Shout Liquid Bleach)

Johnson Products Co., Inc.

Jovan, Inc.

Lamaur, Inc.

Lancome

L'Oreal

Lever Brothers, Inc. (Liquid ALL Laundry Detergent, Concentrated ALL, Dishwasher ALL, Breeze, Drive, Wisk, Final Touch Fabric Softener, Dove Dishwashing Liquid, Lux Dishwashing Liquid, Caress Soap, Dove Soap, Lifebouy Soap, Lux Beauty Soap, Phase III Soap, Shield Deodorant Soap, Pepsodent Toothpaste, Close-Up Toothpaste, Aim Toothpaste, Signal Mouthwash)

*Mary Kay Cosmetics, Inc.

Maybelline

Mennen Co.

*Merle Norman Cosmetics

Neutrogena

Nina Ricci

*Noxell Corp. (Noxzema, Cover Girl Make-up)

Pfizer

Physicians Formula Cosmetics

Proctor & Gamble Co. (Biz, Bounce, Downy, Comet, Comet Liquid, Mr. Clean, Spic'n'Span, Top Job, Camay, Coast, Ivory, Kirk's Castile, Lava, Safeguard, Zest, Bold, Cheer, Tide)

Purex Corp.

Quintessence

Richardson-Vicks, Inc.

Schering-Plough (Maybelline)

Sea & Ski Corp.

Shulton

Squibb

Sterling Drug, Inc.

Syntex
Texize
Vidal Sassoon, Inc.
Warner-Lambert Co.

Wella Corp.
Westwood Pharmaceuticals
Zotos International

Sources: *PETA Factsheet, Animal Experiments,* #7 (revised February 22, 1990), *The PETA Guide to Compassionate Living,* p. 11. Reprinted by permission.

Appendix C

Addresses for government officials

The President
The White House
1600 Pennsylvania Ave., NW
Washington, DC 20500
(202) 456-1414

The Vice President
Office of the Vice President
Old Executive Office Bldg.
Washington, DC 20501
(202) 224-2424

Your Senator
United States Senate
Washington, DC 20510
(202) 224-3121

Your Representative
House of Representatives
Washington, DC 20515
(202) 224-3121

ALABAMA

Governor
State Capitol 100
Montgomery, AL 36130
(205) 261-2500

Senate
State Capitol
Montgomery, AL 36130
(205) 832-3492

House
State Capitol
Montgomery, AL 36130
(205) 261-3100

ALASKA

Governor
State Capitol
P.O. Box A
Juneau, AK 99811
(907) 465-3500

Senate
State Capitol
Pouch V
Juneau, AK 99811
(907) 465-3701

House
State Capitol
Pouch V
Juneau, AK 99811
(907) 465-3701

ARIZONA

Governor
State Capitol
Phoenix, AZ 85007
(602) 255-4331

Senate
State Capitol
Phoenix, AZ 85007
(602) 255-4900

House
State Capitol
Phoenix, AZ 85007
(602) 255-4900

ARKANSAS

Governor	Senate	House
State Capitol	State Capitol	State Capitol
Little Rock, AR	Little Rock, AR	Little Rock, AR
(501) 371-2345	(501) 371-6516	(501) 371-3017

CALIFORNIA

Governor	Senate	House
State Capitol 100	State Capitol	State Capitol
Sacramento, CA 95814	Sacramento, CA 95814	Sacramento, CA 95814
(916) 445-2841	(916) 445-6070	(916) 445-3614

COLORADO

Governor	Senate	House
State Capitol 136	Federal Building	Federal Building
Denver, CO 80203	Denver, CO 80294	Denver, CO 80294
(303) 866-2471	(303) 866-4838	(303) 866-2028

CONNECTICUT

Governor	Senate	House
210 Capitol Ave.	State Capitol	State Capitol
Hartford, CT 06106	Hartford, CT 06106	Hartford, CT 06106
(203) 566-4840	(203) 566-3845	(203) 566-2708

DELAWARE

Governor	Senate	House
Legislative Hall	Legislative Hall	Legislative Hall
Dover, DE 19901	Dover, DE 19901	Dover, DE 19901
(302) 736-4101	(302) 736-4129	(302) 736-4870

FLORIDA

Governor	Senate	House
The Capitol	State Capitol	State Capitol
Tallahassee, FL 32301	Tallahassee, FL 32304	Tallahassee, FL 32304
(904) 488-4441	(904) 488-1621	(904) 488-1157

GEORGIA

Governor	Senate	House
State Capitol 203	State Capitol	State Capitol
Atlanta, GA 30334	Atlanta, GA 30334	Atlanta, GA 30334
(404) 656-1776	(404) 656-5040	(404) 656-1515

HAWAII

Governor
State Capitol 500
Honolulu, HI 96813
(808) 548-5420

Senate
State Capitol
Honolulu, HI 96813
(808) 548-4675

House
State Capitol
Honolulu, HI 96813
(808) 548-7843

IDAHO

Governor
State Capitol 200
Boise, ID 83720
(208) 334-2100

Senate
State Capitol
Boise, ID 83720
(208) 334-2000

House
State Capitol
Boise, ID 83720
(208) 384-2000

ILLINOIS

Governor
Capitol Building 207
Springfield, IL 62706
(217) 782-6830

Senate
State House
Springfield, IL 62706
(217) 782-4517

House
State House
Springfield, IL 62706
(217) 782-8223

INDIANA

Governor
State House 206
Indianapolis, IN 46204
(317) 232-4567

Senate
State Capitol
Indianapolis, IN 46204
(317) 232-9419

House
State Capitol
Indianapolis, IN 46204
(317) 232-9608

IOWA

Governor
State Capitol
Des Moines, IA 50319
(515) 281-5211

Senate
State Capitol
Des Moines, IA 50319
(515) 281-5307

House
State Capitol
Des Moines, IA 50319
(515) 281-5381

KANSAS

Governor
State Capitol
Topeka, KS 66612
(913) 296-3232

Senate
State House
Topeka, KS 66612
(913) 296-2456

House
State House
Topeka, KS 66612
(913) 296-7633

KENTUCKY

Governor
State Capitol
Frankfort, KY 40601
(502) 564-2611

Senate
State Capitol
Frankfort, KY 40610
(502) 564-2611

House
State Capitol
Frankfort, KY 40610
(502) 564-3900

LOUISIANA

Governor	Senate	House
P.O. Box 44004	P.O. Box 44183	P.O. Box 44183
Baton Rouge, LA 70804	Baton Rouge, LA 70804	Baton Rouge, LA 70804
(504) 342-7015	(504) 342-2040	(504) 342-7393

MAINE

Governor	Senate	House
State House	State House	State House
Station 1	Augusta, ME 04333	Augusta, ME 04333
Augusta, ME 04333	(207) 289-1500	(207) 289-1400
(207) 289-3531		

MARYLAND

Governor	Senate	House
State House	State House	State House
Annapolis, MD 21404	Annapolis, MD 21404	Annapolis, MD 21404
(301) 269-3901	(301) 841-3908	(301) 841-3999

MASSACHUSETTS

Governor	Senate	House
Executive Office	State House	State House
State House	Boston, MA 02133	Boston, MA 02133
Boston, MA 02133	(617) 722-1276	(617) 722-2356
(617) 727-3600		

MICHIGAN

Governor	Senate	House
Executive Office	State Capitol	State Capitol
Capitol Building	Lansing, MI 48901	Lansing, MI 48909
Lansing, MI 48909	(517) 373-2400	(517) 373-0135
(517) 373-3400		

MINNESOTA

Governor	Senate	House
130 S. Capitol Bldg.	State Capitol	State Capitol
St. Paul, MN 55155	St. Paul, MN 55155	St. Paul, MN 55155
(612) 296-3391	(612) 296-0504	(612) 296-2314

MISSISSIPPI

Governor	Senate	House
P.O. Box 139	P.O. Box 1018	P.O. Box 1018
Jackson, MS 39205	Jackson, MS 39205	Jackson, MS 39205
(601) 359-3150	(601) 359-3202	(601) 359-3360

MISSOURI

Governor	Senate	House
P.O. Box 720	State Capitol	State Capitol
Jefferson City, MO 65102	Jefferson City, MO 65102	Jefferson City, MO 65102
(314) 751-3222	(314) 751-3766	(314) 751-3829

MONTANA

Governor	Senate	House
Capitol Station, Rm. 204	State Capitol	State Capitol
Helena, MT 59620	Helena, MT 59620	Helena, MT 59620
(406) 444-3111	(406) 444-4880	(406) 444-4822

NEBRASKA

Governor	Legislature (Unicameral)
State Capitol Building	State Capitol
2nd Floor	Lincoln, NE 68509
Lincoln, NE 68509	(402) 471-2311
(402) 471-2244	

NEVADA

Governor	Senate	Assembly
Capitol Building	State of Nevada	State of Nevada
Executive Chambers	Capitol Complex	Capitol Complex
Carson City, NV 89710	Carson City, NV 89710	Carson City, NV 89710
(702) 885-5670	(702) 885-5742	(702) 885-5739

NEW HAMPSHIRE

Governor	Senate	House
208-214 State House	State House	State House
Concord, NH 03301	Concord, NH 03301	Concord, NH 03301
(603) 271-2121	(603) 271-1110	(603) 271-1110

NEW JERSEY

Governor	Senate	House
State House	State House Annex	State House Annex
Trenton, NJ 08625	Trenton, NJ 08625	Trenton, NJ 08625
(609) 292-6000	(609) 292-4840	(609) 292-4840

NEW MEXICO

Governor	Senate	House
State Capitol	State Capitol	State Capitol
Santa Fe, NM 87503	Santa Fe, NM 87503	Santa Fe, NM 87503
(505) 827-3000	(505) 827-4011	(505) 827-4011

NEW YORK

Governor	Senate	Assembly
State Capitol	Legislative Office	Legislative Office
Albany, NY 12223	Building	Building
(518) 474-8390	Albany, NY 12247	Albany, NY 12248
	(518) 455-2800	(518) 455-4100

NORTH CAROLINA

Governor	Senate	House
State Capitol Bldg.	State Capitol	State Capitol
Raleigh, NC 27611	Raleigh, NC 27602	Raleigh, NC 27602
(919) 733-5811	(919) 733-7761	(919) 733-7760

NORTH DAKOTA

Governor	Senate	House
Capitol Building	State Capitol	State Capitol
First Floor	Bismark, ND 58505	Bismark, ND 58505
Bismark, ND 58505	(701) 224-3297	(701) 224-3297
(701) 224-2200		

OHIO

Governor	Senate	House
State House	State House	State House
Columbus, OH 43215	Columbus, OH 43214	Columbus, OH 43214
(614) 466-3555	(614) 466-4900	(614) 466-3357

OKLAHOMA

Governor	Senate	House
State Capitol	State Capitol	State Capitol
Oklahoma City, OK	Oklahoma City, OK	Oklahoma City, OK
73105	73105	73105
(405) 521-2342	(405) 521-2711	(405) 521-2711

OREGON

Governor	Senate	House
State Capitol Bldg.	State Capitol	State Capitol
Salem, OR 97310	Salem, OR 97310	Salem, OR 97310
(503) 378-3111	(503) 378-8168	(503) 378-8880

PENNSYLVANIA

Governor	Senate	House
Main Capitol Bldg.	State Capitol	State Capitol
Harrisburg, PA 17120	Harrisburg, PA 17120	Harrisburg, PA 17120
(717) 787-2500	(717) 787-5920	(717) 787-4610

RHODE ISLAND

Governor
State House
Providence, RI 02903
(401) 277-2080

Senate
State Capitol
Providence, RI 02903
(401) 277-2340

House
State Capitol
Providence, RI 02903
(401) 277-2000

SOUTH CAROLINA

Governor
P.O. Box 11450
Columbia, SC
(803) 734-9818

Senate
P.O. Box 142
Columbia, SC 29202
(803) 758-5937

House
P.O. Box 11867
Columbia, SC 29211
(803) 758-5240

SOUTH DAKOTA

Governor
500 E. Capitol
Pierre, SD 57501
(605) 773-3212

Senate
Pierre, SD 57501
(605) 773-3825

House
Pierre, SD 57501
(605) 773-3842

TENNESSEE

Governor
State Capitol Bldg.
Nashville, TN 37219
(615) 741-2001

Senate
State Capitol
Nashville, TN 37219
(615) 741-2730

House
State Capitol
Nashville, TN 37219
(615) 741-2730

TEXAS

Governor
P.O. Box 12428
Capitol Station
Austin, TX 78711
(512) 463-2000

Senate
P.O. Box 12068
Austin, TX 78711
(512) 475-4271

House
P.O. Box 2910
Austin, TX 78769
(512) 475-5616

UTAH

Governor
State Capitol, Rm. 120
Salt Lake City, UT
  84114
(801) 533-5231

Senate
State Capitol
Salt Lake City, UT
  84114
(801) 533-4710

House
State Capitol
Salt Lake City, UT
  84114
(801) 533-5801

VERMONT

Governor
Pavillion Office Bldg.
Room 500
Montpelier, VT 05602
(802) 828-3333

Senate
State House
Montpelier, VT 05602
(802) 828-2241

House
State House
Montpelier, VT 05602
(802) 828-2247

VIRGINIA

Governor	Senate	House
Capitol Building	State Capitol	State Capitol
Third Floor	P.O. Box 396	P.O. Box 396
Richmond, VA 23219	Richmond, VA 23219	Richmond, VA 23219
(804) 786-2211	(804) 786-2366	(804) 786-8826

WASHINGTON

Governor	Senate	House
Legislative Building	Legislative Building	Legislative Building
Olympia, WA 98504	Olympia, WA 98501	Olympia, WA 98501
(206) 753-6780	(206) 786-7550	(206) 786-7550

WEST VIRGINIA

Governor	Senate	House
Capitol Building	Charleston, WV 25305	Charleston, WV 25305
Charleston, WV 25305	(304) 357-7800	(304) 348-2239
(304) 348-2000		

WISCONSIN

Governor	Senate	House
P.O. Box 7863	State Capitol	State Capitol
Madison, WI 53707	Madison, WI 53702	Madison, WI 53702
(608) 266-1212	(608) 266-2517	(608) 266-1108

WYOMING

Governor	Senate	House
State Capitol	State Capitol	State Capitol
Cheyenne, WY 82002	Cheyenne, WY 82001	Cheyenne, WY 82001
(307) 777-7434	(307) 777-7733	(307) 777-7330

PROPER ADDRESSES AND SALUTATIONS:

Governor:	Senate:	House:
The Honorable (full name)	The Honorable (full name)	The Honorable (full name)
Governor of (State)	(State) Senate	(State) House/Assembly/
(Address)	(Address)	House of Delegates
(City) (State) (Zip)	(City) (State) (Zip)	(City) (State) (Zip)
Dear Governor (surname)	Dear Mr./Ms. (surname)	Dear Mr./Ms. (surname)

Appendix D

A listing of environmental and animal welfare organizations

Not all existing organizations are listed below, but those that are listed are known to be reliable and responsible. However, the organizations listed do not necessarily endorse this book. We suggest that you contact at least one of these groups in order to receive information and learn more about our Earth.

An asterisk indicates that staff, directors, board members, or founders of these organizations have contributed to one of the chapters in this book.

African Wildlife Foundation
1717 Massachusetts Avenue NW
Washington, DC 20036
(202) 265-8394

Animal Protection Institute of
  America
P.O. Box 2250
Sacramento, CA 95822
(916) 422-1921

Animal Welfare Institute
P.O. Box 3650
Washington, DC 20007
(202) 337-2332

American Society for the Prevention
  of Cruelty to Animals (ASPCA)
441 East 92nd Street
New York, NY 10128
(212) 876-7700

Center for Marine Conservation*
1725 DeSales Street NW, Suite 500
Washington, DC 20036
(202) 429-5609

Citizen's Clearinghouse for
  Hazardous Waste
P.O. Box 926
Arlington, VA 22216
(703) 276-7070

The Conservation Foundation
1717 Massachusetts Avenue NW
Washington, DC 20036
(202) 797-4300

Conservation International
1015 18th Street NW, Suite 1000
Washington, DC 20036
(202) 429-5660

Council on Economic Priorities
30 Irving Place
New York, NY 10003
(800) 882-6435

The Cousteau Society
930 West 21st Street
Norfolk, VA 23517
(804) 627-1144

Defenders of Wildlife*
1244 19th Street NW
Washington, DC 20036
(202) 659-9510

Earth First!
P.O. Box 5176
Missoula, MT 59806

East African Wildlife Society
1557 SW Cheyenne Hills Rd.
Topeka, KS 66604
(913) 272-7666

Environmental Defense Fund
1616 P Street NW
Washington, DC 20077
(202) 387-3500

Friends of the Earth
218 D Street SE
Washington, DC 20003
(202) 544-2600

Fund for Animals*
200 W. 57th Street
New York, NY 10019
(212) 246-2096

Greenpeace*
1436 U Street NW
Washington, DC 20009
(202) 462-1177

Humane Farming Association
1550 California Street, Suite 6
San Francisco, CA 94109
(415) 771-2253

Humane Society of the United States
2100 L Street NW
Washington, DC 20037
(202) 452-1100

International Alliance for
  Sustainable Agriculture*
1701 University Avenue SE
Minneapolis, MN 55414
(612) 331-1099

International Wildlife Coalition
320 Giffort Street
Falmouth, MA 02540
(508) 564-9980

Land Stewardship Project
14758 Ostlund Train N
Marine, MN 55047
(612) 433-2770

National Arbor Day Foundation
100 Arbor Avenue
Nebraska City, NE 68410
(402) 474-5655

National Audubon Society
950 Third Avenue
New York, NY 10022
(212) 832-3200

National Coalition Against the
  Misuse of Pesticides
530 7th Street SE
Washington, DC 20003
(202) 543-5450

National Parks and Conservation
  Association
1015 31st Street NW
Washington, DC 20007

National Wildlife Federation
1400 16th Street NW
Washington, DC 20036
(202) 797-6800

Natural Resources Defense Council*
40 W. 20th Street
New York, NY 10011
(212) 737-2700

Nature Conservancy
1815 North Lynn Street
Arlington, VA 22209
(703) 841-5300

People for the Ethical Treatment of
  Animals (PETA)*
P.O. Box 42516
Washington, DC 20015
(202) 726-0156

Rainforest Action Network
301 Broadway, Suite A
San Francisco, CA 94133
(415) 398-4404

Renew America
1400 16th Street NW
Suite 710
Washington, DC 20036
(202) 232-2252

Rocky Mountain Institute
1739 Snowmass Creek Road
Snowmass, CO 81654-9199
(303) 927-3128

Sierra Club
730 Polk St.
San Francisco, CA 94109
(415) 766-2211

Society for Animal Protective
  Legislation
P.O. Box 3719
Georgetown Station
Washington, DC 20007
(202) 337-2334

Trees for Life
1103 Jefferson
Wichita, KS 67203
(316) 263-7294

Union of Concerned Scientists
26 Church Street
Cambridge, MA 02238
(617) 547-5552

United Nations Environment
  Program
DC2-803
#2 UN Plaza
New York, NY 10017
(212) 963-8139

US PIRG (Public Interest Research
  Group)
25 Pennsylvania Avenue SE
Washington, DC 20003
(202) 546-9707

Wilderness Society*
900 17th Street NW
Washington, DC 20006
(202) 833-2300

Wildlife Conservation International
c/o New York Zoological Society
Bronx Park
Bronx, NY 10460
(212) 220-5097

World Resource Institute
1750 New York Avenue NW
Washington, DC 20006
(202) 638-6300

Worldwatch Institute
1776 Massachusetts Avenue NW
Washington, DC 20036

World Wildlife Fund
1250 24th Street NW
Washington, DC 20037
(202) 293-4800

Zero Population Growth*
Suite 320
1400 Sixteenth Street NW
Washington, DC 20077-6640
(202) 332-2200

Notes and Bibliographies

1 / Population Control: Necessary but Insufficient

SUGGESTED READING

Brown, Lester R. "The Changing World Food Prospect: The Nineties and Beyond." *Worldwatch Paper 85,* October 1988.

Daly, Herman E. *Steady State Economics.* San Francisco: W. H. Freeman, 1977.

Daly, H. E., and J. Cobb, Jr. *For the Common Good.* Boston: Beacon Press, 1990.

Ehrlich, Anne H., and Paul R. Ehrlich. *Earth.* New York: Franklin Watts, 1987.

Ehrlich, Paul R., and Anne H. Ehrlich. *The Extinction: The Causes and Consequences of the Disappearance of the Species.* New York: Random House, 1981.

———. *The Population Explosion.* New York: Simon and Schuster, 1990.

Ehrlich, Paul R., and John P. Holdren, "Impact of Population Growth." *Science* 171 (March 26, 1971): 1212–17.

The Global 2000 Report to the President, Washington, DC: US Government Printing Office, 1980.

Hardin, Garrett. "Cassandra's Role in the Population Wrangle." In *The Cassandra Conference: Resources and the Human Predicament,* edited by Paul R. Ehrlich and John P. Holdren. College Station: Texas A&M University Press, 1988.

Holdren, John P., and Paul R. Ehrlich. "Human Population and the Global Environment." *American Scientist* 62 (May–June 1974): 282–92.

Kates, R. W., R. S. Chen, T. E. Downing, J. X. Kasperson, E. Messer, and S. R. Millman. *The Hunger Report: 1988.* Providence, RI: Alan Shawn Feinstein World Hunger Program, Brown University, 1988.

Ornstein, Robert, and Paul R. Ehrlich. *New World / New Mind.* New York: Doubleday, 1989.

Schneider, Stephen H., and Lynn E. Mesirow. *The Genesis Strategy: Climate and Global Survival.* New York: Plenum, 1976.

Vitousek, Peter M., Paul R. Ehrlich, Anne H. Ehrlich, and Pamela Matson. "Human Appropriation of the Products of Photosynthesis." *BioScience* 36:368–73.

United States Commission on Population Growth and the American Future. *Population and the American Future.* (Final report plus eight volumes of research papers.) Washington, DC: US Government Printing Office, 1972. Final report also published by Signet (New York).

World Resources Institute and International Institute for Environment and Development. *World Resources 1988–89.* New York: Basic Books, 1989.

Worldwatch Institute. *State of the World, 1988.* New York: W. W. Norton, 1990.

2 / The Greenhouse Effect: Creation Waits

1. The Episcopal Church, *Book of Common Prayer* (Oxford University Press, New York, 1979), p. 827.

3 / Tropical Forests

SOURCES

Caufield, Catherine. *In the Rainforest: Report from a Strange, Beautiful, Imperiled World.* New York: Alfred E. Knopf, 1985.

————. *Tropical Moist Forest: The Resource, the People, the Threat.* London: Earthscan, 1982.

Friends of the Earth (London). *The Rainforest Times (TRF Times),* Summer Issue, 1988.

Myers, Norman. *The Primary Source: Tropical Forests and Our Future.* New York: W. W. Norton and Co., 1984.

Plotkin, Mark. "Conservation and Ethnobotany in Tropical South America —Report of the First Year." Washington, DC: World Wildlife Fund, 1984.

Rainforest Action Network. *Alert* 3 (1986); 15, 19, 20 (1987); 24 (1988). San Francisco, CA.

Secrett, Charles. *Rainforest: Protecting the Planet's Richest Resource.* London: Russell Press, Ltd., 1984.

Simons, Marlise. *New York Times,* August 12, 1988.

5 / Twentieth-Century Living: Environmental Illness

SOURCES

Altman, Lawrence K., M.D. "Fearful of Outbreaks, Doctors Pay New Heed to Emerging Viruses." *New York Times,* May 19, 1989, p. 24.

Anderson, Alan. "Neurotoxic Follies." *Psychology Today,* July 1982, p. 30.

Bell, Iris. *Clinical Ecology: A New Medical Approach to Environmental Illness.* Colinas, CA: Common Knowledge Press, 1982.

Brown, Michael. "Toxic Wind." *Discover,* November 1987, p. 42.

Coplan, Richard, and Bradford H. Sewell. "Taming the Killer Strawberries." *American Health,* May 1988, pp. 41–45.

Dinsdale, Katherine. "Danger: The Nightmare of a Dallas Family and the Chemical That Is Changing Their Lives." *D Magazine*, April 1985, pp. 88–93, 172–81.

"Don't Go Near the Water." *Newsweek*, August 1988, pp. 42–48.

Faelten, Sharon. *Allergy Self-Help Book.* Emmaus, PA: Rodale Press, 1983.

Godish, Thad. "Formaldehyde and Building Related Illness." *Journal of Environmental Health* 44 (November–December 1981), pp. 116–21.

———. "Formaldehyde—A Physician's Guide." *National Resources Notes*, Winter 1983, pp. 1–8.

Hamilton, Kimberly. "The Latest Food Frights." *Self*, November 1987, pp. 83–88.

Jaffe, Harry. "Dangerous Chemicals: Why the Government Isn't Protecting You." *Family Circle*, May 17, 1984, p. 72.

Loveland, David, and Beth Reichheld. *Safety on Tap.* Washington, DC: League of Woman Voters Education Fund, 1987.

Moeller, Mike. "Straight Talk—Reactions to Pesticide Exposure." *Grassroots.* Texas Department of Agriculture, Fall 1988, pp. 12–13.

Mott, Laurie. "Pesticide Residues in Food: Your Daily Dose." *National Coalition for Alternatives to Pesticides*, Summer 1984, pp. 7–9.

Nero, Anthony, Jr. "Controlling Indoor Air Pollution." *Scientific American*, May 1988, pp. 42–48.

"News Focus." *Journal of Air Pollution Control Association* 35 (March 1985), pp. 270–72.

Olkowski, William. "Biological Control: A Century of Success." *I.P.M. Practitioner* 11 (January 1989), pp. 1–2.

Protecting Texas Groundwater. Austin, TX: Texas Department of Agriculture, Spring 1987.

Rea, William J., and Alfred J. Johnson. "Toxic Volatile Organic Hydrocarbons in Chemically Sensitive Patients." *Clinical Ecology* 5 (1987), pp. 170–73.

Rodgers, Joann E. "Zest, Bran Muffins and Caution." *American Health*, March–April 1983, pp. 39–46.

Stiak, Jim. "Pesticides and Secret Agents." *Sierra*, May–June 1988, pp. 18–21.

Taylor, Ronald. "Now You Can Worry about Bad Air Indoors, Too." *U.S. News and World Report*, September 23, 1985, pp. 71–72.

Toufexis, Anastasis. "The Dirty Seas." *Time*, August 1, 1988, pp. 44–50.

Warner, Bob. "Coping with Toxic Chemicals in the Interiorscape." *New Leaf Press* 3, July 1988.

6 / Silent Spring or Sustainable Agriculture?

Much of the material in this chapter is drawn from:

Terry Gips, *Breaking the Pesticide Habit: Alternatives to 12 Hazardous Pesticides.* The International Alliance for Sustainable Agriculture, Minneapolis, MN, 1987.

"What Is a Sustainable Agriculture" in *Global Perspectives on Agroecology and Sustainable Agricultural Systems,* Agroecology Program, University of California, Santa Cruz, CA, 1988.

1. "The Economics of Pesticides," *EPA Journal,* May 1987, p. 11.
2. Mike Lewis and Allan Woodburn, *Agro-Chemical Service 1984* (London: Wood, Mackensie & Co., 1984), p. 3.
3. Francis Moore Lappé and Joseph Collins, *World Hunger: Twelve Myths* (New York: Grove Press, 1986).
4. *Development/Environment Trends in Asia and the Pacific: A Regional Overview,* Committee on Industry, Technology, Human Settlements (Bangkok: ESCAP, 1983).
5. Robert F. Wasserstrom and Richard Wiles, *Field Duty: U.S. Farmworkers and Pesticide Safety* (Washington, DC: World Resources Institute Study 3, July 1985).
6. C. A. Cohen, C. Eiden, and M. N. Lorber, "Monitoring Ground Water for Pesticides in the U.S.A.," *Evaluating Pesticides in Groundwater,* American Chemical Society, July 1986.
7. Minnesota Department of Health and Minnesota Department of Agriculture, "Pesticides and Groundwater," Surveys of Selected Minnesota Wells," February 1988.
8. Lawrie Mott, with Martha Broad, *Pesticides in Food: What the Public Needs to Know* (San Francisco: Natural Resources Defense Council, March 15, 1984), p. iv.
9. Gips, p. 160.
10. Board on Agriculture, National Research Council, *Regulating Pesticides in Food: The Delaney Paradox* (Washington, DC: National Academy Press, 1987), p. 74.
11. D. Pimentel et al., "Pesticides, Insects in Food, and Cosmetic Standards," *BioScience* 27 (1977), pp. 178–85.
12. World Commission on Environment and Development, *Our Common Future* (Oxford: Oxford University Press, 1987), p. 128.
13. David Pimentel et al., "Land Degradation: Effects on Food and Energy Resources," *Science,* October 8, 1976, p. 150.
14. Lester R. Brown, "The Worldwide Loss of Cropland," *Worldwatch Paper 24* (Washington, DC: The Worldwatch Institute, 1978), p. 24.
15. Wes Jackson, *New Roots for Agriculture* (Lincoln, NE: University of Nebraska Press, 1985).
16. Ibid., p. 18.
17. E. H. Clark et al., *Eroding Soils: The Off-Farm Impacts* (Washington, DC: Conservation Foundation, 1985), p. xviii.
18. Lester R. Brown et al., *State of the World, 1989* (New York: W. W. Norton and Co., 1989), p. 52.
19. Jackson, pp. 23–25.
20. Luis Malaret, *Safe Pest Control: An NGO Action Guide* (Nairobi: Environmental Liaison Center, 1985).
21. Bill Devall, and George Sessions, *Deep Ecology* (Salt Lake City: Peregrine Smith Books, 1985), p. 65.

22. Sarala Devi, *Revive our Dying Planet* (Nainital, India: Gyanodaya Prakashan, 1982), pp. 53–54.

23. Steven Rosen, *Food for the Spirit: Vegetarianism and the World Religions* (New York: Bala Books, 1987), p. 108, Koran, surah 6, verse 38.

24. Dr. Karan Singh, "Hindu Declaration," in "The Environmental Sabbath" information packet. United Nations Environmental Program, 1989.

25. Jeremy Rifkin, with Ted Howard, *Entropy: A New World View* (New York: Bantam Books, 1981), pp. 19–29.

26. Genesis 1:28.

27. Vandana Shiva, *Staying Alive: Women, Ecology and Survival in India* (New Delhi: Kali for Women, 1988).

28. Wendell Berry, *The Unsettling of America: Culture and Agriculture* (San Francisco: Sierra Club Books, 1977), p. 22.

29. Francis Chaboussou, "How Pesticides Increase Pests," *The Ecologist* 16, no. 1 (1986), pp. 29–35.

30. Berry, pp. 7, 39–48.

31. Terry Gips, "$3.45 Million for Minnesota Sustainable Agriculture," *Manna* 5, no. 1–3 (December 1988), p. 1.

32. *Webster's New World Dictionary,* second college ed. (1978), s.v. *sustain.*

33. Terry Gips, "What Is Sustainable Agriculture?" *Manna,* July–August 1984, p. 2.

34. *Websters,* s.v. *sustain.*

35. Richard R. Harwood, "What Is Different about Sustainable Agriculture?" Paper presented to International Institute for Environment and Development Meeting, Washington, DC, July 9, 1985.

36. Paul R. Ehrlich, in Coomer, p. 15.

37. Robert Repetto, *Paying the Price: Pesticide Subsidies in Developing Countries,* Research Report #2 (Washington, DC: World Resources Institute, 1985), p. 1.

38. Gips, *Breaking the Pesticide Habit,* p. 81.

39. *Websters,* s.v. *sustain.*

40. Everett Gendler, "The U.S. Bicentennial and the Biblical Jubilee: The Right We Must Reclaim," *CCAR Journal,* Summer 1975, pp. 85–86.

41. "Sabbatical Year and Jubilee," *Encyclopaedia Judaica* (Jerusalem: Mac-Millan Company, 1977), p. 578.

42. *Facts about Hunger* (Elkhart, IN: Church World Services, 1985).

43. "Women Creating a New World," *Oxfam Facts for Action,* Pub. No. 3 (1985) Oxfam America Pub., Boston, MA.

44. Dr. Marion Moses, "Pesticide Poisonings and North American Farm Workers," Pesticide Action Network, San Francisco, 1988.

45. *Websters,* s.v. *sustain.*

46. Rosen, p. 93.

47. Milton Steinberg, *Basic Judaism* (New York: Harcourt, Brace and World, 1947), p. 100.

48. Ehrenfeld and Bentley, p. 15.

49. Ecclesiastes 3:29.

50. Job 12:7–8.

51. Annie Besant, *Vegetarianism in the Light of Theosophy* (Madras, India: The Theosophical Publishing House, 1919), pp. 18–19.

52. Tom Regan, *The Case for Animal Rights* (Berkeley: University of California Press, 1983), p. 329.

53. Thomas Berry, "The Viable Human," *ReVision* 9, no. 2 (Winter–Spring 1987), p. 78.

54. Jim Mason, "Is Factory Farming Really Cheaper?" *New Scientist*, March 28, 1985.

55. Hill, "'Preventative Pest Control," p. 3.

56. Aldo Leopold, *A Sand County Almanac with Essays on Conservation from Round River* (New York: Ballantine Books, 1984), p. 202.

57. Ibid., p. 251.

58. Wendell Berry, Preface to Masanobu Fukuoka, *The One Straw Revolution* (Toronto: Bantam Books, 1985), p. xiii.

59. Gips, *Breaking the Pesticide Habit*, pp. 86–90.

60. Ibid., pp. 90–92.

61. Brown, p. 4.

62. Keith Schneider, "Farming without Chemicals: Age-Old Technologies Becoming State of Art,"*New York Times*, August 23, 1987, p. 10.

63. Sonia L. Nazario, "Big Firms Get High on Organic Farming," *Wall Street Journal*, March 21, 1989, p. B1.

64. Robin Whyatt, *Intolerable Risk: Pesticides in Children's Foods* (New York: Natural Resources Defense Council, 1989).

65. Nazario.

66. Marian Burros, "Organic Food: Now the Mainstream," *New York Times*, March 29, 1988, p. 17.

67. Nazario.

68. U.S. Dept. of Agriculture, *Report and Recommendations on Organic Farming* (Washington, DC: USDA, 1980), pp. 15–19, 44–46.

69. Dick and Sharon Thompson, "Naturally Healthy Livestock," *The New Farm*, November–December, 1983, in *The Thompson Farm, Nature's Agricultural School* (Emmaus, PA: Regenerative Agriculture Association, 1985), p. 20.

70. Michael O'Keefe, "Regenerative Agriculture in Iowa: An Interview with Dick Thompson," *Manna* 3, no. 1 (January–March 1986), p. 4.

71. Thompson, p. 27.

72. Thompson, pp. 8–10.

73. Gips, "Worldwide Sustainable Agriculture: A Reality."

7 / Air Pollution: Can Our Planet Survive

1. William Longgood, *The Darkening Land* (New York: Simon and Schuster, 1972), p. 81.

2. William Longgood, "Uncertainties Cloud U.S. Debate on Air Pollution Controls," *Washington Post*, July 6, 1981, p. A-6.

3. "Health Effects of Toxic Pollution: A Report from the Surgeon General," and "A Brief Review of Selected Environmental Incidents with a

Potential for Health Effects," reports prepared by the Surgeon General and the Library of Congress for the Committee on Environment and Public Works, US Senate, August 1980, p. 170.

4. *Toxic Chemicals and Public Protection: A Report to the President by the Toxic Substances Strategy Committee* (Washington, DC: Council on Environmental Quality, May 1980), pp. 4, 121–22.

5. Dr. Marc Lavietes, personal communication, March 8, 1989.

6. Steve Sternberg, "Studies Suggest Air Pollution Helps Cancer to Spread," *Atlanta Constitution*, March 28, 1990, p. A-7.

7. Congressman Henry A. Waxman, Letter to *Wall Street Journal*, August 15, 1989.

8. Philip Shabecoff, "Industrial Pollution Called Startling," *New York Times*, April 13, 1989.

9. "Is Breathing Hazardous to Your Health?" *Newsweek*, April 3, 1989, p. 25.

10. Ibid.

11. "EPA Finds Huge Amount, Variety of Toxic Chemicals Polluting Air," *Atlanta Constitution*, March 23, 1989, p. 3-A.

12. Philip Shabecoff, "Air Poisons Called Threat to Public, Chemicals' Effects Are Worse Than Expected," *New York Times*, March 23, 1989, p. 1; idem, "U.S. Only Narrowly Avoided 17 Bhopal-Like Disasters, Study Says," ibid., April 30, 1989.

13. "Air Toxics." National Clean Air Fund, Washington, DC, n.d.

14. Philip Shabecoff, supra note 12.

15. Robert Mendelsohn and Guy Orcutt, "An Empirical Analysis of Air Pollution Dose-Response Curves," *Journal of Environmental Economics and Management*, June 1979, pp. 85–106.

16. "A Brief Review of Selected Environmental Incidents," pp. 162–68, "Before the U.S. Environmental Protection Agency. Petition of the Natural Resources Defense Council, Inc. for Control of Fine Particles," NRDC, Washington, DC, May 29, 1980, pp. 1, 16–17, 20, 33.

17. *Environmental Quality—1979: The Tenth Annual Report of the Council on Environmental Quality,* Washington, DC, December 1979, p. 71; Joanne Omang, "Acid Rain Doesn't Hurt Most Crops...." *Washington Post*, n.d., p. D-7; "Rain Falls Everywhere," editorial, *Washington Post*, July 17, 1980.

18. Dr. Ellis P. Cowline, "Acid Precipitation: A Status Report," US Environmental Protection Agency, Washington, DC, December 1979, p. 1.

19. Roger Peterson, ABC Evening News, June 18 and 19, 1980; Joanne Omang, "Acid Rain: Push toward Coal Makes Global Pollution Worse," *Washington Post*, December 30, 1979, p. A1.

20. *The Global 2000 Report to the President—The Technical Report, Volume Two,* Council on Environmental Quality and the US State Department, July 1980, p. 337.

21. Ibid.

22. Lance Gay, "Storm Brews Among Officials on Solutions to Acid Rain," *Washington Star,* April 10, 1980, p. A2; Press Release, National Clean Air Coalition, Washington, DC, March 6, 1980.

23. David Everett, "Dioxins Found in Isle Royale Lake," *Detroit Free Press,* October 30, 1984, pp. 1A and 13A; Malcolm W. Browne, "Study of Dioxins in Vietnam Is Urged," *New York Times,* April 18, 1986; Robert Cooke, "Dioxins May Pose Greater Hazard Than Suspected," *Atlanta Constitution,* April 17, 1986.

24. US Environmental Protection Agency, United Nations Environment Program, *Effects of Changes in Stratospheric Ozone and Global Climate,* Volume 1—Overview, Volume 4—Sea Level Rise (August 1986).

25. Philip Shabecoff, "Global Warming Has Begun, Expert Tells Senate," *New York Times,* June 24, 1988, p. 1.

26. Ibid.

27. James Gleick, "Even With Action Today, Ozone Loss Will Increase," *New York Times,* March 20, 1988, pp. 1, 17, EPA, supra note 24.

28. Philip Shabecoff, "Cancer Rise Linked to Thinning Ozone," *New York Times,* November 4, 1986; Barry Meier, and Robert E. Taylor, "Bid for Global Chemical Emissions Limit Expected at 40-Nation Meeting on Ozone," *Wall Street Journal,* November 6, 1986; Philip Shabecoff, "Consensus on the Threat to the Ozone," *New York Times,* December 7, 1986.

29. Jeff Nesmith, "Proposed Law Would Slash Production of Chemicals That Deplete Ozone Layer," *Atlanta Constitution,* n.d., 1986.

30. Jane Bryant Quinn, CBS Evening News, December 4, 1986.

31. Philip Shabecoff, "Dozens of Nations Approve Accord to Protect Ozone," *New York Times,* September 17, 1987, p. 1; Sharon Begley, "An Exemplary Ozone Agreement," *Newsweek,* September 28, 1987, p. 8; "The Hole at the Bottom of the World," editorial, *New York Times,* September 19, 1987, p. 18.

32. Ibid.

33. Craig R. Whitney, "12 Europe Nations to Ban Chemicals That Harm Ozone," *New York Times,* March 3, 1989, p. 1; Peter Passell, "Cure for Greenhouse Effect: The Costs Will Be Staggering," *New York Times,* November 19, 1989, p. 1.

34. "Measures Urged to Protect Ozone," *New York Times,* November 30, 1986, p. 21; Jeff Nesmith, "Global Tax Urged to Combat Ozone Depletion," *Atlanta Journal and Constitution,* November 30, 1986, p. 11A.

35. "Close-Up Report: Intensive Confinement—Cruel to Animals, Destroyer of the Environment," The Humane Society of the United States, Washington, DC, February 1990; John Robbins, *Diet for a New America* (Walpole, NH: Stillpoint, 1987); John Robbins, "Realities, 1989" (Santa Cruz, CA: EarthSave Foundation, 1989).

36. Ibid.

37. Robbins, ibid.; "Animal Agriculture Fact Sheet #3: War on the Environment," The Fund for Animals, New York, 1990.

38. Robbins, ibid.

39. Senator Max Baucus, and Senator Joseph Lieberman, "Ask the Asthmatics," *New York Times,* Op-Ed Page, April 22, 1989.

40. A. Myrick Freeman, III, "Benefits of Air and Water Pollution Control: A Review and Synthesis of Recent Estimates," Council on Environmental

Quality, Washington, DC, 1980; Charles Osolin, "CEQ News Release," April 21, 1980.

41. Lewis Regenstein, "Clean Air: Defending a Law in Peril," *New York Times,* Op-Ed Page, August 4, 1981; "Before the U.S. EPA," supra note 16.

42. "Regulatory Impact Analysis on the National Ambient Air Quality Standards for Particulate Matter," US EPA, February 21, 1984; James S. Cannon, *The Health Costs of Air Pollution* (Washington, DC: American Lung Association, 1990, pp. 6–9, 41, 56.

43. "Costs and Benefits of Reducing Lead in Gasoline: Final Regulatory Impact Analysis," US EPA, February 1985; Cannon, pp. 6–9, 56.

44. Mark DeLuchi et al., *A Comparative Analysis of Future Transportation Fuels,* October 1987; Cannon, ibid., pp. 6–9, 56.

45. "Regulatory Impact Analysis on the National Ambient Air Quality Standards for Sulfur Oxides (Sulfur Dioxide)," US EPA, March 1988; Cannon, pp. 6–9, 56.

46. "EPA's Use of Benefit-Cost Analysis: 1981–86," US EPA, 1987; Cannon, p. 29.

47. Denis Hayes, "Energy: The Case for Conservation," The Worldwatch Institute, Washington, DC, 1976.

48. "World Prospects for Z. P. G.," Zero Population Growth, Washington, DC, 1979.

49. *Environmental Quality*—1979, supra note 17; R. Stobaugh, and D. Yergin, eds., *Energy Future* (New York, Random House, 1975).

50. Ibid.

51. Albert Crenshaw, "Curtains for OPEC?" *Washington Post,* June 29, 1980, p. C8.

52. "The Road to Trillion Dollar Energy Savings: A Safe Energy Platform," Public Citizen, Washington, DC, June 1987

53. John H. Cushman, Jr., "Tougher Fuel Economy Rules Planned in Shift from Reagan," *New York Times,* April 5, 1989, p. 1.

54. Sarah Chasis, and Linda Speer, "How to Avoid Another *Valdez,*" *New York Times,* Op-Ed Page, n.d., 1989.

55. "Environmental Quality 1978: The Ninth Annual Report of the Council on Environmental Quality," Washington, DC, 1978.

56. Denis Hayes, "Rays of Hope," The Worldwatch Institute, Washington, DC, p. 155.

57. Philip Shabecoff, "Majority Leader Is Ready to Bring Air Pollution Bill to Senate Floor," *New York Times,* February 28, 1990; idem, "Senators Achieve Accord with Bush on Clean Air Bill," *New York Times,* March 1, 1990, p. A1.

58. Philip Shabecoff, "Health Risk from Smog Is Growing, Official Says, Children Are in Particular Danger from Polluted Air, Doctors Testify," *New York Times,* March 1, 1989.

59. James Gustave Speth, *Environmental Pollution: A Long Term Perspective* (Washington, DC: World Resources Institute, 1988). Philip Shabecoff, "Crop and Tree Damage Are Tied to Air Pollution," *New York Times,* September 11, 1988, p. 14.

60. Shabecoff, supra, note 58.

61. Ibid.

62. Jim Fain, "The Sky Is Falling but Neither Candidate Is Paying Serious Attention," *Atlanta Constitution,* October, 12, 1988, p. A-11.

8 / How We Use and Abuse Water

1. *World Resources 1988–89,* World Resources Institute, International Institute for Environment and Development, and United National Environment Programme.

2. American Water Works Association. Addition information on water use came from Diana C. Gibbons, *The Economic Value of Water* (Resources for the Future, 1986); and Kenneth D. Frederick, *Water Resources: Status, Trends and Policy Needs* (Resources for the Future, 1988).

3. This does not include "in-stream" uses of water for hydroelectric power and other uses. While these uses do not "consume" water, they nevertheless may have profound effects on the water system, for example, by eliminating or damaging habitat for fish and wildlife.

4. Most of the information on the Ogallala aquifer was taken from Ruth Patrick et al., *Groundwater in the United States* (University of Pennsylvania Press, 2d ed., 1987).

5. *New York Times,* March 26, 1989, p. E-6.

6. This century the U.S. Bureau of Reclamation built over 160 water projects and hundreds of dams. In all, the United States has about 80,000 dams, hundreds of thousands of wells, and millions of miles of canals. Frederick, supra, note 2.

7. For more information on federal water projects and subsidies, see *The Broken Promise of Reclamation Reform* (Natural Resources Defense Council, 1987), and *Turning Off the Tap on Federal Water Subsidies* (Natural Resources Defense Council and California Legal Assistance Foundation, 1985).

8. Most of the information on more efficient water use for agriculture, industry, and urban needs was taken from Postel, *Conserving Water: The Untapped Alternative* (Worldwatch Paper 67, 1985).

9. According to one estimate, it would take fifty-three million barrels of oil to replace with petroleum-based fertilizers the amount of nutrients disposed of annually in U.S. wastewater. Sandra Postel, supra.

10. Marcia D. Lowe, "Down the Tubes," Worldwatch, March–April 1989.

11. Marcia D. Lowe, *Newsletter of the Rocky Mountain Institute,* February 1989.

12. EPA, *National Water Quality Inventory* (1987). This estimate is probably low, since EPA does not "count" waters that violate water quality standards less than one out of every ten days. But this is little consolation if your children happen to swim on that tenth day.

13. EPA, Report to Congress, Water Quality Improvement Study (Draft 1988).

14. EPA, 1988 Assessment of Needed Publicly Owned Wastewater Treatment Facilities in the United States.

15. EPA Needs Survey, supra.

16. More information on this problem, and how to solve it, can be found in Thompson et al., *Poison Runoff, A Guide to State and Local Control of Nonpoint Source Water Pollution* (Natural Resources Defense Council, 1989).

17. Paul Thompson, EPA, Results of the Nationwide Urban Runoff Program (1983).

18. Much of the information on groundwater pollution was taken from Patrick, supra, note 4.

9 / Where Are We Going to Put All This Garbage?

SUGGESTED READING

Connett, Paul and Ellen, eds. *Waste Not.* Published by Work on Waste, USA, 82 Judson St., Canton, NY.

Montague, Peter, ed. *Hazardous Waste News.* A weekly newsletter and resource for citizens fighting toxics. Published by the Environmental Research Foundation, P.O. Box 3541, Princeton, NJ 08540.

State of Missouri. *Statewide Resource Recovery Feasibility and Planning Study.* Environmental Improvement and Energy Resources Authority, Missouri Department of Natural Resources. December 1987.

Volland, Craig. "A Critical Review of EPA's Dry Scrubber Standard for Municipal Solid Waste Incinerators," and "Environmental and Financial Risks Associated with Trash Incineration." Published by Spectrum Technologists, 616 E. 63rd St., Kansas City, MO.

11 / The Plight of the Ocean Animals

1. André Carothers, "The Seal Plague: Pollution and the Collapse of the North Sea," *Greenpeace*, November–December 1988, p. 67.

2. David Ehrenfeld, *The Arrogance of Humanism* (New York: Oxford University Press, 1981), p. x.

3. Ted Williams, "The Exclusion of Sea Turtles," *Audubon*, January 1990, pp. 24–33.

4. André Carothers, "And Then There Were None: The Sea Turtle Tragedy," *Greenpeace*, January–March 1987, pp. 13–15.

5. Roger Caras, *Last Chance on Earth: A Requiem for Wildlife* (New York: Schocken Paperback, 1972), p. xiii.

6. Andrew Davis, "Can We Save Marine Mammals?: The Deadly Decline of the Marine Mammal Protection Act," *Greenpeace*, January–February 1988, pp. 11–15.

7. Philip Shabecoff, "Big Tuna Canners Act to Slow Down Dolphin Killings," *New York Times*, April 13, 1990, pp. A1 and A6.

8. Greenpeace direct mail, June 1990.

9. Editorial, *New York Times*, April 5, 1989, p. 26.

10. Greenpeace direct mail, August 1987.

11. *Greenpeace*, May–June 1988, p. 17.

12 / Extinction

1. Paul and Anne Ehrlich, *Extinction* (New York: Ballantine Books, 1985), p. 139.

2. Ibid., p. 151.

3. Lili Sheeline, "Traffic (U.S.A.)," vol. 7, no. 4 (July 1987), World Wildlife Fund, New York, July 1987, p. 1.

4. Ehrlich, p. 145.

5. Ibid.

6. Jim Morris, "Share the Earth News," no. 4 (Spring–Summer 1986), p. 5.

7. "Future in the Wild," 1987, World Wildlife Fund, New York, p. 4.

8. Ibid., p. 10.

9. William K. Stevens, "New Survey Raises Concerns about Recovery of Blue Whale," *New York Times,* June 20, 1989, p. C4.

10. "Future in the Wild," p. 18.

11. Philip Shabecoff, "Where the Planet Is Losing Its Life Forms: An Update on the Destruction of Species," *New York Times,* July 30, 1989, p. E3.

12. George Stanley, "Extinction," *Wichita Eagle-Beacon,* July 5, 1987, p. 9A.

13. Caras, p. xiv.

14. Ehrlich, p. xiv.

15. David Ehrenfeld, *The Arrogance of Humanism* (New York: Oxford University Press, 1981), pp. 207–8.

13 / Toxic Shock: The Pesticide Fix

1. Rachel Carson, *Silent Spring* (New York: Houghton Mifflin Co., 1962), p. 7.

2. Environmental Protection Agency, "Pesticide Industry Sales and US Usage: 1987 Market Estimates," Office of Pesticide Programs, Washington, DC, 1988.

3. A. Maier and G. Zwieg, eds., "Formulation of Pesticides in Developing Countries," United Nations Industrial Development Organization, United Nations, New York, 1983.

4. Environmental Protection Agency, "Pesticides in Groundwater Data Base: 1988 Interim Report," Office of Pesticide Programs, Washington, DC, 1988.

5. United States Department of Agriculture, "USDA Research Plan for Water Quality," Agricultural Research Service and Cooperative State Research Service, Washington, DC, 1988.

6. Robert van den Bosch, *The Pesticide Conspiracy* (Garden City, NY: Doubleday and Co., 1978).

7. D. Pimentel et al., "Pesticides: Environmental and Social Costs," in D. Pimentel and J. H. Perkins, eds., *Pest Control: Cultural and Environmental Aspects* (Boulder, CO: Westview Press, 1980).

8. D. Pimentel et al., "Benefits and Costs of Pesticide Use," *BioScience* 28:772, 778–784, 1978.

9. United States General Accounting Office, "Pesticides: EPA's Formidable Task to Assess and Regulate Their Risks," Resources, Community, and Economic Development Division, Washington, DC, 1986.

10. 7 U.S.C. 136 et seq., Sections 3(c) (5) and 2(bb).

11. S. S. Epstein and S. Briggs, "If Rachel Carson Were Writing Today: *Silent Spring* in Retrospect," *Environmental Law Reporter* 17 (6): 10180–84, 1987.

12. United States General Accounting Office, "Pesticides: EPA's Formidable Task to Assess and Regulate Their Risks," op cit., 1986, p. 20.

13. FIFRA allows for the use of unregistered pesticides, or the use of a product not registered for a specific purpose, under special conditions, such as an emergency caused by a sudden pest outbreak or for experimental use to generate information to be used in obtaining a full registration. FIFRA also allows EPA to issue conditional registrations—registrations that are conditional on the basis of the manufacturer's submission of additional data. These provisions have resulted in the use of pesticides about which too little is known.

14. J. Stiak, "Pesticides and Secret Agents," *Sierra,* 1988 (73) 3:18–21.

15. United States General Accounting Office, "Nonagricultural Pesticides: Risks and Regulation," Resources, Community, and Economic Development Division, Washington, DC, 1986, p. 28.

16. Ibid.

17. J. W. Edwards, "Pretty Poisons," *Sanctuary: The Journal of the Massachusetts Audubon Society,* 1987, 26 (6): 13–16.

18. L. B. Hunt, "Kinetics of Pesticide Poisoning in Dutch Elm Disease Control," US Fish and Wildlife Service Circ., 1965, 226:12–13.

19. E. H. Dustman in *Scientific Aspects of Pest Control,* National Academy of Sciences, National Research Council: Washington, DC, 1966, pp. 343–51.

20. W. L. Reichel, E. Cromartie, T. G. Lamont, and B. M. Mulhern, *Pesticide Monitor Journal,* 1969, 3:142–44.

21. M. L. Flint and R. van den Bosch, *Introduction to Integrated Pest Management* (New York: Plenum Press, 1981).

22. R. J. Hall, "Impact of Pesticides on Bird Populations," pp. 85–111 in G. J. Marco et al., eds., *Silent Spring Revisited* (Washington, DC: American Chemical Society, 1987).

23. Pierre Beland, "Witness for the Prosecution," *Nature Canada,* 1988, 17 (4):28–36.

24. Terry Gips, "The Consumer and the World: Influencing International Pesticide Use," *Journal of Pesticide Reform,* 1986, 6 (1):2–5.

25. M. Pallemaerts, "The International Effort to Protect Trade of Banned and Severely Restricted Pesticides," *Journal of Pesticide Reform,* 1986, 6 (1): 23–27.

26. V. H. Freed, "Pesticides: Global Use and Concerns," pp. 145–58 in G. J. Marco et al., eds., *Silent Spring Revisited.*

27. M. O'Brien, "Chlorpyrifos," *Journal of Pesticide Reform,* 1989, 8 (4):42–44.

28. R. Balcom, "Secondary Poisoning of Red-shouldered Hawks with Carbofuran," *Journal of Wildlife Management,* 1983, 47 (4):1129–32.

29. C. E. Grue et al., "Assessing Hazards of Organophosphate Pesticides to Wildlife," transcript from North American Wildlife and Natural Resource Conference, 1983, 48:200–220.

30. C. J. Henny et al., "Case Histories of Bald Eagles and other Raptors Killed by Organophosphorous Insecticides Topically Applied to Livestock," *Journal of Wildlife Dis.,* 1987, 23 (2):292–95.

31. E. W. Odenkirchen, and R. Eisler, "Chlorpyrifos Hazards to Fish, Wildlife, and Invertebrates: a Synoptic Review," US Fish and Wildlife Service, *Contaminant Hazard Reviews,* 1988, Report No. 13, Washington, DC.

32. G. J. Smith, "Pesticide Use and Toxicology in Relation to Wildlife: Organophosphorus and Carbamate Compounds," US Fish and Wildlife Service, Resource Publication 170, 1987, Washington, DC.

33. W. Stone, "Poisoning of Wild Birds by Organophosphate and Carbamate Pesticides," *New York Fish and Game Journal,* 1979, 26 (1):37–47.

34. Environmental Protection Agency, "Carbofuran Special Review: Technical Support Document" (Office of Pesticides and Toxic Substances: Washington, DC, 1989).

35. Environmental Protection Agency, "Preliminary Determination to Cancel All Registrations of Granular Carbofuran," *Federal Register,* 1989, 54:3744–49.

36. G. Payne, Pesticide Residues in Wildlife: Violating Legal Standards?" *Journal of Pesticide Reform,* 1988, 7 (4):18–19.

37. Ibid.

38. Ibid.

39. Ibid.

40. Ibid.

41. J. Serfis et al., "The Environmental Protection Agency's Implementation of the Endangered Species Act with Respect to Pesticide Registration" (Center for Environmental Education: Washington, DC, 1986).

42. S. S. Epstein, and S. Briggs, "If Rachel Carson Were Writing."

43. Ibid.

44. L. Weiss, "Keep Off the Grass: A Review of the Health Effects of Pesticides Most Commonly Used by the Lawn Care Industry" (Public Citizen's Congress Watch, Washington, DC, 1989).

45. D. R. Bottrell, "Integrated Pest Management" (Council on Environmental Quality: Washington, DC, 1979), p. iv.

46. S. Daar, "Least-toxic Pest Management for Lawns" (Bio-integral Resource Center: Berkeley, CA, 1986).

47. Ibid.

48. Ibid.

49. M. Dover and B. Croft, *Getting Tough: Public Policy and the Management of Pesticide Resistance* (Washington, DC: World Resources Institute, 1984).

50. J. E. Horne, Testimony submitted to the Committee on Government Operations, "Low Input Farming Systems: Benefits and Barriers" (Washington, DC: US Government Printing Office, 1988).

51. Ibid.

52. Terry Gips, "Breaking the Pesticide Habit: Alternatives to 12 Hazardous Pesticides," International Alliance for Sustainable Agriculture, Publ. no. 1987–1.

14 | Wetlands: America's Endangered Habitat

SOURCES

Berkman, Richard L., and W. Kip Viscusi. *Damming the West.* New York: Grossman Publishers, 1973.

Campbell, Joseph, with Bill Moyers. *The Power of Myth.* New York: Doubleday and Co., 1988.

"Colorado Gov. Buckles to Two Forks Pressure." *Audubon Activist,* January–February 1989, The Audubon Society, p. 10.

Environmental Protection Agency. *Wetlands Action Plan,* Office of Wetlands Protection, Washington, DC, January 1989.

Farrar, Jon. "The Rainwater Basin—Our Vanishing Wetlands." Nebraska Fish and Game Commission, Lincoln, NE, n.d.

Gibney, Frank, Jr. "Louisiana's Bayou Blues." *Newsweek,* June 22, 1987, p. 54.

Huevelmans, Martin. *The River Killers.* Harrisburg, PA: Stackpole Books, 1974.

Krapu, Gary. "The Last Watering Holes on the Prairie." *Natural History,* January 1989, p. 67.

Kusler, Dr. Jon A. "Our National Wetland Heritage." The Environmental Law Institute, Washington, DC, 1983.

Laycock, George. "What Water for Stillwater?" *Audubon,* November 1988, p. 14.

Lenssen, Nicholas. "Where Have the Ducks Gone?" *World Watch,* January–February 1989, p. 9.

"Massive Loss of Coastal Wetlands Shrinks Louisiana." *Audubon Activist,* November–December 1988, p. 1.

"Nebraska Not Spot for Sandhill Cranes." *Salina Journal,* April 13, 1986, p. 31.

Protecting America's Wetlands: An Action Agenda. Walford, MD: The Conservation Foundation, Harper Graphics, 1988.

Rude, Kathleen. "An Age-Old Image Problem." *Ducks Unlimited,* September–October 1987, p. 80.

———. "Silent Spring Phase Two." *Ducks Unlimited,* November–December 1988, p. 30.

———. "A Weighty Decision." *Ducks Unlimited,* January–February 1989, p. 13.

The Platte River Whooping Crane Habitat Maintenance Trust. *Habitat Monitoring Plan,* Grand Island, NE.

Steinhart, Peter. "Empty the Skies." *Audubon,* November 1987, p. 71.

Tiner, Ralph W., Jr. *Wetlands of the United States: Current Status and Recent Trends.* Washington, DC: U.S. Government Printing Office, March 1984.

United States General Accounting Office. *Wetlands: The Corps of Engineers Administration of the Section 404 Program.* Washington, DC: U.S. Government Printing Office, July 1988.

Vogt, Bill. "Now, the River Is Dying." *National Wildlife,* June–July 1978, p. 4.

"Wetlands Saving on Sewage Treatment." *The Manhattan Mercury,* December 1, 1988, p. B-12.

Wildlife Management Institute. *Outdoor News Bulletin,* December 2, 1988, p. 2.

Wildlife Management Institute. *Outdoor News Bulletin,* December 16, 1988, p. 3.

Wildlife Management Institute. *Outdoor News Bulletin,* February 10, 1989, p. 2.

Wildlife Management Institute. *Outdoor News Bulletin,* January 13, 1989, p. 2.

Wildlife Management Institute. *Outdoor News Bulletin,* December 15, 1989, p. 1.

Wildlife Management Institute. *Outdoor News Bulletin,* March 2, 1990, pp. 1–2.

15 / Animal Rights: A More Compassionate Life-style

1. Transcript of the "CBS Evening News with Dan Rather" (Bob Schieffer substituting), December 27, 1988.

2. Ibid.

3. Milt Freudenheim, "Beef Dispute: Stakes High in Trade War," *New York Times,* January 1, 1989, p. 1.

4. Roger Caras, "We Must Find Alternatives to Animals in Research," *Newsweek,* December 26, 1988, p. 57.

5. Stephen Kaufman, M.D., in *Boston Globe,* June 13, 1987.

6. Jean Deurlinger, "Computerized Human Body Advances Ecology Research," *New York Times,* November 12, 1985, p. C-3.

7. Arthur Klausner, "Tissue Culture for Improved Toxicology," *Biotechnology* 5, p. 779.

8. "The Growing Furor over Fur: A Brutal Status Symbol?" *Newsweek,* December 26, 1988, p. 52.

9. Merritt Clifton, "The Battle to Stomp Out an Abominable Industry," *The Animal's Agenda,* January–February 1987.

10. Merritt Clifton, interview by Kathryn Fisher, PETA, October 1988.

11. Greta Nilsson et al., *Facts about Furs* (1980), p. 141.

12. Ibid., p. 129.

13. Ibid., p. 180.

14. Dan Dinello, "Women, Is That Fur Coat Worth All the Suffering That Animals Endure?" *Chicago Sun-Times,* October 5, 1987.

15. Ibid.

16. "PETA's Guide to Compassionate Living," People for Ethical Treatment of Animals, Washington, DC, 1988, p. 6.

17. Robert Baker, testimony prepared for the Maryland Senate Rules Committee, March 11, 1986.

20 / *The Religious Foundations of Ecology*

1. Donald Worster, *Nature's Economy: The Roots of Ecology* (San Francisco: Sierra Club Books, 1977).
2. Huston Smith, *The Religions of Man* (New York: Harper and Row, 1958).
3. Ibid.
4. Ibid.
5. Ibid.
6. Ibid.
7. The Venerable Lungrig Namgyal, "Assisi Declarations," 1986.
8. Father Lanfrancho Serrini, "Assisi Declarations," 1986.
9. His Excellency Dr. Karan Singh, "Assisi Declarations," 1986.
10. His Excellency Dr. Abdullah Omar Nasseef, "Assisi Declarations," 1986.
11. Rabbi Arthur Hertzberg, "Assisi Declarations," 1986.
12. Robert Meye, *Tending the Garden* (Grand Rapids, MI: Eerdmans, 1987).
13. David Ehrenfeld, "Nature in the Jewish Tradition," Au Sable Forum Papers, Au Sable Institute, Mancelona, MI, 1982.
14. William Dyrness, "Stewardship of the Earth in the Old Testament," Au Sable Forum Papers, Au Sable Institute, Mancelona, MI, 1984.
15. David Ehrenfeld, "Nature in the Jewish Tradition."
16. Howard Snyder, "The Economy of God: the Ecology of the Church," Au Sable Forum Papers, Au Sable Institute, Mancelona, MI, 1981.
17. Wesley Granberg-Michaelson, "Toward a Theology of Earthkeeping: A Call to Global Sanctification," Au Sable Forum Papers, Au Sable Institute, Mancelona, MI, 1982.
18. Dennis Testerman, "Missionary Earthkeeping—An Overview," Au Sable Forum Papers, Au Sable Institute, Mancelona, MI, 1985.
19. Donald Worster, *Nature's Economy: The Roots of Ecology* (San Francisco: Sierra Club Books, 1977).

21 / *The Wages of Greed*

1. Albert Gore, "An Ecological Kristallnacht. Listen," *New York Times,* March 19, 1989, p. E-7.
2. Robert Lekachman, *Greed Is Not Enough: Reaganomics* (New York: Pantheon Books, 1982), p. 110.
3. Ibid.
4. Ibid., pp. 110–11.
5. Lewis Regenstein, *How to Survive in America the Poisoned* (Washington, DC: Acropolis Books, 1986), p. 143.
6. Lynn Davidson. A letter: "Greenpeace Campaign against Offshore Drilling." *Greenpeace,* August 1987.

7. Regenstein, p. 207.

8. Ibid.

9. US PIRG (Public Interest Research Group), "Poisoned Policy: How the Pesticide Lobby Spreads the Wealth in Washington," *Pesticide Control,* Winter 1987, p. 4.

10. Ibid.

11. Ibid.

12. Philip M. Stern, *The Best Congress Money Can Buy* (New York: Pantheon Books, 1988), p. 10.

13. Ibid.

14. "Where's the Limit?" in cover story "A Game of Greed," *Time,* December 5, 1988, p. 67.

15. Ibid.

16. James Robertson and André Carothers, "The New Economics: Accounting for a Healthy Planet," *Greenpeace,* January–February 1989, p. 12.

17. Dan Dignam, "After 2-Year Wait, Virgin Grand Breaks Ground," *Tour & Travel News,* January 19, 1989, p. 36.

18. Karl Menninger, M.D., *Whatever Became of Sin?* (New York: Hawthorn Books, 1977), p. 156.

19. "Where's the Limit?"

20. Gene Smith, "Visit to a Prairie Dog Town," *Topeka Capitol-Journal,* August 14, 1988, p. 2-F.

21. Ibid.

22. Regenstein, *The Politics of Extinction* (New York: Macmillan Publishing Co., 1975), p. 214.

23. Ibid., p. 223.

24. Loudon Wainwright, "A Need for Caring," *Life,* November 1988, p. 32.

25. "Shades of Buffalo Bill," *Time,* February 20, 1989, p. 41.

26. *Mid-County Advertiser,* San Benito, TX, February 16, 1989, p. 3.

27. *National Wildlife,* National Wildlife Federation, Leesburg Pike, VA, June–July, 1988.

28. Joe McCarthy, *Papal Bulls and English Muffins* (New York: Paulist Press, 1974), p. 62.

29. Robert van den Bosch, *The Pesticide Conspiracy* (Garden City, NY: Doubleday & Co., 1978), p. 49.

Contributors

ROBERT W. ADLER is a Senior Attorney and Director of the Clean Water Project at the Natural Resources Defense Council (NRDC). Before coming to NRDC, Mr. Adler was the Executive Director of Trustees for Alaska, an Anchorage-based environmental group, and an attorney with the Pennsylvania Department of Environmental Resources. Mr. Adler has a B.A. in ecology from the Johns Hopkins University (1977) and a law degree from the Georgetown University Law Center (1980).

GEORGE BAGGETT is founder of Liquid Products, Inc., a company involved in the recycling of inorganic industrial chemicals. He studies toxic industrial chemicals and air and water pollution, and publishes a newsletter entitled "Toxic News." He is a member of many environmental organizations, but is most active in Citizens for Recycling, a grassroots organization founded to promote recycling and to oppose garbage incinerators in Missouri, Kansas, Nebraska, and Arkansas. He is a founder of The Grass Roots Alliance for Solid Waste Solutions, a national organization of local environmental groups opposing the proliferation of solid waste and hazardous waste incinerators.

THE REVEREND THOMAS BERRY is director of the Riverdale Center for Religious Research in the Bronx. Father Berry is also an ecologist and has written numerous books and articles. His latest work is *The Dream of the Earth* published by Sierra Club Books in 1988.

ANDRÉ CAROTHERS is the editor of *Greenpeace* magazine. ANDREW DAVIS is assistant media director for Greenpeace USA. Greenpeace is recognized world wide as one of the foremost environmental organizations. Greenpeace maintains offices in Argentina, Australia, Austria, Belgium, Canada, Costa Rica, Denmark, France, Luxembourg, the Netherlands, New Zealand, the Soviet Union, Spain, Sweden, Switzerland, Germany, the United Kingdom, and the United States.

DR. CALVIN B. DEWITT is professor of Environmental Science at the University of Wisconsin, Madison. He is founder and Director of Au Sable Institute, a center for the study of environmental science and religious values. He is also Chair of the North American Conference on Christianity and Ecology and has written extensively on the subject of religion and ecology.

317

PAUL R. EHRLICH is Bing Professor of Population Studies, and ANNE H. EHRLICH a senior research associate, in the Department of Biological Sciences at Stanford University. Both have written extensively; their latest book is entitled *The Population Bomb* (Simon and Schuster, 1990), upon which this chapter is based. Paul Ehrlich is also a correspondent for NBC TV and Anne Ehrlich was recently selected for The United Nation's Global 500 Roll of Honour for Environmental Achievement.

JAN GARTON is graduate of Kansas State University with degrees in history, journalism, and mass communications. She is president of the Kansas Audubon Council. She has received numerous conservation awards for her work on behalf of the Cheyenne Bottoms, including the National Audubon Society's William Dutcher Award, 1990, and the Chevron Conservation Award, 1990.

TERRY GIPS is an agricultural economist trained at the University of California, Davis, and the Yale School of Organization and Management. He has worked for the Cooperative Extension Service in California; Cargill, Inc.; the White House Executive Office; and the United States Congress, where he was responsible for agriculture and pesticide policy for the United States Representative John Krebs, a member of the House Agriculture Committee. Gips is author of *Breaking the Pesticide Habit: Alternatives to 12 Hazardous Pesticides* and cofounder of the International Alliance for Sustainable Agriculture.

CAROLYN GORMAN is Director of Health Education at the Environmental Health Center in Dallas. She received her B.A. from Southern Methodist University and her M.A. from Texas Woman's University in the field of health education.

SUSAN HAGOOD was a member of the staff of Defenders of Wildlife, a national, nonprofit wildlife conservation organization, for eight years. As Defenders' Washington Representative for Wildlife Protection, her specialties included the effects of pesticides on wildlife and federal predator control programs. She attended Stephens College and Louisiana State University, majoring in biology and wildlife management.

THE REVEREND WARREN G. HANSEN was born and raised in Denver. His education includes a B.A. in biology and chemistry, a M.A. in anatomy and physiology, and a Ph.D in biochemistry and pathology. He taught at St. Louis University, Washington University, St. Louis College of Pharmacy, and Purdue University. Convinced that any real progresss toward a safer, cleaner, sustainable world would have to come from the spiritual conversion of large numbers of people, he qualified himself through seminary studies for the ministry and was ordained priest in St. John's Episcopal Church, Lafayette, IN, in 1971. He has since served several parishes. Although recently retired, he serves part-time at Trinity Church, St. James, MO.

MIKE LARUE, a graduate of the University of Kansas, is assistant director of the World Famous Topeka Zoo. He serves on the North American Propagation Group for Orangutan Species Survival Plan and is the North American

Studbookkeeper of the Mandrill Baboon. LaRue was involved in the development of the Conservation/Propagation Center for the World Famous Topeka Zoo, a facility dedicated to the survival of endangered species. He has written for *Zoo* magazine and numerous conservation publications.

SUSAN MEEKER-LOWRY is an author and an editor of *Catalyst*, a newsletter she started in order to report on opportunities for investing in social change. She is interested in the possibility of a Gaean, or Earth-based, economy and cofounded the Institute for Gaean Economics (now *Catalyst*) located at 64 Main Street, Montpelier, VT 05602.

INGRID E. NEWKIRK is cofounder and National Director of People for Ethical Treatment of Animals, the largest animal rights organization in the United States. Newkirk's campaigns to save animal lives have made the front pages of the *Washington Post* and other national newspapers. She has appeared on many national television and radio shows, including "The Today Show," "Phil Donahue," "The Oprah Winfrey Show," "West 57th Street," and "20/20." Newkirk has spoken internationally on animal rights issues, from the steps of the Canadian Parliament to the streets of Calcutta, India. She has travelled extensively in the US and teaches activists how to eliminate animal suffering in their own neighborhoods. Named "Washingtonian of the Year" in 1981, Newkirk is the author of numerous articles on the social implications of our treatment of animals in factory farms and laboratories, including "Animal Rights and the Feminist Connection."

KATHRYN J. O'HARA is director of the Marine Pollution Program of the Center for Marine Conservation. She specializes in developing educational materials and presentations on the subject of marine debris. She was the principal investigator on a study commissioned by the Environmental Protection Agency which outlined the types, quantities, sources, and impacts of marine debris. The study was published as *Plastics in the Ocean: More Than a Litter Problem*. Ms. O'Hara is also the primary author of *A Citizens' Guide to Plastics in the Ocean*, and *Marine Wildlife Entanglement in North America*. She has also written numerous articles and professional papers on the subject of marine debris and wildlife entanglement. She has a master's degree in Marine Science from the Charleston (SC) Higher Consortium and a bachelor's degree in zoology from Duke University.

LEWIS G. REGENSTEIN is Director of the Interfaith Council for the Protection of Animals and Nature in Atlanta, Georgia, an affiliate of the Humane Society of the United States, and author of *Replenish the Earth: A History of Organized Religion's Treatment of Animals and Nature, Including the Bible's Message of Conservation and Kindness toward Animals* (Crossroad). He is the author of several books on conservation, including *How to Survive in America the Poisoned* and *The Politics of Extinction*, both of which were nominated for the Pulitzer Prize. He serves on the Council of the American Lung Association in Atlanta and is vice-president of H.O.P.E. (Help Our Planet Earth), an environmental-products firm.

ANDY RUDIN is married with three children. He lives in Philadelphia and works with nonprofit agencies to reduce their energy costs so they will have more money for community service. He has a B.A. in biology from Clark University and a M.A. in ecology from the University of Vermont. He serves on ASHRAE (American Society of Heating, Refrigerating and Air Conditioning Engineers) committees for energy conservation standards in existing buildings and on the Illuminating Engineering Society committee on lighting houses of worship.

JUDITH S. SCHERFF, has been an environmental and animal welfare volunteer for twenty years. She holds a B.A. and a M.S. in political and social science from Pittsburg State University and is currently enrolled in the graduate division of environmental studies at the University of Kansas. She is an environmental stewardship representative for the Episcopal Church.

DOUGLAS B. TRENT is an American ecologist from Kansas living in Brazil. He and his wife, Nancy, own and operate Focus Tours, Brazil's most respected nature tour company. Focus Tours is used to promote their goal of educating the public about tropical forests and other environmental issues, as well as raising money for conservation projects in Brazil. Their conservation work has been endorsed by the National Audubon Society, Friends of the Earth (London), Dr. Norman Myers, Catherine Caufield, and Dr. Ghillean T. Prance. Mr. Trent can be contacted at: Focus Tours, Rua Grao Mogol, 502; Sion 30.330; Belo Horizonte, MG; Brazil.

T. H. WATKINS is editor of *Wilderness,* the quarterly magazine of the Wilderness Society. Richard Hoppe is Assistant Director of Public Affairs and Gail Backman-Love is on the staff.